The Legal Guide to E-Business

THE LEGAL GUIDE TO E-BUSINESS

Jacqueline Klosek

Westport, Connecticut
London

Library of Congress Cataloging-in-Publication Data

Klosek, Jacqueline, 1972–
    The legal guide to e-business / Jacqueline Klosek.
      p. cm.
    Includes bibliographical references and index.
    ISBN 1–56720–403–1 (alk. paper)
      1. Electronic commerce—Law and legislation—United States—Popular works.
I. Title.
  KF390.5.C6K59   2003
  343.7309′944—dc21   2003052891

British Library Cataloguing in Publication Data is available.

Library of Congress Catalog Card Number: 2003052891
ISBN: 1–56720–403–1

First published in 2003

Praeger Publishers, 88 Post Road West, Westport, CT 06881
An imprint of Greenwood Publishing Group, Inc.
www.praeger.com

Printed in the United States of America

The paper used in this book complies with the
Permanent Paper Standard issued by the National
Information Standards Organization (Z39.48–1984).

10 9 8 7 6 5 4 3 2 1

This book is intended to provide information regarding the law applicable to the
Internet. However, legal information is not the same as legal advice. The information
provided in this book cannot and does not attempt to apply the law to any individual's
specific circumstances. Although I have aimed to provide information that is accurate
and useful, I recommend that you consult a lawyer if you desire professional assurance
that the information contained herein and your interpretation of it is appropriate to your
particular situation.

This book is dedicated to my parents for fostering my adventurous spirit and encouraging me to explore the world and to my Aunt Mary for providing me with her boundless support and valuable guidance.

I would also like to thank Mary Hildebrand and Kristin Bissinger for being mentors, as well as friends, and Patrice King for making me laugh and keeping me sane.

CONTENTS

Chapter 1

INTRODUCTION

THE IMPORTANCE OF LEGAL ISSUES IN WEB-BASED BUSINESSES

Despite what some recent economic events may suggest, the Internet is still, and will continue to be, an extremely important force in international commerce. Today a vast number of enterprises, both in the United States and abroad, use Web sites as important business tools in their daily operations. Many companies use Web sites to provide information and to promote their products and services; many other companies use their Web sites for buying goods and services. Although the Internet provides businesses with a number of benefits, it is also a legal minefield, fraught with potential liabilities.

A number of factors are contributing to the legal complexities facing today's Web site operators. First, there has been a rapid and comprehensive evolution in the laws governing Internet issues. During the past several years, while the technology that enables today's Web sites was evolving, so too was the legal framework governing the operation of such sites. Second, because the Internet is a medium that crosses state and national boundaries, Web sites may be subject to many different laws and regulations. Despite some efforts at harmonizing national legislation applicable to the Internet,[1] there continue to be important differences from country to country. Accordingly, entities operating Web sites in the current era have a large and complex body of law with which to comply.

The fact that there is a large and rapidly evolving body of law applicable to Web sites means that operators will frequently have to evaluate their sites to ensure that they comply with all applicable laws. When creating a new Web site, or evaluating an existing one, a common tendency among many companies is to place the focus on the business-related aspects of the site. While it is certainly important to examine business issues, such as whether one's site is attractive to Web surfers and whether the site offers an appropriate selection of products and services, it is essential that concern about business-related aspects of the site does not result in a neglect of the essential legal issues. Focusing on business issues may facilitate the creation of a highly enticing and popular Web site. However, if a site is improperly constructed from a legal standpoint, it can breed lawsuits and even create liability risks that can result in the closure of businesses.

INTRODUCTION TO SIGNIFICANT LEGAL ISSUES

The Development of U.S. Law

The law of the Internet is still in its relative infancy. Nonetheless in recent years there has been a momentous evolution in the law pertaining to the Internet, and there is a growing body of law that will have to be considered when developing a new Web site or evaluating an existing one. For instance, the law currently limits the ability of Web site operators to collect personally identifiable information from children who visit their Web sites and requires operators to obtain verifiable parental consent before doing so.[2] Also, designating an agent and complying with the relatively simple requirements of the Digital Millennium Copyright Act could help to protect a Web site operator from liability based on allegations that the content on the site infringes someone's copyright.[3] These are just two examples of the many recently enacted Internet-specific laws and regulations with potential relevance to Web site operations.

In addition to complying with such specific Internet laws, it is also essential to ensure that on-line activities are undertaken in accordance with any other applicable non-Internet laws. For instance, if a Web site offers on-line trading functions, the operator must ensure that the site complies with regulations of the Securities and Exchange Commission (SEC) and any other applicable laws pertaining to securities. Likewise, when advertising or selling various consumer goods via the Internet, Web site operators will have to ensure that their offerings comport with the requirements of the Federal Trade Commission (FTC).

In recent years, many bodies of law that are not specific to the Internet have also been changing to fit the evolving technology. The SEC, for example, has issued interpretations pertaining to the posting of certain financial information on-line.[4] In an April 28, 2000, Interpretive Release, the SEC unambiguously stated that "the federal securities laws apply in the same manner to the content of . . . websites as to any other statements made" through a different medium. Accordingly, "issuers are responsible for the accuracy of their statements that can reasonably be expected to reach investors or the securities markets regardless of the medium through which the statements are made, including the Internet."[5]

The FTC has also been active in reminding Web site operators that their use of the Internet does not in any way reduce their obligation to comply with traditional off-line requirements such as truth-in-advertising disclosures. In a recent report on the necessity of proper disclosures in on-line advertising, the FTC noted: "But cyberspace is not without boundaries, and fraud and deception are unlawful no matter what the medium. The FTC has enforced and will continue enforcing its consumer protection laws online to ensure that products and services are described truthfully in online ads and that consumers get what they pay for."[6]

These are just two of the numerous examples of how traditional legal requirements and regulations are being applied in the new on-line world. These examples demonstrate that a review of one's on-line practices will necessitate a review not only of new, Internet-specific legislation but also of revisions and updates to generally applicable law.

The International Dimension

An important fact that must be considered when creating a new Web site or evaluating an existing Web presence is that using the Internet has profound international implications.[7] Clearly, posting an advertisement on the Internet is immensely different from placing an advertisement in a newspaper, even a major, globally read newspaper such as the *Wall Street Journal*. The reality is that when information is placed on the Internet, it becomes available throughout the entire world in a very rapid fashion. At the same time, the Web site operator who has made such information available also becomes subject to a number of different national and local laws and regulations.

The Internet has made significant contributions to improving the practicality and feasibility of small business-to-consumer transactions on-line. Consumers are making good use of this new opportunity to purchase foreign goods and services directly from vendors in other countries. The Internet eliminates the necessity of intermediaries and helps to reduce transaction costs, resulting in lower prices for consumers.

Because sending information via the Internet is substantially less expensive than other forms of communication and because the time for delivery of information via the Internet is not impacted by the geographic separation of the parties, the growth of Internet-based commerce is likely to result in a significant increase in cross-border transactions. While the international nature of the Internet has been advantageous to many, it has also raised new international legal issues. Although the Internet has certainly made it easier for an Australian national residing in Tokyo to contract with a vineyard in Bordeaux to obtain her favorite wine, it has not helped to reduce the complications resulting from her dissatisfaction with her purchase. In fact, it has compounded them. What does the Australian in our example do when the expensive wine she has ordered arrives looking and tasting very much like grape juice?

The situation may be even worse for the wine distributor in Bordeaux. As an on-line seller, the vineyard faces the unpleasant and uncertain prospect of a number of different national legal systems claiming jurisdiction over its distribution business based on its Web presence and sales through the Internet. The situation has become much more complicated than it was a few years ago, when the vineyard restricted its sales to national consumers. Although its customer base and revenue were smaller when it engaged exclusively in local, off-line transactions, the vineyard could at least count on the predictability of the French legal system.[8] Now, the vineyard's potential client base has widened, but so has its scope of potential liability.

The global availability of the Internet and the large number of different legal systems throughout the world have exacerbated the already difficult task of determining the relevant rules and laws pertaining to one's proposed endeavor on the Internet. To some extent, Web site operators will need to be aware about the laws existing in all countries. Obviously, it will be impossible to be cognizant of all the requirements in all the countries around the world. However, by making one's Web site available on the Internet, operators will be making the site available to individuals throughout the world. As such, it is important that Web site operators become aware of the principal laws of the regions in which they will make their products and services available. In conjunction with such an investigation, Web site operators should also consider limiting the legal availability of their site and its services to those countries in which the operator has a high degree of awareness and legal certainty.

Web Site Operators That Do Business Overseas

Operators that do business overseas through their Web site or are interested in working to develop an international clientele will have to be sensitive to the various rules and legal requirements of those countries in which services will be made available. Even if the company and its servers are physically based in the United States, the Web site operator can still be subject to the jurisdiction of a foreign country for its Web-based activities.

Failing to ensure that one's Web site is in compliance with the relevant laws of the countries in which products and services will be offered could leave the operator exposed to a number of unforeseen consequences. Consider, for instance, the European Data Protection Directive, which will be the subject of more substantial analysis in chapter 4. Pursuant to the terms of this directive, in certain circumstances, European authorities are empowered to block transfers of personal data from inside the European Union to third countries. Now, imagine the consequences if all of a company's customer data from Europe were suddenly blocked because the company failed to provide its European customers with adequate notice and guarantees concerning the protection of their personal information. Becoming well versed in the relevant legal principles of the international jurisdictions in which a Web site will be made available may help to prevent problems such as these.

Web Site Operators That Do Not Do Business Overseas

Web site operators that do not do business overseas and have no intention of pursuing an international presence will have substantially simpler tasks. Instead of focusing on the national laws from a host of different countries and international conventions, domestic operators will be required to focus their energies on ensuring that their site complies with the relevant state and federal laws, rules, and regulations. While doing so, however, it will also be important to include disclaimers and possibly even implement technical means to prevent individuals from countries outside the United States from having access to the site and its services.

THE PURPOSE OF THIS BOOK

The aim of this book is to provide an overview of many of the legal issues involved in creating and operating an e-commerce Web site. It is intended both for companies that do not yet have a large on-line presence and for those that are currently on-line but have concerns about the legal issues involved with Internet commerce and the application of recently passed laws pertaining to the Internet.

Chapter 2, "Getting Started," will provide information about some of the many legal pitfalls that one might encounter when setting up a Web site. In particular, this chapter will explain Web site development and hosting agreements. It will also offer information about the various legal issues that are likely to arise when negotiating such agreements and tips about how small companies can better protect their interests when concluding these types of agreements. Also included in this chapter will be a discussion of domain names. This brief overview of domain names will discuss issues such as selecting and registering a domain name, as well as handling disputes over domain names.

Chapter 3, "Managing Risks through Web Site Terms of Use," will discuss one of the main agreements that all Web site operators should consider developing—a terms-of-use agreement. A properly drafted agreement can help operators control many of the legal risks that are likely to arise through the development and operation of a Web site. Through terms of use, for example, operators can establish conditions under which the materials available on their Web site can be used. Terms of use can also specify who is entitled to access the site. For instance, through terms of use, operators can limit access to the site to individuals who are over the age of eighteen and residents of the United States.

In examining the importance of terms-of-use agreements, this chapter will also examine the enforceability of on-line agreements and provide specific information about the legal treatment of electronic documents and electronic signatures in a number of jurisdictions around the world. This is important because, due to the nature of the Internet, Web sites have a global presence. Accordingly, when offering products and services through a Web site to individuals in other countries, it will be essential to ensure that any agreements concluded with such individuals, including the terms that will govern their use of the Web site, will be valid and enforceable.

Chapter 4, "Internet Privacy Issues," will devote special attention to understanding the affect that the Internet has on the protection of personal information. While the protection of the privacy of personal information has long been an important issue to many individuals, the use of the Internet has complicated existing concerns about the collection, use, and distribution of personally identifiable information. At the same time, personal data has also become an important commodity and, as such, is often at the heart of many Internet-related agreements such as co-branding contracts and on-line marketing deals. This chapter will examine how American and European regulators are responding to the increased privacy risks posed by the Internet. Attention will be devoted to providing Web site operators with techniques to better ensure that they are providing Web site visitors with an adequate level of personal privacy protection.

Chapter 5, "On-Line Advertising and Marketing," will examine the legal issues of advertising and marketing on the Internet. This chapter will provide detailed information about some of the pitfalls involved with advertising on-line and will explore a number of issues including the distribution of unsolicited commercial e-mail. Once again, the legal and regulatory frameworks of a number of different legal jurisdictions will be presented to convey an understanding of the legal issues that may arise when working in a borderless medium such as the Internet.

Chapter 6, "Protecting Property On-Line," explores the various methods that Web site operators can use to better ensure the protection of property on-line. This chapter will include information concerning the ways in which Web site operators can protect their intellectual property that is exposed on-line. It will also include information about protecting one's Web site from computer crime and abuse. In each instance, legal responses to the threat of on-line property theft will be discussed and analyzed.

Chapter 7, the conclusion, will present practical techniques for reviewing one's own Web site to determine if it complies with the main laws and regulations applicable to a particular Web-based endeavor. This chapter presents a useful starting point for examining whether the construction and presentation of a Web site will be exposing the operator to legal risks.

Chapter 2

GETTING STARTED

WHY HAVE A WEB SITE?

There are many reasons to develop a commercial Web site. Today, entities of all types and sizes are finding that a Web site is a productive way to communicate with real and potential customers, suppliers, and business partners. In a short time, the Internet has become an indispensable means for companies to provide information about their products and services and to reach potential customers.

Once the decision to have a Web site has been made, it will be essential to ensure that sufficient resources are devoted to the development and maintenance of the site. One of the most notable aspects of the Internet is that it is highly interactive in nature. When individuals access a Web site—as opposed to hearing an advertisement on the radio or seeing one on television—they have made an affirmative choice to view what that site has to offer. With the competition just a click away, it will be important for businesses to take advantage of this opportunity.

Setting up an Internet Web site has become a key strategy for any business or organization hoping to capitalize on the increasing range of commercial activity occurring on-line. Through the use of Web sites, companies can publicize their products and services, permit users to order their products or services, provide customer services, and facilitate communications between groups of diverse users.

Although creating a Web site can create a number of new and interesting business opportunities, it can also create new liabilities risks for a company. Accordingly, it is essential to adequately address all the special legal issues implicated by the development of a Web site. With this in mind, this chapter will examine some of the key issues likely to arise in some of the preliminary stages of Web site development and launch. Specifically, this chapter will address Web site development, hosting, and domain name selection and registration.

CREATING YOUR WEB SITE

Practical Issues

Once the decision is made to develop a Web site for commercial purposes, it will be time to consider the practical issues involved in moving the site from the planning stage to the functional stage. Just as the precise content and organization of a given Web site will depend on the kind of site that is desired, the scope of the site development and hosting services for which a company will contract will also depend on its needs and intentions for the site. At an elementary level, one of the most basic services a company will require in the context of developing a Web site is file conversion. This will involve converting non-HTML files into HTML and scanning photos or graphics and saving them as GIF or JPEG files. Beyond file conversion, companies are also likely to require services in Web design. This normally involves designing the look and feel of the Web site, including logos and banners, navigation bars or tools, page layout and object placement.[1] Web design will also involve code development, including coding HTML pages, CGI scripts, Java applets, and other applications.

Many entities will also require some system integration services. Insofar as Web sites are concerned, system integration will involve integrating the site with one or more third-party applications, such as chat rooms, search engines, electronic commerce storefronts, and other related activities. Additionally, many companies will require services to integrate the new Web site with the old back-end systems.

It is advisable to determine exactly what will be required from the Web site developer before the developer is actually engaged. Of course, it is often necessary to make alterations to the specifications for the Web site as the development work progresses. However, the more detail that is worked out beforehand, the better.

As a final practical matter, it should be recalled that there is a wide variety of developers performing Web development services. With the tremendous growth of e-commerce, there has also been a growth of related service providers, including Web site developers. Today, companies seeking Web site development services can choose between solo developers and large corporate enterprises and everything in between. Whereas smaller companies may be in better positions to negotiate some of the significant legal issues with solo practitioners, they may find more choices and options with larger companies. Opting for the services of a large company may also prove beneficial in the event that something goes wrong during the development process and it becomes necessary to obtain legal recourse. Determining which type of developer to use will be another key factor in the overall development process.

Legal Issues: A Dissection of Web Site Development Agreements

While one way to obtain Web development services is by assigning the company's employees to perform the desired services, many small or start-up enterprises will not have the resources or the need to employ Web site developers on a full-time basis. Furthermore, many larger companies that have the resources to perform their own development work may opt to engage the services of professional Web site developers. Accordingly, many companies will contract with a developer to develop their Web site on an independent contractor basis. While the use of such independent contractors is a common practice, it also raises a host of legal issues that need to be addressed in the Web site development agreement.

Once an appropriate Web site developer is located, substantial time and effort will have to be devoted to reviewing and revising the Web site development agreement that will establish the terms and conditions for the development work. Most developers' Web site development agreements will be very short and will often fail to address many of the important issues that will be in the company's interests to address. As such, the company's review of the developer's proposed Web site development agreement will necessitate more than simply reviewing the existing language. Instead, in most cases it will also necessitate the addition of certain key provisions.

There are several key issues to consider when examining an agreement presented by a Web site developer. One of the most important issues in a Web site development agreement is that of ownership. It is also the issue that is likely to cause the most contention when negotiating the agreement. The recommended starting point for most customers is that all development work will be performed as work made for hire, with the customer having all ownership rights.

It is likely that many Web site developers will resist this approach. Often Web site developers will be concerned that accepting such broad ownership provisions will negatively affect their ability to use various materials, tools, and concepts employed in creating one company's Web site when performing work for other customers. However, by insisting that the work performed will be a "work made for hire," the customer's objective is not to limit the developer from using its tools and preexisting materials in developing other Web sites. As such, a company obtaining Web development services may respond to Web site developers' concerns about the ownership issue by insisting that all of the development work will be performed as a work made for hire, with sole and exclusive ownership of the deliverables reserved to the customer, but excluding all of the developer's tools and preexisting materials from the customer's ownership.

Regardless of where the parties ultimately arrive in negotiating the issue of ownership, it is essential that the agreement clearly define such rights. For the company engaging the services of the Web site developer, it is crucial that the development agreement actually spell out that the work is being performed as a "work made for hire," as the term is construed under U.S. copyright laws,[2] and that the company owns work product prepared by the developer in the course of performing the services under the agreement. Failing to include such a provision could have disastrous results for the company, since without it, the developer can retain all intellectual property rights in the developed work product. In addition to including the "work for hire" language, companies retaining the services of Web site developers should also ensure that the agreement takes the belts-and-suspenders approach and specifies that in the event that any portion of the work product is not a "work for hire," then the developer assigns all rights in the developed product to the company. The inclusion of such language should provide the company with further assurances that it will own all intellectual property rights in the developed works. Box 2.1 presents an example of ownership language that is favorable to the customer obtaining the services of a Web site developer.

It should be noted that the customer-favorable language contained in box 2.1 is basic language designed to target the singular issue of the ownership of the works that are developed by the developer while performing the Web site development services. A more complete ownership section will often address additional issues such as excluding any of the developer's preexisting software and other tools from the list of works

Box 2.1
Customer-Favorable Ownership Section

Ownership of the Works

The Services provided by Developer and the Developed Works shall constitute "works made for hire" for Customer, as that phrase is defined in Section 101 of the Copyright Act of 1976 (Title 17, United States Code). Customer shall be considered the author and shall be the copyright owner of the Developed Works. If any of the Developed Works do not qualify for treatment as "works for hire," Developer hereby grants, assigns, and transfers to Customer ownership of all United States and international copyrights and all other intellectual property rights in the Developed Works, free and clear of any and all claims for royalties or other compensation. Developer agrees to give Customer, and its representatives, any assistance required to perfect the rights defined in this Section, including, but not limited to, executing and delivering all documents requested by Customer.

owned by the customer and granting a license to the customer for use of those preexisting works.

In addition to the paramount issue of ownership, in negotiating a Web site development agreement, it is important to ensure that the agreement adequately addresses concerns about timing. Time will usually be of the essence for companies engaging the services of Web site developers. The Internet changes at an extremely rapid pace, and the longer that companies wait for the completion of their development work to finish, the greater the likelihood that such companies will be placed at a competitive disadvantage. To ensure that concerns about timing are met, the agreement should contain a rigorous schedule along with appropriate remedies should the developer fail to meet the timetable.

Many customers obtaining Web development services also desire the inclusion of an acceptance clause. Such a provision would specify, for instance, that all of the developed works are subject to the acceptance of the customer. The clause would also provide for certain corrective procedures if the customer does not deem the developed works to be acceptable. Additionally, the acceptance clause should specify that any payment obligations or other responsibilities of the customer will not commence until after the customer's acceptance of the developed works. Box 2.2 provides a sample of a customer-friendly acceptance provision.

Considerable attention should also be directed to the pricing and payment terms of the agreement. Often, Web site developers are interested in being paid on an hourly basis as they complete the work. It is in the customer's interest, however, to pay the developer a flat fee for its work

---

Box 2.2
Customer-Favorable Acceptance Section

Acceptance

All Developed Works are subject to Customer's Acceptance. Customer is not required to pay for any Developed Works deemed unacceptable by Customer. Customer shall notify Developer of its Acceptance or rejection of all Developed Works within thirty (30) days of Customer's receipt thereof. In the event of a rejection of any Developed Works, Developer shall have five (5) days to correct any deficiencies and resubmit the Developed Work(s) to Customer. As used herein, "Acceptance" shall means the receipt by Customer of written notice from Customer that the Developed Works have been reviewed and accepted by Customer.

---

and to defer as much of the payment as possible. Ideally, a large portion of the payments should be deferred until after the customer has had an opportunity to review and accept the developer's work. Being able to hold back some of the payments may also prove valuable in the event that the developer is unable to meet the agreed-on project deadlines.

Before the developer begins work, it is necessary to select the platform on which the Web site will reside. Furthermore, the company contracting the developer must also determine if the Web site will be optimized for a particular browser and if the Web site will offer certain features that cannot be accessed by certain browsers.

For the customer obtaining Web site development services, it will be important to pursue contractual measures that will restrict the service provider from making unauthorized modifications to the site. At a minimum, if the developer is given the right to make some modifications to the site, the customer will want an opportunity to review and approve these modifications before the Web site actually goes "live."

Some Final Tips

When reviewing a draft of a Web site development agreement, it is important to ensure that the agreement is sufficiently thorough to address the most significant concerns. It will usually be to the company's advantage to spend adequate time reviewing and revising the agreement prior to the commencement of the development services rather than to attempt to respond to and address problems that arise after the development work has commenced. In this regard, several important questions should be considered when evaluating the negotiated Web site development agreement.

- What are the responsibilities of each party?
- What are the procedures for feedback, corrections, and change orders?
- What is the acceptance procedure?
- Are the customer's payment obligations tied to acceptance?
- What are the pricing issues?
- Who will own the rights in the developed site and related materials such as drafts and specifications?
- What are the developer's rights and obligations with regard to customer data collected through the site?
- Are milestones and deadlines laid out clearly in the agreement?
- What are the remedies for delay or failure?

By the time the negotiations of the agreement have been completed, the responses to these questions should be clear within the text of the agreement. If upon final review of the agreement, the responses to these questions are not clear, further revision of the agreement should be considered.

OBTAINING HOSTING SERVICES

Practical Issues

After the Web site has been developed, the company must choose an appropriate service provider to furnish hosting services for the site, if this has not already been done.[3] Some companies will host their own sites, but many small and medium-size enterprises do not have the resources to maintain their own server to host their site or have other reasons for selecting a third-party host. This section will examine some of the primary practical and legal issues that are likely to arise when contracting for hosting services.

The term "hosting" is used frequently when discussing various different services provided to Web site operators. While "hosting" is often used in a generic sense, it is important to note that the term can actually encompass a number of distinct services. First, the term can be used to refer simply to the hosting of the Web site on the service provider's servers. In a typical hosting relationship, the service provider provides the servers and software in addition to the connection to the Internet. In some hosting arrangements, the customer is solely responsible for managing the site's content, while in others, the service provider may agree to update some or all of the content on a regular basis. Whichever arrangement is chosen, the specifics of the parties' obligations should be outlined clearly in the agreement. Unfortunate consequences could arise if the customer assumes that the hosting service provider is responsible for updating the site content and subsequently discovers that the service agreement provides otherwise.

The term "hosting" can also include collocation. Collocation, another form of hosting, occurs when the customer locates customer-owned servers at the service provider's facility. In the collocation scenario, it is the service provider's responsibility to connect the servers to the Internet and, usually, to ensure that the servers are operable. In a simple collocation relationship, the service provider will not manipulate content on the servers. Often service providers providing collocation services offer additional services, such as reselling equipment or software.

Co-branding arrangements can also be considered as a form of Web site hosting. In a typical co-branding scenario, the Web site owner would co-brand pages of its Web site on a third party's servers. It is possible to conceptualize these co-branded pages as being hosted by the third party.

Another option for obtaining necessary hosting services is to outsource one or more functions of the Web site to a third-party service provider. Outsourcing shares some similarities with co-branding in that the service provider is operating software for the customer. However, in an outsourcing relationship, the Web site operator becomes dependent on the service provider for the particular function that has been outsourced.

Finally, it is also important to note that in addition to straight hosting services, many service providers offer additional services such as search engine registration, domain name registration, and on-line promotional activities. Normally these are additional offers that can be accepted or declined depending on the company's circumstances and the terms of the deal that the service provider is offering.

Regardless of which types of hosting services are desired, it will be important to conduct a thorough investigation of the prospective service provider. Today, many different companies offer Web hosting services. While there may be a tendency to select a service provider that offers the most reasonably priced services, Web site operators will need to search for a hosting service provider that can provide reliable, secure, uninterrupted, redundant, and high-speed access to the Internet.

Legal Issues: A Dissection of Web Hosting Agreements

The agreement that a company enters into with the hosting service provider will be of great importance. The hosting agreement will govern significant issues such as the uptime of the site. Most companies will seek to compel the service provider to ensure that the Web site will be operational 24 hours a day, seven days per week, without exception. Having the site inaccessible for even a small period of time can cause the site operator to lose valuable Web traffic and can lead to lowered consumer perceptions of the site. With this in mind, this section will examine some of the most important provisions in a Web hosting agreement.

Performance Standards

Preeminent among the provisions in a typical Web site hosting agreement is the issue of performance standards. To ensure that the provider of the Web hosting services does so in accordance with the site operator's needs, the hosting agreement should specify that the hosting entity must host the site in accordance with specific service level standards. The precise content of these service level standards, which will depend on the characteristics of the Web site and the needs of the site operator, should be specified clearly within the agreement. The agreement should also contain language indicating that the service level standards will apply regardless of the cause of any disruptions in service and even if the disruption is caused by matters beyond the control of the host. Although certain service providers may demonstrate an initial reluctance to include such service guarantees, they are actually quite common, and most customers should not experience too much difficulty in ensuring that guarantees are included in the hosting agreement. At a minimum, the service level standards should address the following issues: (1) availability of the Web site, (2) response time, (3) bandwidth, and (4) security, each as discussed in further detail hereafter.

Availability Uptime is one of the crucial considerations in Web site hosting agreements. Loss of operational time is detrimental to a company's business, especially when potential customers can access competitive products and services by clicking on the next site. There are a number of ways to address the issue of uptime contractually. It is customary to pursue guarantees of Web site availability, all of which can be considered by companies obtaining Web hosting services. For instance, customers could contemplate compelling the service provider to represent and warrant that the Web site will be made available to users a certain percentage of time during any 24-hour period or any seven-day period. In this regard, it is important to note that specifying a time period to measure the availability of the Web site will be essential. After all, maintaining that the Web site will be available 95 percent of the time during every 24-hour period is different from maintaining that the site will be available 95 percent of the time during the year.

When including provisions providing that the Web site will be available for a certain percentage of time in a given time period, it will also be useful to further provide that there will be no period of interruption in accessibility to the Web site that exceeds a certain number of continuous hours. In each of these cases, the exact numbers for availability percentages and for permitted downtime will depend on the characteristics of the Web site, the needs of the site operator, and the parties' respective bargaining power.

Response Time Response time is another immensely important issue when negotiating a Web hosting agreement. It is essential to conclude contracts that will help to ensure that individuals who access the Web site will receive a response within an appropriate time period. Slow response time can translate into long waits for Web site visitors, causing them to become frustrated and to look elsewhere for the desired product, service, or information. The guarantees pertaining to response time should apply when the Web site is being used at high capacity levels.

Bandwidth Web site operators should also ensure that the Web hosting agreement specifies that the service provider will provide the operator with a certain amount of dedicated bandwidth at all times. In this context, bandwidth refers to the amount of data that can be transmitted in a fixed amount of time. It can be thought of as the width of the pipe through which the information will travel. In addition to specifying the amount of bandwidth, the hosting agreement should also specify that the bandwidth will be fully dedicated, switched, and redundant through all Internet access points.

Security Security is an extremely important issue for Web site operators of all sizes and industries. Individuals who are uncertain about a Web site's security, especially if the site is offering e-commerce services, may be less likely to visit that site and may be reluctant to provide that site with their personal information and credit card information. Furthermore, there is a growing body of laws that requires entities that process personally identifiable information to implement certain security measures to protect such information. That being said, it is not always the service provider that will have control over the site's security. Whether the service provider has such control and whether the provider should be obligated to ensure the security of the site will depend on the system configuration and on the allocation of responsibilities between the parties.

In situations where the service provider does have some control of security issues, the Web site operator should seek to oblige the provider contractually to take proactive steps to prevent security breaches and to develop processes for fixing known security breaches once identified. At minimum, Web site operators should compel their service providers to notify them when security breaches or security holes are identified.

Other Considerations In addition to these primary concerns, many Web site operators may wish to consider pursuing other contractual provisions to protect their site and their interests. System redundancy, for instance, is another issue that site operators may wish to address. To reduce the likelihood of negative consequences resulting from server problems, it is in a Web site operator's interests to compel the provider to mirror servers or to connect customers' servers via multiple Internet service providers.

The agreement with the party providing hosting services should also obligate the service provider to continuously monitor the Web site and the Internet to ensure proper load balancing and traffic routing. In this regard, the parties can also agree to an escalation procedure, whereby the service provider will agree to take certain predefined steps to correct server and traffic irregularities. At a minimum, such escalation procedures should consist of (1) immediate notification of the identified problem to the Web site owner, (2) a system that tracks the correction procedures taken and their status, and (3) a guarantee that only certified technicians will be used to correct software-based errors.

It may also be advantageous to pursue assurances about user support. "User support" is a broad term, and it will take effort to clarify the parties' respective obligations with respect to inquiries by, and concerns of, the Web site's users. For instance, the site operator may be in the best position to respond to substantive customer service inquires, such as "I did not receive my order for the black boots I bought on-line three weeks ago," whereas the service provider may be in the best position to respond to inquiries involving technical issues, such as the failure of a certain URL to load correctly or the failure of a correct password to work. Accordingly, the agreement should clearly identify the respective obligations of each party in this area. Additionally Web site operators will wish to include standards for professionalism and promptness when responding to customer service inquiries that fall within the host's range of responsibility. The agreement should also specify any escalation procedures for instances in which the service provider's efforts are ineffective. Without such guarantees, the reputation of the company can be damaged by the negative behavior of the customer service representatives of the hosting service provider.

An additional and highly controversial area of potential concern is that of user data. In this increasingly networked age, customer data have become an important commodity. At the same time, legislative requirements and customer demands are making the privacy of customer data a very sensitive issue.[4] Accordingly, the issue of ownership and control of personal data will arise in many agreements, including agreements between the Web site operator and its service providers. Because the service provider's servers are collecting information from or about users, as a first step, Web site operators will be interested in compelling the service provider to provide copies of the server logs applicable to the Web site. Most service providers now provide raw, unprocessed server logs at no additional cost, but reports derived from the server logs may have a separate price tag. In any event, it is crucial for businesses to get this data so that they can learn more about the site's users.

To prevent any potential disputes about privacy, it is important to limit the ability of the service provider to use or transfer such data. If a company loses control of the personally identifiable data that it has collected, it can have profound effects on the company's business—potentially leaving the site's users exposed to unsolicited commercial e-mail, or spam, providing the company's competitors with a targeted list of potential customers for their own goods or services, educating the company's competitors about the true inner workings of the Web site, and leaving the company exposed to potential lawsuits and liability. Moreover, as will be discussed in further detail in chapter 4, companies are under increasing legal pressure to maintain the security and confidentiality of the personally identifiable data that they collect. For all of the foregoing, it is best for the Web site operator to ensure that it has exclusive ownership of all user data. Additionally, exclusive ownership rights should be backed up with confidentiality provisions limiting the ability of the hosting service provider to disclose user data.

The agreement should also specify the service provider's post-termination responsibilities. Many agreements prepared by service providers will be silent with regard to the provider's responsibilities in the event of a termination of the relationship between the Web site operator and the service provider; however, this is an important issue that the site operator should address in the agreement.

The operator should ensure that it has the greatest control over termination and endeavor to minimize the number of circumstances in which the provider can unilaterally shut down the Web site or otherwise stop performing under the agreement. Additionally, the site operator should pursue the inclusion of a procedure for the service provider to transfer the Web site to a new provider and to cooperate with all aspects of such a transition. This procedure should include time periods and effective remedies for failure to perform the transition services. Ideally, the service provider's obligation to provide transition should apply even if the termination of the agreement is due to the customer's breach. An example of simple transition language is presented in box 2.3. This language merely compels the service provider to provide the customer with commercially reasonable assistance in transferring the hosted Web site either to the customer's server or to a third-party server. Depending on the particular nature of the deal, the customer may require a much more elaborate transition services provision.

There are other steps that Web site operators should take to prevent potential difficulties at termination. For instance, to reduce the likelihood that a service provider will hold the customer's Web site hostage, the customer should plan for eventual transition of the site by obtaining a complete copy of the Web site periodically during the course of the relationship. Where feasible, the service provider should deliver a complete copy frequently, often on a monthly basis, so that a minimal amount of data will be lost if a customer makes a forced emergency transition. Without the inclusion of provisions obliging the hosting service provider to provide termination services, there is a risk that the Web site operator's business and reputation can be damaged severely by the delay tactics of the service provider.

Some Final Tips

When reviewing a draft of the Web hosting agreement, it is important to ensure that the agreement is sufficiently thorough to address the most significant concerns of the company seeking such services. It will usually be to the advantage of the company obtaining the hosting services to spend additional time reviewing the agreement at the start rather than responding to and attempting to address problems that arise after the execution of the agreement. In this regard, there are several important

---

Box 2.3
Simple Transition Services Provision

Transition of Web Site
Upon termination of the Agreement, Service Provider shall provide Company with commercially reasonable assistance to transfer the Web site from Service Provider's Server to Service Provider or a third party designated by Company.

questions that companies should consider when evaluating the negotiated Web site development agreement.

- Have concerns about (1) availability, (2) response time, (3) bandwidth, and (4) security of the Web site been addressed adequately?
- What are the payment terms?
- Are the parties' responsibilities with respect to customer service delineated clearly?
- What are the parties' rights and obligations with respect to user data?
- Does the agreement compel the hosting service provider to provide sufficient transition services?

By the time the negotiations of the hosting agreement have been completed and the parties are ready to execute the agreement, the customer should be able to answer the foregoing questions. If upon final review of the agreement, the responses to these questions, as well as all other key issues, are not clear, further revision of the agreement should be considered.

SELECTING AND REGISTERING YOUR DOMAIN NAME

Choosing a Domain Name

Selecting an appropriate domain name is an important part of the development of a successful Web site. The importance of a domain name to a Web site is analogous to the location of a physical business in the off-line world. A high-impact, easily accessible domain name can help to draw visitors to one's Web site. Accordingly, many companies devote considerable resources to selecting and promoting their domain names.

The quest to obtain an ideal domain name has become increasingly difficult. As the use and popularity of the Internet has grown, so too has the number of individuals and entities registering their domain names. The result of this is that there are fewer domain names available. Businesses attempting to register a new domain name at this stage in the game may find that they will be required to either negotiate with, or even commence a legal action against, the current rights holder.

The choice of a domain name will depend on a number of factors, including the company's name, industry, and products and services. Most companies will desire to register some variation of their name and may also register some of their lead products or services. There are a number of other tips that should be considered when selecting a domain name. Box 2.4 presents a summary of several important tips that should be considered when selecting a domain name.

Registering a Domain Name

Once the domain name is selected, it will be necessary to register the name with a domain name registration entity. However, prior to registering a domain name, it may be useful to have some knowledge about the Domain Name System. The Domain Name System is set up to make regular words map to Internet protocol (IP) addresses.[5] Domain names are organized hierarchically. At the highest level is the top-level domain (TLD). At present, three TLDs are commonly used worldwide: .com, .org, and .net. According to the original plan of the domain system, the .com TLD is reserved for commercial firms, .org for nonprofit organizations, .net for computer networks, .edu for educational institutions, and .gov for federal governmental bodies. Under current practices, however, most entities register their domain names across all of the TLDs except for .gov and .edu. A less common TLD is the designation .us. This is the country code for the United States. Anyone can register a domain name in .us, but because of the cumbersome naming convention required,

---

Box 2.4
Key Tips in Selecting a Domain Name

- The characters eligible for use are alphabetic (a–z), numeric (0–9), minus sign (–), and period (.).
- The name can comprise a maximum total of 26 characters, including the top-level designation.
- The first character must be alphabetic.
- Periods have special uses, so do not use them unless you desire one of the special uses.
- The last character cannot be a minus sign or a period.
- There can be no spaces in a domain name.
- Single-character names are not allowed.
- Do not use the word "gateway," unless the server is actually a gateway.
- Avoid domain names that are confusing or possibly offensive.
- Do not infringe on someone else's trademarked name.

the .us TLD is mostly used by schools, libraries, counties, and other state and local governmental jurisdictions. For example, the URL for the Department of Community and Economic Development of the State of Alaska is http://www.dced.state.ak.us, and the Web site for the New York state division of the budget is located at http://www.budget.state.ny.us.

After a number of proposals to increase the number of TLDs, on November 16, 2000, the board of directors of the Internet Corporation for Assigned Names and Numbers (ICANN) announced its selection for the new TLDs as (1) .aero, (2) .biz, (3) .coop, (4) .info, (5) .museum, (6) .name, and (7) .pro.[6]

Although the Internet is a global medium, the vast majority of domain name registrations, at least initially, occurred in the United States. Recently, however, as the global use of the Internet has increased, foreign governments and organizations have increased the use and development of country code domains. Internationally, domain name authorities have designated numerous additional TLDs, referred to as country codes. Examples include .fr for France, .be for Belgium, and .ch for Switzerland. There are several domain name registrars that specialize in international country codes. However, many national domain name registrars have a number of prerequisites that will have to be met before an individual or entity can register a domain name using their country code. For instance, many national registrars require that the registrant have a physical presence in the country. Polices for such local physical presence vary widely from one country to another. Still, the trend does appear to be moving away from stringent national regulation of country codes. In recent years, a number of localities, including, for instance, Belgium, have liberalized their systems to allow for registrations from entities that lack a physical presence within the territory. Appendix 1 presents a list of the current country codes, along with the means for contacting the national registrars in each of the jurisdictions.

The costs and procedures involved in registering a domain name will vary depending on the precise domain registration entity. When the Domain Name System was first set up, Network Solutions, under a contract with the U.S. government, was given responsibility for assigning domain names. The Web site for Network Solutions is located at www.networksolutions.com, and the company will register a domain name for one year for $35. However, the yearly fee decreases as the term of registration increases. For instance, a ten-year registration is $150, or $15 per year.[7] Registering a domain name with Network Solutions is an easy process. Its Web site is very user friendly, and visitors are able to verify the availability of their selected domain name from the home page of the site. If the name is available, the prospective registrant will be able to register the name by completing five steps: (1) name the site; (2) choose and additional services to accompany the domain name registration; (3) review the shopping cart: (4) provide the information; and (5) pay and check out.

Recently, however, ICANN began to accredit other companies to register domain names in the United States and abroad.[8] Additionally, many of the companies that are offering domain name registration services also offer other services such as Web site hosting and e-mail forwarding. One of the biggest advantages of these registrars is that they often allow the user to register a domain name across a number of different TLDs. Table 2.1 contains a list of some of the numerous ICANN-approved U.S.-based registrars. This is not intended to be an all-inclusive listing of companies providing such registration services, nor is the listing of any company in Table 2.1 intended to represent any endorsement or recommendation of the company.

Disputes over Domain Names

With the growing number of Web sites, there has been increased competition for domain names, resulting in a number of disputes over domain names.[9] While some of the disputes over domain names have been a result of pure competition for limited resources, there have also been a number of instances in which individuals have intentionally registered another company's trademarked name with the hopes of then selling that name back to the company for a large profit. Such individuals are often referred to as "cybersquatters" or "cyberpirates."

In response to concerns about cybersquatting,[10] on November 29, 1999, Congress passed the Anticybersquatting Consumer Protection Act (the "Anticybersquatting Act"). The Anticybersquatting Act was passed as an amendment to the Lanham Act and provides a separate cause of action against those who register a domain name with a "bad faith intent to profit."[11] Pursuant to the legislation, the domain name at issue must be identical or confusingly similar to a distinctive or famous mark or dilutive of a famous mark.[12] Before the passage of the Anticybersquatting Act, many owners of trademark registrations seeking to recover a domain name registration from a cybersquatter commenced court actions alleging traditional causes of action such as unfair competition and trademark infringement.

In determining "bad faith," the act sets forth nine nonexhaustive factors for courts to consider.[13] The first factor is meant to identify situa-

Table 2.1
A Sampling of U.S.-based Registrars

Registrar Name	URL	Accredited Top-Level Domains
Address Creation	http://www.addresscreation.com	.biz, .com, .info, .name, .net, .org
Amazon Registrar, Inc.	http://registrar.amazon.com	.biz, .com, .info, .net, .org
BulkRegister.com	http://bulkregistrar.com	.biz, .com, .info, .name, .net, .org, .pro
Catalog.com	http://catalog.com	.biz, .com, .info, .name, .net, .org
DomainName, Inc.	http://domainname.com	.biz, .com, .info, .name, .net, .org
DomainPro, Inc.	http://domainpro.com	.biz, .com, .info, .name, .net, .org
DomainRegistry.com Inc.	http://domainregistry.com	.biz, .com, .info, .net, .org
DomainZoo.com, Inc.	http://domainzoo.com	.com, .net, .org
Dotster, Inc.	http://dotster.com	.biz, .com, .info, .name, .net, .org
Hosting-Network, Inc.	http://hosting-network.com	.biz, .com, .info, .name, .net, .org
Intercosmos Media Group, Inc.	http://directnic.com	.biz, .com, .info, .name, .net, .org, .pro
Namesecure.com, Inc.	http://namesecure.com	.biz, .com, .info, .name, .net, .org
Register.com, Inc.	http://register.com	.biz, .com, .info, .name, .net, .org, .pro
Stargate.com, Inc.	http://stargateinc.com	.biz, .com, .info, .net, .org
USA Webhost	http://usawebhost.com	.biz, .com, .info, .name, .net, .org
Wild West Domains, Inc.	http://wildwestdomains.com	.biz, .com, .info, .name, .net, .org

tions where there are two (or more) rightful trademark owners both asserting rights to a particular domain name. Such a situation could arise, for instance, if the name of one company was the same as the name of a key product of another company. In such a case, both entities may desire the domain name, but obviously only one can have it.

The second factor examines the extent to which the domain name is the same as the registrant's own legal name or name by which a person is identified. Such a case could arise if, for instance, an individual named John Cisco registered the name "Cisco," not intending to infringe on the rights of the company with the same name but simply because Cisco was indeed his name.

The third factor to be considered concerns the registrant's prior use of the domain name in the offering of goods or services.[14] The purpose of this factor appears to be twofold. First, it can be used by courts to recognize a legitimate business owner who has a bona fide interest in the domain name and is not attempting to trade off of the goodwill created by the trademark holder. Second, it can also be used in determining whether the registrant had been previously marketing goods or services under the trademarked name without causing confusion.

According to the fourth factor, the act instructs courts to examine whether the registrant has put up a Web site that is accessible under the domain name and makes legitimate or fair use of the name.[15] The crux of this factor will be determining whether there is any bad-faith intent to profit.

For the fifth factor, the analysis shifts to an assessment of whether there are indicators of bad faith.[16] When conducting this analysis, courts will look at whether the registrant intended to divert customers from the trademark owner's site either for commercial gain or to tarnish or disparage the mark by causing confusion about its source or affiliation. There have been a number of examples of this, including the registration of whitehouse.com by a pornography site.

The sixth factor is intended to catch "traditional" cybersquatting. As such, it looks at whether the registrant has offered to transfer, sell, or otherwise assign the domain name to the mark owner or any other party for more than out-of-pocket expense without having used the domain name in the bona fide offering of goods or services or has engaged in a pattern of similar conduct in past situations.[17]

Pursuant to the seventh factor, the courts will determine whether the registrant has used false contact information when registering the domain name.[18] According to the eighth factor, courts should consider if the registrant has engaged in a pattern of acquiring multiple domain names that are identical to, confusingly similar to, or dilutive of others' marks, without regard to the goods and services offered.[19] Finally, the courts will look at the extent to which the mark incorporated in the domain name is distinctive and famous under § 43(c)(1) of the Lanham Act.[20]

The Anticybersquatting Act provides aggrieved parties with two major weapons: election of statutory money damages in lieu of traditional Lanham Act damages[21] and in rem jurisdiction.[22] As to the first weapon, the statute provides for monetary damages of $1,000 to $100,0000 per domain name.[23] As for the second weapon, the act also provides for in rem jurisdiction when the abusive domain name registrant cannot be found.[24] The in rem action is filed against the name itself in the juris-diction in which it was registered.[25]

Although the Anticybersquatting Act provides aggrieved parties with useful weapons, it is not the only way for trademark holders to pursue their rights. Instead of, or in addition to, the Anticybersquatting Act, trademark holders can file a complaint under the ICANN Uniform Dis-pute Resolution Policy (UDRP). All accredited registrars of Internet do-main names follow the UDRP.

The arbitration proceeding pursuant to the UDRP is quick and rela-tively inexpensive. Additionally, a review of past UDRP findings sug-gests that the process may be geared toward favoring the trademark holders. To be successful under the UDRP, the party bringing the claim must demonstrate (1) that the domain name is identical or confusingly similar to a trademark or service mark, (2) that the registrant has no rights or legitimate interest in the domain names, and (3) that the domain name has been registered and is being used in bad faith. In instances in which there is manifested bad faith, such as a case of cybersquatting, the UDRP provides for an expedited administrative proceeding where the holder of trademark rights may initiate a complaint by filing a com-plaint with an approved dispute-resolution provider.

Whether one should chose to litigate or arbitrate the matter using the UDRP will depend on a number of factors. Clearly there are a number of pros and cons to both of the procedures. Relying on the UDRP is usually less expensive and more expedient. On the other hand, with its provisions on injunctive relief and statutory damages ranging from $1,000 to $100,000 per domain name, the Anticybersquatting Act should also be an effective tool against cybersquatters.

CONCLUSION

This chapter has examined some of the most significant legal com-ponents of the initial development of a Web site: Web site development agreements, Web site hosting agreements, and the registration of a do-main name. A company's selection of Web site developers and hosting service providers, along with the negotiation of the relevant agreements in both these areas, will have substantial implications for how the Web site will look and operate in the days and months to come. When ne-gotiated effectively, Web site development and hosting agreements define all of the operational and functional specifications for the Web site, pro-vide for predictability, allocate responsibilities for errors and downtime, and establish the parties' respective rights and responsibilities. As such, it is essential that businesses devote sufficient energy and attention to this process. While it may appear to be less burdensome and less costly to accept whatever form agreement the prospective developer or host may offer, in the long run such an approach is likely to be disadvantageous.

In chapter 3, the discussion will move on to some of the most important contractual issues that arise when operating an e-commerce Web site. Whether a business is in the process of developing a new Web site or revising an existing one, contractual issues are likely to come into play. Even if the intended Web site will be solely informational and will not provide users with the opportunity to purchase goods or services, contractual issues will still arise if you desire to compel users to become bound by Web site terms and conditions, a practice that is recommended.

Chapter 3

MANAGING RISKS THROUGH WEB SITE TERMS OF USE

WEB SITE TERMS OF USE

The Need for Terms of Use

It is clear that the use of a Web site can contribute significantly to a company's commercial success, irrespective of whether such company is itself involved in the technology industry. In fact, the Web site has become such a commonly used business tool that the inherent legal risks involved with using a Web site are often not given the attention that they deserve. While it is true that a Web site can bring new business and revenues to a company, it can also result in losses to the company if steps are not taken to manage the liability risks that often result from the operation of a Web site. One effective way to respond to some of the legal risks that can result from operating a Web site is to develop and post a terms-of-use agreement (hereafter "Terms of Use") and require all Web site visitors to consent to the Terms of Use before being allowed to use the site. Such Terms of Use will establish the terms and conditions under which the site may be accessed and the information therein may be used.

While all companies operating Web sites share similar risks, there is no single form Terms of Use that will work for all Web sites. Instead, the scope and contents of a Terms of Use will depend on a number of factors, including the company's scope of operations, the materials and services available on or through the Web site, the target audience of the given Web site, and the company's level of risk tolerance. While each company is likely to have its own specific requirements for its Terms of Use, most companies are likely to have similar reasons for requiring a Terms of Use on their Web sites. For one, developing and posting a Terms of Use can help to ensure compliance with applicable law. A Terms of Use may also be necessary to establish terms and conditions to protect the intellectual property available on the Web site. Through clauses pertaining to disclaimers of warranties and limitations of liability, the Terms of Use can also help the Web site operator to manage liabilities that arise in connection with the operation of the site. Terms of Use can also be used to establish other conditions and restrictions on the use of the Web site and its materials and content. Finally, Terms of Use can help to improve user confidence and use of the site.

Top Reasons for Posting a Terms of Use

1. Ensure compliance with applicable law.
2. Protect intellectual property.
3. Manage potential risks and liabilities.
4. Establish conditions and restrictions on the use of the Web site and its materials.
5. Improve user confidence and encourage Web site usage.

Consider first the importance of complying with applicable law. Operating a Web site on the Internet, a medium without national boundaries, has the potential of implicating many different laws. In some instances, having a properly drafted Terms of Use can help to reduce the risk that a company operating a Web site will be held liable for violating applicable law by virtue of its operation of the site. A number of laws and regulations, including the U.S. export regulations and certain privacy laws, impose criminal penalties on violators, some of which may even involve prison sentences. Accordingly, it is important to ensure that the Web site does not violate any laws. While ensuring compliance with applicable law will surely necessitate a full review of the entire Web site, the drafting of the Terms of Use should also take legal and regulatory compliance into consideration. For instance, ensuring compliance with applicable law may also entail putting users on notice that the Web site is available for use only in particular jurisdictions.[1] As will be discussed later in this chapter, if there is uncertainty regarding the legal requirements of a certain foreign jurisdiction, it is often best to prohibit users from that jurisdiction from being able to access the Web site.

The Terms of Use can also contribute significantly to protecting intellectual property. Posting the Terms of Use can help a Web site operator achieve two important goals related to intellectual property. First, by identifying and reserving the owner's rights to the intellectual property available on the Web site, the Terms of Use can protect the site operator's intellectual property from unauthorized actions such as copying. Second, by inserting proper disclaimers and warnings, a Terms of Use can insulate the operator from potential liability that may result from allegations that the site is infringing a third party's intellectual property rights or breaching the terms of the licensed agreement pursuant to which such content was procured. Both of these issues will be discussed in further detail later in the chapter.

Terms of Use also permit a Web site owner to manage potential liabilities through a number of means, such as a disclaimer of warranties regarding the operation and function of the site and the goods and services available on the site. For example, an operator providing information should consider posting Terms of Use disclaiming any inaccuracies or errors in the information, whether the information is provided by the site operator or by third parties. This is particularly important if the information provided consists of stock quotes, for instance, or other information that individuals rely on in making investment decisions.

Terms of Use are also necessary to establish other conditions and restrictions on users that are necessary in the course of business or that provide important legal protections to the Web site operator. These conditions and restrictions include many of the same types of provisions that are needed in off-line agreements, including forum selection, choice of law, the establishment of conditions in which linking and framing may be permitted, the establishment of indemnification obligations, and the reservation of the Web site operator's right to disclose information if required by law.

Finally, irrespective of the relevant legal considerations, many Web site operators will include a Terms of Use as part of good business practices. While it is true that lengthy Terms of Use agreements may appear intimidating to some users, the inclusion of Terms of Use can actually be reassuring to Web site users. By reviewing a carefully drafted Terms of Use, users will have a clear idea about the policies and practices of the Web site operator and may thus feel more comfortable using the site.

Drafting the Terms of Use

Although there is no effective "one size fits all" approach to developing the Terms of Use, certain provisions will be useful for most Web site operators.[2] Initially, the Terms of Use should introduce the Web site visitor to the company and its site. This introductory paragraph can also set forth definitions and other terms that are used throughout the Terms of Use and indicate the last date on which the Web site was updated. While there are many different formulas that can be used to accomplish this purpose, an example introductory paragraph is contained in box 3.1.

If the Web site for which the Terms of Use have been developed is protected by passwords or other security measures, it will also be advantageous to include a brief statement concerning the distribution of user IDs and passwords. Such a provision also explains the obligation of the Web site user to maintain the confidentiality of his or her user ID and password and, depending on the nature of the Web site, can specify that the Web site user will be responsible for all activity and transactions conducted under his or user ID and password.

After introducing the user to the Terms of Use, it will be useful to provide an explanation of the permitted uses of the Web site and any materials available through the Site. Such an explanation will depend to a great extent on the kinds of information and services that are available on the Web site. For instance, because of obligations imposed in the agreements with its content providers, a Web site that offers compilations of news from a number of different sources may have to place considerably more conditions and restrictions on the use of the information available on the site than a Web site that simply offers its own brochureware.

The site operator should also consider including an indemnification clause. There are a number of ways through which a Web site user's use of a Web site can result in third-party claims against the site operator, and the Web site operator should act to protect itself against such claims.

Box 3.1
Sample Introductory Paragraph

Welcome to the Company X Web site at [URL of Web site] (the "Site"). Company X (referred to as "CX," "we," "us," or "our," as applicable) provides you with access to the Site subject to the terms and conditions contained in this Terms of Use Agreement (the "Terms of Use"). These Terms of Use were last updated on December 1, 2003.

A clause compelling the user to indemnify the site operator against such third-party claims and damages will be of assistance in this respect. Box 3.2 contains a sample indemnification clause.

The sample indemnification language in box 3.2 is rather general in nature. The precise contents of the indemnification clause and whether it will be included at all will depend on the content of the Web site as well as the views and risk tolerance of the site operator. Additionally, it should be pointed out that the body of law pertaining to the enforceability of Terms of Use is in its relative infancy. However, based on the small body of case law, some of which will be discussed further in this chapter, it does not appear that Web site operators may improve their ability of enforcing their Terms of Use by ensuring that user assent is obtained and avoiding the inclusion of unreasonable provisions. Such caveats should be kept in mind when considering the contents of indemnification clauses.

Another important provision to be included in the Terms of Use is the disclaimer of warranties. The content of the disclaimer of warranties will depend on a number of factors, including the content of the Web site and the law that governs the agreement. It is beyond the scope of this chapter to examine the intricacies of warranties; however, very generally speaking, companies may be found to have actually made certain warranties if such warranties are not properly disclaimed. A sample of a general disclaimer of warranties is contained in box 3.3. It must be emphasized, however, that this is a rather generic disclaimer of warranties. The precise nature of the disclaimer of warranties that should be included

---

Box 3.2
Sample Indemnification Clause

In the event that any legal action is taken resulting from (1) your use of the Content or Web site, or (2) any unsolicited information provided by you, you agree to defend, indemnify, hold harmless, and pay any reasonable legal and accounting fees without limitation incurred by Company X, its affiliates, its and their directors, officers, employees, agents, investors, or licensers. Company X shall provide notice to you promptly of any such claim, suit, or proceeding. Company X shall have the right, at its option and expense, to participate in the defense and/or settlement of any claim or action, or to assume the exclusive defense and control of any matter otherwise subject to indemnification by you without relieving your indemnification obligations. In no event shall you settle any suit or claim imposing any liability or other obligations on Company X without its prior written consent.

Box 3.3
Sample Disclaimer of Warranties

The site and the content are provided on an "as is," "as available" basis, without warranties of any kind. There may be delays, omissions, or inaccuracies in the content and the site. Company X and its affiliates do not warrant the accuracy, completeness, timeliness, noninfringement, title, merchantability, or fitness for a particular purpose of the content or the site itself, and we hereby disclaim any such express or implied warranties. Company X does not represent or warrant that the content of this site is free of viruses, worms, or other code that may manifest contaminating or destructive properties. Because some jurisdictions do not permit the exclusion of certain warranties, these exclusions may not apply to you.

in a Terms of Use will depend on the nature of the Web site and the kinds of materials that are available on the site. For instance, a Web site that contains content from a number of different sources may need to be more concerned about disclaiming any warranties for such information than a site operator who is only posting information that he or she has authored. The nature of the disclaimer will also depend on the nature of the content displayed on the Web site. For example, Web site operators that display stock quotes and other time-sensitive financial information need to pay careful attention to disclaiming warranties concerning the accuracy and timeliness of such information.

The language in box 3.3 is intended to represent a general disclaimer of warranties provision. Of course, each company's ability to disclaim warranties may be limited by applicable legislation, particularly when the company is contracting with consumers. In the United States, of particular significance is the Magnuson Moss Warranty Act, along with applicable state legislation.

In addition to a general disclaimer of warranties, if the Web site contains hyperlinks to Web sites not under the control of the Web site operator, it will also be important to disclaim liability for the content of the linked sites, as well as the conduct of the operators of those sites. When Web site users access third-party sites through hyperlinks available on one site, they may not always be aware that they are accessing another Web site operated by a different company with different policies, procedures, and Terms of Use. If the Web site user has a negative experience or a dispute with one of the linked-to sites, the user may attempt to hold the original Web site through which the linked sites were accessed responsible. At a minimum, unless clear distinctions are made between the original Web site and the site to which links have been established, the user's impressions of the original site may become colored by such user's experiences with the linked site. Accordingly, it is important to make clear to the user that when accessing hyperlinks, he or she will be accessing sites that are not under the control of the Web site that has provided such links. Box 3.4 contains some sample language intended to disclaim liability for third-party Web sites accessible through hyperlinks.

Similarly, if the Web site will contain a considerable number of banners and other advertising or promotional materials from third-party sources, it will be to the site operator's advantage to include a specific provision regarding the site user's dealings with advertisers. The purpose of such a provision is to remind users that the Web site operator is not responsible for the actions or conduct of any advertiser. Box 3.5 contains sample language to this effect.

Web site operators should also consider including a limitation-of-liability clause in their Terms of Use agreements. The use and operation

---

Box 3.4
Sample Third Party Link Disclaimer

This Site contains hyperlinks to other Web sites that are not operated by Company X (the "Third Party Sites"). This Terms of Use applies only to this Site and not to the Third Party Sites. The hyperlinks to the Third Party Sites are provided for your reference and convenience only and do not imply any review or endorsement of the material on these Third Party Sites or any association with their operators. Company X does not control these Third Party Sites and is not responsible for their content. The Third Party Sites may contain information that is inaccurate, incomplete, or outdated. Your access and use of the Third Party Sites is solely at your own risk.

Box 3.5
Sample Advertising Disclaimer

Your correspondence or business dealings with, or participation in promotions of, advertisers found on or through the Site, including payment and delivery of related goods or services, and any other terms, conditions, warranties, or representations associated with such dealings, are solely between you and such advertiser. You agree that we are not responsible, nor shall we be liable, for loss or damage of any sort incurred as a result of any such dealings or as the result of the presence of such advertiser on the Site.

of a Web site can bring a number of advantages to a business, but it can also create liabilities. Accordingly, it is important to establish contractual limitations on potential liability just as would be done in most off-line agreements. Once again, the precise contents of the limitation-of-liability clause that is ultimately used in a Terms of Use agreement will vary considerably based on the Web site operator's goals and level of risk tolerance.

The Terms of Use should also contain a general section that sets forth typical general clauses such as governing law and venue, severability, and the provision of notices. The general clause should also contain information regarding the parties' ability to assign the agreement. In most cases, the Web site operator will desire to restrict the user's ability to assign the Terms of Use agreement while reserving full assignment rights for itself. In this clause, the Web site operator may also choose to place limitations on the amount of time during which any claims may be brought and specify that the Terms of Use represent the entire agreement between the Web site operator and the Web site user concerning the subject matter.

Finally, there are a number of additional provisions that Web site operators may wish to include in their Terms of Use. For instance, the Terms of Use may be an appropriate place to explain the operator's policy concerning the use of links to the Web site and set forth restrictions on the use of frames on the site. The precise framing and linking policy that is set forth in the Terms of Use will depend on the views of the company. While links are sometimes viewed as favorable because of the increased traffic they bring to the Web site, they can also be detrimental if, for example, they result in an undesirable association between the company that is doing the linking and the operator of the Web site to which links are being provided. Accordingly, it is often advisable to have companies that wish to provide links agree to a standard set of terms and conditions governing that linking arrangement. On the other hand, because of framing's tendency to mislead and confuse Web site visitors, the use of framing should be prohibited altogether in absence of a specific agreement governing its terms.

Depending on the nature of the Web site and its features, it may also be necessary to include a provision concerning any unsolicited information and materials that are provided to the Web site. The kinds of unsolicited materials that are provided to the Web site will vary to a great extent depending on the nature of the Web site, and the provision that is drafted concerning such unsolicited materials will depend on their specific nature. Nonetheless there are some general points to consider.

The Web site user should be notified that any information that he or she provides to the site will be nonconfidential and that the site operator will have a perpetual, royalty-free, and irrevocable right and license to use, reproduce, modify, adapt, publish, translate, distribute, transmit, publicly display, publicly perform, sublicense, create derivative works from, transfer, and sell such unsolicited information. While the term "unsolicited information" is a broad one and may seem a bit vague, there are a number of circumstances in which a Web site operator may receive unsolicited information. For instance, if a Web site user sends an e-mail that is extremely complimentary of the products or services of the site operator, the Web site operator may wish to include an excerpt of that complimentary information in its brochures or other publicity materials.

The sample clauses examined in this section are intended to illustrate some of the issues that should be addressed in a Terms of Use agreement. They are not intended, however, to embody a conclusive list of clauses to be included in the Terms of Use. As mentioned at the outset, there really is no effective "one size fits all" approach where Terms of Use are concerned. While form agreements may function well in some other areas of the law, such as apartment leasing, there is no standard "form" that should be used when developing a Web site Terms of Use. Instead of representing a complete list of provisions for a Terms of Use, this section is intended to encourage reflection regarding the different types of provisions to include when drafting a Terms of Use.

Presenting Terms of Use

While it is important to have a Terms of Use, such an agreement will be worthless unless it is enforceable. In recent years, a number of courts have addressed the enforceability of on-line Terms of Use agreements. A review of this body of case law is useful when considering how to ensure that the Web site's Terms of Use will be enforceable. One way for an entity operating a Web site to improve the likelihood that it will be considered to have obtained the user's consent to the Terms of Use agreement is to require the user to click through the Terms and Use and indicate his or her assent, usually through an "I agree" button, before proceeding. Such agreements are often referred to as "click-wrap" agreements.[3]

While the use of click-wrap agreements is highly recommended, especially for transactional Web sites, not all Web site operators are willing to take this step. In the absence of a click-wrap agreement, to improve the likelihood that a Terms of Use will be enforceable, Web site operators should take steps to ensure that (1) the user has reasonable notice of the agreement and (2) the user has assented to the agreement.

The concept of "reasonable notice" is rather logical—a Web site user cannot be bound by an agreement unless the party has notice of the terms of the agreement.[4] Whether a user has been given reasonable notice of a Terms of Use agreement depends on how the Terms of Use agreement is presented on a Web site. For example, in a case involving Ticketmaster and the operator of the Web site located at Tickets.com, the United States District Court for the Central District of California found that the display of a link to a Web site's Terms of Use failed to give a user adequate notice of the provisions of the Terms of Use.[5]

This case arose after Ticketmaster commenced an action after Tickets.com had made "deep" links into the internal pages of the Ticketmaster Web site.[6] At the time the case arose, the home page of Ticketmaster's Web site contained user instructions and a directory of subsequent pages. By scrolling down to the bottom of the home page, a visitor was also able to read the site license, labeled "Terms and Conditions," which provided that anyone going beyond the home page agreed to the terms and conditions set forth. These terms and conditions set forth, among other provisions, that the information on Ticketmaster's Web site was for personal use only and could not be used for commercial purposes. In addition, the terms and conditions also prohibited the use of deep links to the Web site.

Ticketmaster filed suit against Tickets.com in the District Court for the Central District of California for ten separate causes of action,[7] including breach of contract, copyright infringement, and unfair competition. In its complaint, Ticketmaster alleged, in part, that through the use of deep linking, Tickets.com had copied Ticketmaster's interior Web pages and then extracted basic event information from them.

At the time the case arose, Tickets.com operated a Web site that performed services similar to those provided on the Ticketmaster Web site. Namely, the Tickets.com site provided information on various events, including description, time, date, venue, and ticket prices. In contrast to the Ticketmaster Web site, however, Tickets.com offered only a limited number of tickets for sale through its Web site. In the instances in which Tickets.com was not selling tickets to a particular event itself, it offered a place where visitors could click for a reference to another ticket broker or another Internet ticket seller. In many instances, the users of the Tickets.com Web site would be transferred by deep link from the Tickets.com site to an interior page of the Ticketmaster Web site, bypassing the Ticketmaster home page.

In this case, the court drew attention to the fact that the Web site's Terms of Use were not posted conspicuously and did not require any confirmation from the user that they had been read and acknowledged.[8] The court stated that instead of being "open and obvious and in fact hard to miss" as shrink-wrap licenses generally are, Ticketmaster's Terms and Conditions were not sufficiently prominent.[9] In questioning the prominence of the Terms and Conditions, the court highlighted the fact that Web site visitors would need to scroll down to the bottom of the home page to view a link to the Terms and Conditions.

Another similar case was decided in July 2001. This case, *Specht v. Netscape Communications Corp.,* arose after a group of Internet users commenced a class action against Netscape and its parent company, America Online, alleging that the use of Netscape's SmartDownload transmits private information about the user's file transfer activity to Netscape in violation of law.[10] Netscape made a motion to compel arbitration arguing that all disputes concerning the software were subject to a binding arbitration clause in the license agreement for the software.

The court found against Netscape and, applying California law, concluded that because of the manner in which the license agreement was presented, there was no assent to that agreement. The court contended that Netscape never obtained the user's assent to the agreement. It observed:

> The only hint that a contract is being formed is one small box of text referring to the license agreement, text that appears below the screen used for downloading and that a user need not even see before obtaining the product:
>
>> Please review and agree to the terms of the Netscape Smart-Download software license agreement before downloading and using the software.
>
> Couched in the mild request of, "Please review," this language reads as a mere invitation, not as a condition. The language does not indicate that a user must agree to the license terms before downloading and using the software. While clearer language appears in the License Agreement itself, the language of the invitation does not require the reading of those terms or provide adequate notice either that a contract is being created or that the terms of the License Agreement will bind the user.[11]

The court concluded that it could not compel the plaintiffs to submit to arbitration because there was no mutual assent to the software license agreement.

The *Ticketmaster* and *Specht* cases are quite significant because they provide further support for the notion that if an entity desires its Terms of Use to be enforceable, it should not merely bury a link to the Terms of Use at the bottom of the home page. In many cases, especially for Web sites that are conducting transactions or are offering highly regulated products and services, it is advisable to use a click-wrap agreement. Where the use of a click-wrap agreement is not desired, other efforts must be made to ensure that the user has had notice of the Terms of Use and has consented to it. While the attainment of notice and consent will depend on the specific features and organization of the Web site, among other factors, generally, it will be useful to ensure that the link to the Terms of Use appears in a prominent location, above the fold of the Web page. If choosing this option, it will be important to combine the links to the Terms of Use with appropriate language in the Terms of Use. Box 3.6 contains sample language intended to put Web site visitors on notice that the Terms of Use will govern their use of the Web site.

The enforceability of a particular Terms of Use is also likely to depend on its contents. This point is illustrated by the case of *America Online, Inc., v. Mendoza,*[12] in which a California appeals court upheld the decision of the lower court, which found that the click-wrap user agreement of America Online (AOL) was unfair because its forum selection clause required that all suits arising as a result of such agreement be heard in Virginia. In reaching its determination, the court referenced the California Consumers Legal Remedies Act,[13] which contains a provision that voids any purported waiver of rights under the act as against the public policy of California.[14] The appellate panel reviewing the case concluded that the enforcement of AOL's forum selection clause would be tantamount to a contractual waiver of the consumer protection provisions contained in the California Consumers Legal Remedies Act and, accordingly, would be prohibited under California law.

This case highlights the great importance of being aware of the intricacies of state law when attempting to develop a Terms of Use that will

---

Box 3.6
Sample Language Informing of the Binding Nature of the Terms of Use

These Terms of Use set forth the terms and conditions for your use of this Site. You should carefully review these Terms of Use before using the Site. Your use of the Site will signify your assent to be bound by these Terms of Use. If you do not agree to be legally bound by these Terms of Use, you should exit this Site immediately.

be applicable to users from all over the country. Of course, the task will be even more complicated when one is developing a Terms of Use that will apply to a Web site that will be used by individuals from all over the world. While having knowledge of local legal requirements is always important, it will be even more significant when individual consumers are the target audience of the Web site, because many jurisdictions have enacted strict consumer protection laws, many of which apply to Internet-based transaction.[15]

In this regard, it is useful to consider the case of *Williams v. America Online, Inc.* In this case a Massachusetts court ruled that AOL could not enforce the venue clause contained in its click-wrap agreement and thus could not force its users residing in Massachusetts to move their lawsuit to Virginia.[16] In this case, the court concluded that it was unfair to force the plaintiffs to use the forum selection clause because of the mechanism used to obtain the users' acceptance. AOL had used a procedure whereby users seeking to upgrade to version 5.0 of the AOL software were presented with the forum selection clause and other terms and conditions only after the software upgrade was downloaded and installed on the users' computers. However, the plaintiffs contended that their cause of action actually arose during the installation process (i.e., before they were given the opportunity to review and consent to the terms of use).

The court also objected to the ways in which AOL presented its users with the opportunity to accept the terms and conditions of the user agreement. Upon the completion of the installation process, the user was presented with the option of selecting "I agree" or "Read now." If a user selected "Read now," he or she was presented with a second set of choices stating "Okay, I agree" and "read now" but was not presented with the actual user agreement. Only if the user selected "read now" a second time was he or she presented with the user agreement.

Furthermore, as in *America Online v. Mendoza,* the *Williams* court also expressed concern about the reasonableness of the forum selection clause. The clause at issue required plaintiffs seeking to represent a class of Massachusetts residents in a class action to litigate in Virginia. Accordingly, similar to *Mendoza,* the *Williams* case also emphasizes the importance of not offending the court's notions of reasonableness when drafting the contents of the Terms of Use or devising the methods for presenting the Terms of Use and obtaining the user's consent.

Just as it is essential to obtain the Web site user's consent to the Terms of Use the first time he or she uses the Web site, so it is also important to obtain the user's consent to any subsequent modifications of the Terms of Use. The method for obtaining such consent often depends on a number of factors including the nature of the Web site, the risk tolerance of the site operator, and the significance of the changes. Ideally, to have a high level of certainly that the consent to the changes will be deemed to be valid, it is useful to contact every Web site user, provide notification of the changes to the Terms of Use, and obtain the users' consent to be bound by the revised Terms of Use.

At the other end of the spectrum, some Web site operators will opt for the inclusion of a statement in the Terms of Use specifying that they can be modified at any time by the site operator and that the revised Terms of Use will be posted on the Web site. While this practice is currently used by a number of Web sites, its enforceability is not fully clear. At the least, entities using this technique may face public relations issues if Web site users feel that the company is changing the Terms of Use frequently without sufficient notice. Box 3.7 contains sample language intended to reflect this technique.

The concern about using this method is that Web site users may not receive actual notice of any changes to the Terms of Use unless they decide to view the Terms of Use again. Accordingly, the site operator may improve its ability to enforce revised terms by taking an affirmative step to inform users of changes by e-mail notification or by requiring users to agree to the revised Terms of Use each time a change is made.

CONTRACTING ELECTRONICALLY

Using Electronic Contracts

Another way to improve the enforceability of Web site Terms of Use agreements is to use electronic signatures for the execution of such agreements. In the past several years, legislative developments in the United States and abroad have helped to advance the legal recognition and en-

---

Box 3.7
Sample Language Concerning Changes to the Terms of Use

Company X reserves the right to amend these Terms of Use at any time and will notify you of any such changes to these Terms of Use by posting the revised Terms of Use on the Site. Unless otherwise specified, such changes shall be effective upon posting. You have the obligation to review changes in these Terms of Use. Your continued use of the Site constitutes your agreement to be bound by any such changes to these Terms of Use.

forceability of electronic signatures. As such, companies conducting business on-line may wish to evaluate whether using electronic signatures and contracts will bring benefits to them through reduced transaction and increased transaction speed. This section will examine some of the legalities and practicalities of using electronic signatures—both in the Terms of Use agreement and beyond.

What Are Electronic Signatures and Electronic Agreements?

Electronic Signatures

When considering electronic transactions, it is useful to examine the potential value of electronic signatures. Electronic signatures can be used in the electronic world in much that same way as traditional signatures are used in the paper-based world.

The term "electronic signature" is a generic one that can mean many different things depending on the context in which it is used. Today most laws concerning electronic signatures take a broad view when defining electronic signatures. Such a broad view is usually desirable because it may help to ensure that rapidly developing technology does not render the legislation obsolete.

As an example of the broad way in which electronic signatures are being defined, consider the European Community Directive 1999/93/EC on a Community Framework for Electronic Signatures (the "European E-signature Directive"),[17] which defines an electronic signature as "data in electronic form which are attached to or logically associated with other electronic data and which serve as a method of authentication."[18] The European E-signature Directive distinguishes ordinary electronic signatures from "advanced electronic signatures," which are defined as any electronic signatures that meet the following requirements: "(a) is uniquely linked to the signatory; (b) is capable of identifying the signatory; (c) is created using means that the signatory can maintain under his sole control; and (d) is linked to the data to which it relates in such a manner that any subsequent change of the data is detectable."[19] As another example, the Model Law on Electronic Signatures of the United Nations Commission on International Trade Law defines an electronic signature as "data in electronic form, affixed to, or logically associated with, a data message, which may be used to identify the signatory in relation to the data message and indicate the signatory's approval of the information contained in the data message."[20] Another example of a broad definition of electronic signature is contained in the Finnish Act on Electronic Service in the Administration, which defines electronic signatures as "a set of data that confirms the integrity and originality of an electronic message by a method that is open to public inspection."[21]

Electronic Agreements

An electronic contract is simply an agreement that is created and "signed" in electronic form. One example of an electronic agreement is the click-wrap agreement, where a party to an on-line agreement is required to review the agreement and click on the "I agree" button, indicating consent, usually before being provided with access to a Web site, software, or other products or services. Also, an electronic contract can result where one individual uses her computer to create an agreement and then e-mails such agreement to a business associate, who uses his computer to "sign" the agreement and indicate his assent thereto and then e-mails it back with his electronic signature.

The Legal Response

Given the advantages and usefulness of electronic signatures, a number of countries and states have proposed or passed legislation intended to give legal effect to electronic signatures. Today, some years after electronic signatures first began to be used, a great number of jurisdictions specifically recognize the legal validity of electronic signatures, at least in some circumstances. The following sections will examine a few key laws governing the recognition and use of electronic signatures in the United States and select foreign jurisdictions.

The United States

As a result of the Electronic Signatures in Global and National Commerce Act (the "E-sign Act"),[22] since October 1, 2000, electronic contracts and electronic signatures have been recognized as legally enforceable in the United States. The enactment of the E-sign Act has helped to remove the legal uncertainty that has hindered the use of electronic signatures in electronic contracts.[23] Although there were a number of initiatives prior to the E-sign Act, it was the first comprehensive legislation to give legal effect to electronic signatures at the federal level.

The E-sign Act provides that "with respect to any transaction in or affecting interstate or foreign commerce,"[24] "a signature, contract or other record relating to such transaction may not be denied legal effect, validity, or enforceability solely because it is in electronic form,"[25] and "a contract relating to such transaction may not be denied legal effect, validity, or enforceability solely because an electronic signature or electronic record was used in its formation."[26]

While the E-sign Act provides for the legal recognition of electronic signatures and documents, it does not compel any consumer to use or accept the use of electronic signatures or documents. The legislation requires that where information about a commercial transaction is required by law to "be provided or made available to a consumer in writing, the use of an electronic record to provide or make available (whichever is required) such information satisfies the requirement that such information be in writing,"[27] as long as "the consumer has affirmatively consented to such use and has not withdrawn such consent."[28] However, even before any such consent can be granted, the consumer must be informed of (1) "any right or option . . . to have the record provided or made available on paper or in nonelectronic form" and "the right . . . to withdraw the consent to have the record provided or made available in electronic form and or any condition, consequences (which may include termination of the parties' relationship), or fees in the event of any such withdrawal";[29] (2) the procedures that must be used to withdraw consent;[30] and (3) how, after consent, the consumer may, upon request, obtain a paper copy of a record and whether any fees will be charged for the copy.[31] Further, the consumer must also be informed of "the hardware and software requirements for access to and retention or the electronic records,"[32] and the consumer must give his or her consent electronically "in a manner that reasonably demonstrates that the consumer can access information in the electronic form that will be used to provide the information that is the subject of the consent."[33] For example, if the records in question would be sent to the individual in .pdf format, perhaps the individual would receive an e-mail with instructions contained in an attached .pdf file indicating how to indicate consent. If the consumer was able to indicate consent, it would mean that he or she was able to access the instructions in .pdf format and thus that he or she would be able to access the records delivered in .pdf format.

Despite the existence of rather extensive consumer protection provisions, it should be noted that the E-sign Act does allow businesses to collect additional fees from individuals who require the use of paper. The E-sign Act provides individuals with the ability to opt out of using electronic contracts if so desired. Additionally, even if an individual consents to the use of electronic signatures and records, the individual can change his or her mind and revoke his or her consent. Should this occur, the company would have to respect that decision and provide copies of documents and agreements in paper.

While the E-sign Act is generally applicable, it does contain certain exceptions, as follows:[34]

- wills, codicils, and testamentary trusts
- documents relating to adoption, divorce, and other family law matters
- court orders, notices, and other court documents such as pleadings or motions
- notices of cancellation or termination of utility services
- notices of default, repossession, foreclosure, or eviction
- notices of cancellation or termination of health or life insurance benefits
- product recall notices affecting health or safety
- documents required by law to accompany the transportation of hazardous materials

One interesting aspect of the E-sign Act concerns its stance on the preemption of state law. The E-sign Act will not override any state laws on electronic transactions provided that the state law is "substantially similar" to the federal law or the state has adopted the Uniform Electronic Transactions Act (UETA), which also establishes the legal validity of electronic signatures and contracts.[35] In plainer language, this means that if a state law is more or less the same as the E-sign Act, it will remain in force. Otherwise, the state law will be trumped by the E-sign Act.

The E-sign Act is an important development in electronic commerce. It makes significant contributions by providing a uniform national legitimacy to electronic contracts, records, and other documents. It provides Web site operators with the opportunity to reduce transaction costs and increase the speed of transactions and the distribution of information by using electronic contracts and records. Accordingly, Web site operators find it beneficial to take advantage of the provisions of the act when obtaining user consent to Web site Terms of Use agreements and when concluding other on-line agreements or distributing electronic records. At the same time, while enhancing the ability of businesses to engage in electronic transactions, the E-sign Act also endeavors to provide adequate protection to consumers.

Internationally

Today a large number of countries afford electronic signatures some form of legal recognition. In some jurisdictions, such as the European

Union, the legal recognition afforded to electronic signatures is broad based. In other jurisdictions, such as the United Arab Emirates, the legal recognition of electronic signatures is evolving on a sectoral basis.[36] The following sections will present further information on legislative approaches toward electronic signatures that have been adopted in other countries.

The European Union

The European E-signatures Directive was adopted on November 30, 1999. Its stated purpose is "to facilitate the use of electronic signatures[37] and to contribute to their legal recognition."[38] The legislation was also intended to contribute to efforts to develop electronic commerce throughout the European Union. The directive endeavors to create a harmonized framework for the legal recognition of electronic signatures throughout the European Union. The necessity of this legislation was made evident by the fact that at the time of the initial proposal, many Member States of the European Union[39] had announced that they had either adopted or were in the process of adopting their own national legislation governing electronic signatures.[40] As such, to prevent potential difficulties resulting from divergent regulatory regimes in the different Member States of the European Union, efforts were directed towards adopting a cohesive legislative approach for electronic signatures.[41] In attempting to create a harmonized pan-European approach, the directive sets guidelines for the recognition of electronic signatures,[42] defines the responsibilities and liabilities of certification authorities,[43] and outlines the requirements for signature creation devices. Significantly, it also contains provisions for the recognition of electronic signatures originating outside of the European Union.[44] The directive can best be understood by examining the following issues: legal recognition, free circulation, liability, technology-neutral framework, scope, and international issues.

The European E-signatures Directive provides that an electronic signature cannot be legally discriminated against solely on the grounds that it is in electronic form.[45] As long as certain requirements are met, Member States must afford electronic signatures with the same legal validity as handwritten signatures. It also provides that electronic signatures can be used as evidence in legal proceedings.[46]

Pursuant to the European E-signatures Directive, all products and services related to electronic signatures can circulate freely and are subject to the legislation of only the country of origin.[47] Furthermore, Member States are prohibited from making provision of services related to electronic signatures subject to mandatory licensing.[48]

The directive establishes minimum liability rules for service providers who, in particular, would be liable for the validity of a certificate's content.[49] Specifically, the directive provides that a certification service provider[50] is liable for damage caused to any entity or legal or natural person who reasonably relies on that certificate (1) with regard to the accuracy at the time of issuance of all information contained in the qualified certificate and with regard to the fact that the certificate contains all the details prescribed for a qualified certificate; (2) for assurance that at the time of the issuance of the certificate, the signatory identified in the qualified certificate held the signature-creation data corresponding to the signature-verification data given or identified in the certificate; and (3) for assurance that the signature-creation data and the signature-verification data can be used in a complementary manner in cases where the certification service provider generates them both. However, the certification service provider will not be held liable if it proves that it has not acted negligently. It is likely that such an approach was taken in hopes that it would help to ensure the free movement of certificates and certification services within the internal market as well as to build consumer trust.

Like the U.S. E-sign Act, the European E-signatures Directive is technologically neutral. It provides for the legal recognition of electronic signatures irrespective of the technology used. This is important, for if the directive were not technologically neutral, there would be a chance that it could be rendered obsolete shortly after its effective date.

The European E-signatures Directive also includes provisions designed to promote electronic commerce on a global level.[51] It includes mechanisms for cooperation with third countries on the basis of mutual recognition of certificates and on bilateral and multilateral agreements. Specifically, the directive provides that Member States are required to ensure that certificates that are issued as qualified certificates to the public by a certification service provider established in a third country are recognized as legally equivalent to certificates issued by a certification service provider established within the European Union if (1) the certification service provider fulfills the requirements laid down in the directive and has been accredited under a voluntary accreditation scheme established in a Member State; or (2) a certification service provider established within the European Union that fulfills the requirements laid down in the directive guarantees the certificate; or (3) the certificate or the certification service provider is recognized under a bilateral or multilateral agreement between the European Union and third countries or international organizations.[52]

While the European E-signatures Directive was being debated, American authorities remained highly concerned about the possibility that the directive would call for specific technical standards for electronic signatures.[53] During the debate and since the passage of the directive, European authorities have stressed that it is technologically neutral and provides for the legal recognition of electronic signatures irrespective of the technology used. This is a factor that has been very important for American businesses. If the directive were not technologically neutral, there would be a chance that it could be restrictive and discriminatory against the technology now being used or being developed by American businesses.

Although the directive does not clearly specify a certain technology that is to be used, certain of its provisions do still raise some concerns. Particular attention should be drawn to Recital 16 of the directive, which states: "A regulatory framework is not needed for electronic signatures exclusively used within systems, which are based upon voluntary agreements under private law between a specified number of participants; the freedom of parties to agree among themselves the terms and conditions under which they will accept electronically signed data should be respected to the extent allowable by national law."[54] There is some justifiable concern that the phrasing of this recital could permit Member States as they develop their own laws implementing the European E-signatures Directive to authorize the creation of individual licensing regimes that specify technology-specific requirements for electronic signatures.

There is also a risk that the directive might be implemented inconsistently among the European Union's fifteen Member States. Under European law, directives serve to define the minimum standards that must exist within the laws of each of the Member States. While each Member State may implement the basic terms of a directive into its own national law, they are often afforded considerable liberty in doing so. As this directive has been characterized as being somewhat vague,[55] there is a strong likelihood that significant divergences may emerge among the different Member States once the directive is fully implemented into national law. As such, even after the directive has been implemented fully into the national laws of the Member States, American businesses may still find it necessary to thoroughly review each national law instead of focusing only on the directive itself.

Table 3.1 contains further information regarding the national laws that have been enacted in order to implement the European E-signatures Directive.

Table 3.1
Key European Union Electronic Signatures Legislation

Country	Key Electronic Signatures Legislation
Austria	Act on Electronic Signatures 1999
	Ordinance of the Federal Minister on Electronic Signatures 2000
	Ordinance of the Federal Minister on the Suitability of Confirmation Offices 2002
Belgium	Act of October 20, 2000 Introducing the Use of Telecommunications Tools and the Electronic Signatures in Judicial and Extra Judicial Proceedings
	Act of July 9, 2001 Introducing a Legal Framework for Electronic Signatures
Denmark	The Danish Act on Electronic Signatures of May 21, 2000
	The Danish Executive Order of May 10, 2000
Finland	Government Bill 197/2001 on Electronic Signatures and Certificates
France	Act of March 13, 2000 Introducing a Legal Framework for Electronic Signatures
	Decree of March 20, 2001 Relative to the Electronic Signature
	Decree of April 18, 2002 Relative to Certification Devices and Providers
Germany	Law Governing Framework Conditions for Electronic Signatures and Amending Other Regulations
	Law Adjusting Legal Form in German Law to the Efforts of Electronic Communications and Commerce
	Law Implementing the Electronic Form in the Public Sector
Greece	Presidential Decree 150/2001
	Regulation of the National Telecommunications and Post Commission on the Provision of Certification Services for Electronic Signatures
Ireland	Electronic Commerce Act 2000
Italy	Legislative Decree Number 10
	Presidential Decree Number 445
Luxembourg	Law of August 14, 2000 Relating to Electronic Commerce, Transposing Directive 1999/93 Relating to a Community Framework for Electronic Signatures, Directive 2000/31/EC Relating to Certain Legal Aspects of Information Society Services and Certain Provisions of 97/7/EC Concerning Distance Selling of Goods and Services Other Than Financial Services
	Law of March 22, 2000 relating to the creation of a National Accreditation Registrar, a National Council for Accreditation, Certification, Standardization and Quality Promotion
	Grand-Ducal Regulation of June 1, 2001 Relating to Electronic Signatures, Electronic Payment and Implementation of the Electronic Commerce Committee
Netherlands	Adaptation of Chapter 3 and 6 of the Civil Code, the Telecommunications Act and the Economic Offenses Act Regarding Electronic Signatures, Effecting Directive 1999/93/EU of the European Parliament and the Council of the European Union of 13 December 1999 on a Community Framework for Electronic Signatures
Portugal	Decree-Law 290-D/99 of August 2, 1999
	Decree-Law 375/99 of September 18, 1999
Spain	Law 14/1999 of September 17, 1999
Sweden	Act on Qualified Electronic Signatures
	Act Concerning Technical Conformity Assessment
United Kingdom	Electronic Communications Act 2000
	Electronic Signatures Regulations 2002

Some Business Tips

The fact that electronic signatures and electronic agreements have been afforded legal recognition in many jurisdictions means that companies that conduct business on-line have a number of new opportunities for streamlining their operations and providing their services. In the United States, as a result of the E-sign Act, as well as in many other countries, as a result of similar legislation, businesses and consumers will be able to buy virtually any goods or services over the Internet without ever concluding a handwritten agreement. Such a new way of doing business may result in substantial savings for companies, which can be passed on to consumers.

At the same time, however, divergent approaches between the United States and other countries can lead to uncertainties about whether e-signatures will be considered legal and enforceable in a particular jurisdiction. The lack of a harmonized legislative regime governing electronic signatures on a global level can give rise to a number of problems for businesses. If different jurisdictions have conflicting laws pertaining to electronic signatures, companies may find themselves caught up in a jurisdictional quagmire. When using e-signatures in a borderless medium such as the Internet, businesses must be aware of divergent national legislation or limit the sale of products and services to countries about which there is a high level of legal certainty.

JURISDICTIONAL ISSUES: DECIDING WHERE TO OFFER YOUR PRODUCTS AND SERVICES

The Problem

A discussion of managing risks through a Web site Terms of Use would not be complete without considering jurisdictional issues. The Internet raises new and challenging issues regarding jurisdiction because the Net is truly a medium without national boundaries. When a small bait-and-tackle company in Connecticut develops a Web site as a convenience to its local customers, as soon as the site goes on-line, it becomes accessible to individuals around the world. While this could benefit Bob's Bait and Tackle by bringing the small company many more customers than it had ever anticipated, it could also bring trouble if the company finds itself subject to criminal liability after violating some obscure advertising regulation in a country in which it had never intended to do business.

Although there has been debate over the general topic of Internet jurisdiction ever since the Net came into existence, concern over facing civil or criminal liability in foreign jurisdiction because of the content of one's Web site is a relatively new issue, fostered in large part by the experiences of Yahoo! in France.[56] This case commenced in April 2000 when the International League against Racism and Anti-Semitism and the Union of French Jewish Students objected to the fact that certain Nazi material was being made available through Yahoo!'s on-line auction service hosted out of the United States. The groups claimed that the availability of such memorabilia in France constituted a violation of Article R. 645-1 of the French Penal Code, which prohibits the exhibition or sale of racist materials.[57]

In response to the claim, a French judge initially ordered Yahoo! to take measures to make it impossible for Web surfers in France to reach any Nazi memorabilia through the Yahoo! site or pay fines in the amount of Fr 100,000 per day.[58] Since the issuance of the French order in 2000, the case involving Yahoo! has become increasingly more complex. In December 2000, Yahoo! filed for a judgment in a U.S. federal court that would declare that the French government has no jurisdiction over the company's operations. In November 2001, the U.S. District Court for the Northern District of California ruled that Yahoo! would be shielded from the judgment of the French court. This, however, did not end the legal battles of Yahoo!. More recently, the Association of Auschwitz Deportees commenced a case against the former head of Yahoo!. Such case sought to hold this individual personally liable for (1) justifying a crime against humanity and (2) exhibiting a uniform, insignia, or emblem of a person guilty of crimes against humanity, each as as result of the fact that Nazi-related memorabilia was made available through the Yahoo! Web site. In early 2003, however, the judges ruled that neither charge had been proved.

The initial decision of the French court in the Yahoo! case was widely criticized. Many free-speech advocates contended that the decision would stifle free speech by causing publishers in the United States to place limitations on their own expression based on the laws of other countries. Likewise, proponents of a free Internet argued that the decision would lead to increased restrictions and boundaries in Internet use.

While the Yahoo! case generated a significant amount of media attention and should serve as a kind of wake-up call to many Web site operators,[59] it is not representative of the kinds of risks with which Web site operators should be concerned. In fact, operators may find themselves running afoul of foreign laws for things much more mundane than offering Nazi materials. There are many, many examples of how domestic U.S. Web sites can find that they have violated the law of one country by virtue of the kinds of materials they have placed on their sites. In the early days of the Internet, for example, CompuServe decided to deny its subscribers worldwide access to certain sex-related discussion groups because of the potential for liability under German antipornography laws.[60] Similarly, in 1996, a number of German Internet service providers attempted to block out American and Canadian Web sites that contained neo-Nazi material.[61] As national and local governmental authorities continue to enact laws and regulations concerning the Internet, conflicts such as these are likely to continue and even intensify.

Possible Solutions

Once a decision is made concerning the number of jurisdictions from which Web site users will be accepted, a number of methods can be used to discourage individuals from prohibited jurisdictions from entering and using the Web site. First, the Terms of Use can specify that the Web site is intended for use only by residents of certain countries, such as, for example, the United States, Japan, and Canada. Additionally, some Web site operators may choose to require Web site users to enter their postal code or country of residence on the home page. If the user enters a postal code or the name of a country in which the Web site operator does not intend to submit to jurisdiction, the individual will not be able to proceed into the Web site. Additionally, some Web site operators may require a user to click on an on-line box indicating that he or she is not from certain prohibited jurisdictions.

The main problem with such procedures is that they can easily be defeated by most users. If, for example, an individual residing in the United States wished to access a Web site in France but was aware that the site was off-limits to American users, she could just simply enter false information regarding her location of residence. Additionally, the legal effect of such methods is not fully certain, especially in jurisdictions outside the United States. In some circumstances, especially where the content of the Web site or the conduct of the site operator is viewed as particularly egregious under the national law of the foreign country, the foreign country may attempt to exercise jurisdiction over the Web site operator regardless of its use of these various methods.

When attempting to address jurisdictional issues, some Web site operators may find that they do not have to prohibit individuals in certain countries from accessing the Web site altogether, but they may have to control the use of certain parts of the site. This scenario arises frequently for operators of on-line trading services. Such Web sites may contain news and other information that can be viewed freely by individuals from all jurisdictions. However, the on-line trader may wish to enable only individuals who are residents in the United States to open on-line trading accounts. Often the best way to proceed in such a situation is to develop a layered Web site with all individuals being able to access the site's public areas and only individuals who are residents in the United States and have completed off-line account agreements having access to the trading portions of the site.

Going forward, it is likely that the technological measures that can be used to limit jurisdictional accessibility will be improved. At the same time, however, individuals' ability to overcome such technological restrictions will likely also improve. A more promising solution would be for nations to pursue a more harmonized approach for regulating the Internet. However, until the regulation of the Internet becomes more harmonized, Web site operators should consider a combination of technical and legal measures to limit the jurisdictional accessibility of their sites.

CONCLUSION

This chapter has examined how Web site operators may reduce the legal risks inherent in operating a Web site by developing and posting Terms of Use agreements. It has also presented information regarding the means for obtaining user assent to the Terms of Use, such as through the use of electronic signatures. Finally, it has also examined some of the legal risks involved with making a Web site accessible internationally, as well as the methods that can be used to control such risks.

The next chapter will shift to a subject of growing importance in the area of Internet business: privacy. The increased use of the Internet for business purposes has raised new concerns about the protection of individual privacy and has also motivated the enactment of new laws and regulations.

Chapter 4

INTERNET PRIVACY ISSUES:
THE LAW'S ALL OVER THE MAP

During the past few years, privacy has become an extremely prominent topic, particularly within the context of electronic commerce. While concerns about privacy and the protection of personal data have long existed, such concerns have been heightened with the advent of the Internet and related technologies. As a result of the Internet, companies have become better equipped to transmit large amounts of data across great distances and to multiple recipients with immense speed. At the same time, the ability of companies to collect personal information from individuals without their full knowledge, through cookies, spyware, and other technologies, has also been enhanced.

As a result of all the new risks to the privacy of personal information, a number of jurisdictions have enacted rules and regulations designed to protect individual privacy. While many of these laws have similarities, there are important differences between the approaches taken by many of them. This reality adds to the complexity of engaging in commerce and other activities that involve the collection, use, and transfer of personal data and requires entities to analyze more than one body of law when considering the development of their operations.

This chapter will explore the timely subject of privacy and examine how the regulation of privacy and the protection of personal data impact the ability of companies to conduct business on-line. The chapter commences with a review of relevant law both in the United States and in several key jurisdictions abroad. From there, the discussion will center on how companies can operate successful Internet-based ventures in light of this growing body of regulation.

THE UNITED STATES

Federal Laws and Regulations

In sharp contrast to other jurisdictions, such as the European Union, which has a broad-based regime for the protection of personal information, in the United States, the protection of personal information is based on a patchwork of federal, state, constitutional, statutory, and case law. With respect to federal law, the United States has adopted an approach that is largely sectoral in nature. Therefore, while there are certain protections for, among other things, the privacy of video rental records[1] and driving records,[2] there is not a singular law providing for the privacy of all different types of personal data. The following sections will explore several key federal laws concerning data privacy that have implications for entities that operate Web sites.

The Children's Online Privacy Protection Act

One of the most important laws concerning data privacy is the Children's Online Privacy Protection Act (COPPA).[3] COPPA was signed into law on October 21, 1998. The stated goals of the act are (1) to enhance parental involvement in order to protect the privacy of children in the on-line environment; (2) to help protect the safety of children in on-line forums such as chat rooms, home pages, and pen pal services in which children may make public postings of identifying information collected on-line; and (3) to limit the collection of personal information from children without parental consent.[4]

Pursuant to the act, operators[5] of Web sites directed to children under age 13 or who knowingly collect personal information from children under age 13 on the Internet must

- provide parents notice of their information practices;
- obtain prior, verifiable parental consent[6] for the collection, use, and disclosure[7] of personal information from children (with certain very limited exceptions);
- upon request, provide a parent with the ability to review the personal information collected from his or her child;
- provide a parent with the opportunity to prevent the further use of per-

sonal information that has already been collected, or the future collection of personal information from that child;

- limit collection of personal information for a child's on-line participation in a game, prize offer, or other activity to information that is reasonably necessary for the activity; and
- establish and maintain reasonable procedures to protect the confidentiality, security, and integrity of the personal information collected.[8]

The passage of COPPA is further evidence of the commitment on the part of U.S. legislators and regulators to afford protection to the privacy of children. The FTC has long demonstrated an interest in protecting children from unfair information collection practices on-line. Even before the entry into force of COPPA, the FTC was active in investigating and even commencing enforcement actions against companies that were alleged to have engaged in unfair or deceptive information collection practices involving children. For example, in 1998, the FTC commenced a proceeding against GeoCities for deceptive practices in connection with GeoCities' collection and use of personal identifying information.[9] In addition, around the same time, the FTC also commenced an action against Liberty Financial Co. based on allegations that the company was collecting data from children and using the data in a manner that was inconsistent with the company's stated policies.

Since the enactment of COPPA, the FTC has commenced six enforcement actions against entities alleged to have violated the act. On April 19, 2001, one year after the entry into force of COPPA, the FTC announced the settlement of the first three COPPA cases. These cases involved three companies, Monarch Services and Girls Life, operators of www.girlslife.com; Bigmailbox.com and Nolan Quan, operators of www.bigmailbox.com; and Looksmart, operator of www.insidetheweb.com.[10] The three companies were charged with illegally collecting personally identifying information from children under 13 years of age without parental consent.

In an aim to settle the FTC charges, the companies together agreed to pay a total of $100,000 in civil penalties. Moreover, they also agreed to comply with COPPA in connection with any future on-line collection of personally identifying information from children under 13 and to delete all personally identifying information collected from children on-line at any time since the effective date of COPPA.

Since the settlement of these three initial cases, the FTC has commenced several additional enforcement actions. All indications are that there will be additional cases. In April 2002, for example, the FTC sent notices to more than 50 Web site operators warning them to bring their sites into compliance with COPPA.[11]

The Gramm-Leach-Bliley Act

Also significant to a discussion of data privacy is Subtitle A of Title V[12] of the Gramm-Leach-Bliley Act (GLB Act).[13] The GLB Act contains provisions concerning the privacy of the nonpublic information of individuals who are consumers[14] or customers of financial information.[15] These provisions place restrictions on the ability of financial institutions to disclose a consumer's personal financial information to nonaffiliated third parties. They also require financial institutions to provide notices to their customers about their information-collection and information-sharing practices and to give individuals the opportunity to opt out if they do not wish for their information to be shared with nonaffiliated third parties.

The GLB Act provides specific exceptions under which a financial institution may share customer information with a third party and the consumer may not opt out. For instance, a financial institution may disclose nonpublic personal information to nonaffiliated third parties under several exceptions where consumers and customers do not have the right to opt out of such sharing and, in some cases, will get no notice of the disclosure. For example, the financial institution must provide notice, but not the right to opt out, when it provides nonpublic personal information to a third-party service provider that provides services for the financial institution or other financial institutions with whom the financial institution has entered into a joint marketing agreement.

A third-party service provider may market the financial institution's own products and services or the financial products or services offered under a "joint marketing agreement" between the financial institution and one or more other financial institutions.

A joint marketing agreement with other financial institution(s) means a written contract pursuant to which those institutions jointly offer, endorse, or sponsor a financial product or service. However, to take advantage of this exception, the financial institution must

- provide the initial notice as required to consumers and customers; and
- enter into a contract with the third-party service provider or financial institution under a joint marketing agreement that prohibits the disclosure or use of the information other than for the purpose for which it was disclosed.

There are also certain exceptions to the notice and opt-out requirements.[16] These exceptions are disclosures

- made to effect, administer, or enforce a transaction that a consumer requests or authorizes;[17]
- made in connection with servicing or processing a financial product or service that a consumer requests or authorizes; maintaining or servicing a consumer's account; or a proposed or actual securitization, secondary market sale (including the sale of servicing rights), or similar transactions;
- made with consumer consent;
- made to protect the confidentiality or security of records;
- made to protect against or prevent actual or potential fraud;
- made for required institutional risk control or for resolving consumer disputes or inquires;
- made to persons holding a legal or beneficial interest relating to the consumer;
- made to persons acting in a fiduciary or representative capacity on behalf of the consumer (i.e., the consumer's attorney);
- made to provide information to insurance rate advisory organizations, persons assessing compliance with industry standards, or the financial institution's attorneys, accountants, or auditors;
- made to law enforcement entities or self-regulatory groups (to the extent permitted or required by law);
- made to comply with federal, state, or local laws;
- made to comply with subpoena or other judicial process;
- made in response to summons or other requests from authorized government authorities;
- made pursuant to the Fair Credit Reporting Act, to a consumer reporting agency, or from a consumer report reported by consumer reporting agency; and
- made in connection with a proposed or actual sale, merger, transfer, or exchange of all or a portion of a business or operating unit.

Aside from these exceptions, all financial institutions are required to provide individuals with a notice and opt-out opportunity before they may disclose information to nonaffiliated third parties outside of what is permitted under the exceptions.

The GLB Act also contains significant security provisions. The act requires the FTC and certain other federal agencies to establish standards with which financial institutions must comply in order to protect the security of their customers' nonpublic information. The FTC recently issued its final rule on Standards for Safeguarding Customer Information.[18] This rule will require financial institutions to develop, implement, and maintain a comprehensive information security program that contains administrative, technical, and physical safeguards. As part of this security program, each financial institution must

- designate an employee or employees to coordinate the information security program;
- identity reasonably foreseeable internal and external risks to the security, confidentiality, and integrity of customer information that could result in the unauthorized disclosure, misuse, alteration, destruction, or other compromise of information and assess the sufficiency of any safeguards in place to control the risks;
- ensure that contractors or service providers are capable of maintaining appropriate safeguards for the customer information and requiring them, by contract, to implement and maintain such safeguards; and
- adjust the information security program in light of developments that may materially affect the entity's safeguards.

The Health Insurance Portability and Accountability Act

Another piece of legislation with potential relevance to Internet privacy is the Health Insurance Portability and Accountability Act of 1996 (HIPAA).[19] HIPAA is extremely comprehensive health legislation. Of significance to the current discussion, HIPAA contains detailed provisions relating to the privacy of certain kinds of health information.

The obligation to comply with regulations on Standards for Privacy of Individually Identifiable Health Information (the HIPAA Privacy Rule)[20] issued pursuant to the HIPAA became effective for most covered entities on April 14, 2003. The exception to this is small health plans with $5 million or less in annual receipts, which will have until April 14, 2004 to comply with the HIPAA Privacy Rule.

The HIPAA Privacy Rule establishes a number of rules and requirements relative to the privacy and security of individually identifiable health information, which is defined as

[I]nformation that is a subset of health information, including demographic information collected from an individual, and: (1) Is created or received by a health care provider, health plan, employer, or health care clearinghouse; and (2) Relates to the past, present, or future physical or mental health or condition of an individual; the provision of health care to an individual; or the past, present, or future payment for the provision of health care to an individual; and (i) that identifies the individual; or (ii) with respect to which there is a reasonable basis to believe the information can be used to identify the individual.[21]

The requirements of the HIPAA Privacy Rule apply to health plans, health care providers and health care clearinghouses (collectively, Covered Entities). Among its many requirements, the HIPAA Privacy Rule mandates the creation and distribution of privacy policies that explain how all individually identifiable health information is collected, used and shared. The HIPAA Privacy Rule also establishes strict controls on the use and disclosure of individually identifiable health information. Entities that are subject to the requirements of the HIPAA Privacy Rule are not permitted to use or disclose individually identifiable health information except as permitted by such privacy rule.

While the requirements of the HIPAA Privacy Rule set forth the security standards and apply specifically to Covered Entities, the HIPAA Privacy Rule may also impact other types of entities because, subject to certain limited exceptions, the HIPAA Privacy Rule requires Covered Entities to execute Business Associate agreements with all third party service providers that will be provided with access to individually identifiable health information by the Covered Entity. Accordingly, entities that are not Covered Entities may still need to be aware of the requirements of the HIPAA Privacy Rule in order to negotiate effectively the terms and conditions of Business Associate agreements.

On February 13, 2003, the department of Health and Human Services announced the adoption of the final rule on Security Standards issued pursuant to HIPAA[22] (the HIPAA Security Rule). While announced in February 2003, the HIPAA Security Rule has an effective date of April 21, 2003. Most covered entities will have until April 21, 2005 in order to comply with the requirements of this rule. However, small health plans will have until April 21, 2006 to comply.

Section 164.306 of the HIPAA Security Rule sets forth the security standards and requires covered entities to

- ensure the confidentiality, integrity, and availability of all electronic protected health information created, received, maintained, or transmitted by the Covered Entity;
- protect against any reasonably anticipated threats or hazards to the security or integrity of such information;
- protect against any reasonably anticipated uses or disclosures of such information that are not permitted or required by the HIPAA Privacy Rule; and
- ensure compliance by the workplace.

The remainder of the HIPAA Security Rule sets forth the standards and specifications required to implement the general security standards. In doing so, the HIPAA Security Rule focuses on administrative safeguards, technical safeguards, business associate agreements and policies, procedures and documents.

The provisions pertaining to administrative safeguards focus on the security management process.[23] These sections of the HIPAA Security Rule mandate risk analysis, risk management, sanction policy, and information system activity review.[24]

Technical safeguards are covered in 45 C.F.R. 164.312. Pursuant to this section of the statute, Covered Entities must implement

- technical policies and procedures for access control on systems that maintain electronic protected health information;
- transmission security, including integrity controls and encryption;
- hardware, software, and/or procedural methods for providing audit controls;
- policies and procedures to protect electronic protected health information from improper alteration or destruction to ensure data integrity;
- person or entity authentication, which requires the covered entity to implement procedures that verify that a person or entity seeking access to electronic protected health information is the one claimed to be doing so.

Also of interest are the provisions of 45 C.F.R. 164.316, which require covered entities to implement reasonable and appropriate policies and procedures to comply with the standards, implementation specifications, or other requirements of the HIPAA Security Rule. Three required implementation specifications complete this standard, requiring that the covered entity must

- maintain the documentation for six years from the date of its creation or the date when it last was in effect, whichever is later;
- make the documentation available to those persons responsible for implementing the procedures to which the documentation pertains; and
- review documentation periodically, and update as needed, in response to environmental or operational changes affecting the security of the electronic protected health information.

Like the HIPAA Privacy Rule, Section 164.314 of the HIPAA Security Rule requires a Business Associate agreement. For relationships where a third party is used to create, receive, maintain, or transmit electronic protected health information on the covered entity's behalf, the Security Rule requires the business associate to

- implement administrative, physical, and technical safeguards that reasonably and appropriately protect the confidentiality, integrity and availability of the covered entity's electronic protected health information;
- ensure that its agents and subcontractors to whom it provides electronic protected health information meet the same standard;
- report to the covered entity any security incident of which it becomes aware; and
- ensure that the contract authorizes termination if the business associate has violated a material term.

Other Privacy Laws

There are a number of other federal privacy laws in addition to those discussed in the foregoing sections. Special attention was paid to those laws because they may be of particular importance to a company's Web-based operations. Nonetheless, there are a number of other laws that can also be of relevant when collecting personally identifiable information from individuals on-line.

One example is the Fair Credit Reporting Act (FCRA),[25] which imposes duties on consumer reporting agencies.[26] The FCRA requires every consumer credit reporting agency to take appropriate measures to prevent any inappropriate disclosure of information. For their part, prospective users of information must identify themselves, certify the purposes for obtaining the information, and certify that the information will not be used for any unauthorized purposes. Under the act, consumers have the right to opt out of receiving preapproved credit card offers in the mail. Consumers can call to remove their names from lists for prescreened offers of credit by informing any one of the large credit bureaus. A phone call will remove consumers from this list for two years. However, consumers who fill out a written form will be removed from the list forever.

Another interesting piece of legislation is the Electronic Communications Privacy Act (ECPA),[27] which places restrictions on the interception of electronic communications and creates privacy protections for stored electronic communications.[28] ECPA is broken down into individual titles that cover different areas related to electronic communications. Title I of ECPA concerns acquisition and disclosure of communication streams.[29] This title of the act is concerned with protecting both voice and data communications while in transit. The act's coverage of wire communications is limited to aural transfers made through cable, wire, and similar transmission media maintained by persons engaged in the business of providing or operating facilities for interstate or foreign communications.[30] ECPA prohibits the interception of oral, wire, and electronic communications by private and public parties unless specifically authorized by statute or by a court order. While e-mail is not directly mentioned in ECPA, it is included in the scope of its general protection of electronic communications.[31]

Title II of the act governs both the acquisition and disclosure of stored information.[32] The provisions of ECPA pertaining to stored communications prohibit the unauthorized access to, or use of, stored communications. These provisions also prohibit electronic communications service providers from disclosing the content of such stored communications except in certain limited circumstances.[33] Permissible disclosures include disclosures that are authorized by the sender or receiver of the message, disclosures that are necessary for the effective rendition of the service or system, and disclosures that pertain to the commission of a crime or law enforcement.[34]

Title III concerns the acquisition and disclosure of transactional information.[35] The provisions of this title contain restrictions on the use of mobile tracking devices, pen registers, and trap and trace devices. However, it is beyond the scope of this book to discuss these restrictions in substantial detail.

The statute authorizes individuals or entities that are aggrieved by any intentional violation of ECPA to commence a civil action. Appropriate relief for individuals or entities damaged as a result of a violation of the statute may include preliminary, equitable, or declaratory relief, as appropriate,[36] actual damages,[37] attorney's fees, and court costs.[38]

Also of potential interest is the Video Privacy Protection Act.[39] Subject to certain limited exceptions, this act prohibits videotape service providers[40] from disclosing personally identifiable information[41] about individuals who rent or buy videos to third parties.[42] The act provides that customers may bring an action against any video store that discloses personally identifiable information.[43] Actual damages are recoverable under the act but must not be less than liquidated damages in the amount of $2,500. In addition, punitive damages, as well as reasonable attorney's fees and litigation costs, may be awarded, and "preliminary and equitable" relief may be ordered as deemed appropriate. There is a two-year statute of limitations on proceedings brought pursuant to the act.

Furthermore, it is important to note that there continues to be a strong possibility of new federal legislation governing privacy. Each year brings a great number of proposals for new legislation concerning privacy, especially Internet privacy in the broad sense. In the 107th Congress, for example, the House of Representatives proposed H.R. 89 Online Privacy Protection Act of 2001 (a measure that would prescribe regulations to protect the privacy of personal information collected from and about individuals who are not covered by COPPA), H.R. 91 Social Security On-Line Privacy Protection Act (a measure to regulate the use by interactive computer services of Social Security account numbers and related personally identifiable information), H.R. 112 Electronic Privacy Protection Act (a proposal that would prohibit the making, importation, exportation, distribution, sale, offer for sale, installation, or use of an information collection device without proper labeling or notice and consent), and H.R. 237 (a bill that would protect the privacy of consumers who use the Internet), among many other proposals. Privacy-related proposals in the Senate included S. 324 Social Security Number Privacy Act of 2001 (a bill that would amend the GLB Act to prohibit the sale and purchase of the Social Security number of an individual by financial institutions and to include Social Security numbers in the definition of nonpublic personal information), S. 536 Freedom from Behavioral Profiling Act of 2000 (a proposal that would amend the GLB Act to provide for a limitation on sharing of marketing and behavioral profiling information), and S. 1055 Privacy Act of 2001 (a proposal that would require the consent of an individual prior to the sale and marketing of such individual's personally identifiable information), along with numerous other proposed initiatives.

State Laws

While there are a number of laws at the federal level that can impact the way a company does business on-line, there is also a growing body of state privacy laws that can be of concern to companies that may be collecting personal information on-line. Many states specifically guarantee the right of privacy in their constitutions.[44] However, although a number of state constitutions contain provisions that protect individual privacy, a great number of these provisions focus on protecting the individual from governmental intrusions of privacy.[45]

A number of states have enacted legislation concerning specific matters of privacy protection such as unsolicited commercial e-mail, the protection of consumer credit information, school records, and financial data.[46] Other states have adopted more general privacy protection legislation. A good example is California's Personal Information and Privacy Protection Act.[47] This legislation mandated the creation of an Office of Privacy Protection within the department of consumer affairs and provided that the duties of the office would be to protect "the privacy of individuals' personal information in a manner consistent with the California Constitution by identifying consumer problems in the privacy area and facilitating development of fair information practices."[48] The Personal Information and Privacy Act contains a number of other interesting provisions concerning privacy, including the requirement that all state department and agencies enact and maintain permanent privacy policies.

U.S.-Based Self-Regulatory Initiatives

In addition to federal and state laws and regulations, there are a number of self-regulatory initiatives in place in the United States. Entities may find that their participation in such initiatives can demonstrate to their customers and business partners that they are serious about privacy and have taken concrete steps toward providing adequate privacy protections. Seal programs are among the most popular self-regulatory initiatives. The basic premise of such programs is that entities that agree to abide by certain rules when collecting, using, and transferring personal data are preauthorized to display a seal or other mark on their Web site indicating their participation in the program and their compliance with its terms.

TRUSTe offers one of the most prominent privacy seal programs. TRUSTe is a nonprofit organization that was formed by two other nonprofits, the Electronic Frontier Foundation and Commerce Net.[49] The TRUSTe initiative was officially launched in 1997. Today it is the most widely used program of its kind. In July 2002, TRUSTe was said to have more than 1,300 participants.[50] In addition to its general privacy seal programs, TRUSTe also offers a European Union Safe Harbor Privacy Seal program for Web sites that comply with the Safe Harbor program and a children's privacy seal program that coincides with COPPA.

Another self-regulatory initiative has been put forth by the Better Business Bureau Online (BBBOnline), a subsidiary of the Council of Better Business Bureaus.[51] BBBOnline officially launched its seal program in 1999. Participants in the BBBOnline program must operate and maintain a U.S.-based Web site and adopt a privacy policy concerning required elements. As of July 2002, BBBOnline listed several hundred entities as participating in its privacy seal program.[52]

While TRUSTe and BBBOnline represent two of the most popular privacy seal programs, there are a number of other programs, including the Web Trust program that was jointly developed by the American Institute of Chartered Public Accountants and the Canadian Institute of Chartered Accountants[53] and the PriceWaterhouse Cooper's Better Web program.[54] Moreover, it appears likely that the development and expansion of seal programs will continue. Such programs provide entities with another mechanism for enhancing consumer confidence regarding their privacy practices and policies.

Summary of the U.S. Approach

As has been demonstrated from the previous discussion, in the United States, privacy protections are somewhat piecemeal in nature. What privacy legislation exists tends to focus on specific types of data or specific industries. For instance, U.S. legislators have demonstrated a particular propensity for protecting certain types of data such as medical records, financial records, Social Security numbers, consumer credit data, and personal information concerning children.

Unlike the other countries that will be examined in this chapter, the United States does not have a broad and comprehensive data privacy law that applies to all data, irrespective of the particular industrial sector that is involved in the processing of such data. Each year there are a number of proposals for legislation that would bring legal protection to the privacy of a broad class of data or at least require Web site operators to post and implement accurate on-line privacy policies. Thus far, however, none of these initiatives have passed.

The next section will focus on privacy protection in Europe, an area of the world where privacy is viewed quite differently than it is in the United States. While many European countries have been revising data privacy laws to take into account new concerns brought about by the Internet age, the vast majority of western European countries have had comprehensive data privacy laws in place for more than 20 years. In many European countries, privacy has long been viewed as a fundamental human right. This interpretation of privacy is evident in the case law and legislation of European countries, as well as in key multinational instruments such as the Guidelines on the Protection of Privacy and Transborder Flows of Data of the Organization for Economic Cooperation and Development.[55] The next section will examine the current European data privacy rules in close detail and explore what they might mean to entities operating globally accessible Web sites.

THE EUROPEAN UNION

Background

The European Data Protection Directive was passed on October 24, 1995, and came into effect on October 25, 1998.[56] It is extremely comprehensive legislation that concerns all aspects of personal data processing. Because the Data Protection Directive was passed in 1995, a time when the Internet was really just beginning to develop as a significant commercial force, the directive did not really focus on specific Internet issues related to data protection. Instead it treated the protection of personal data from a broad perspective. Also significantly, "personal data" are defined broadly under the directive as "any information relating to an identified or identifiable natural person."[57]

The Data Protection Directive, as other European Community directives, is not a law directed at individual entities. Instead it is a set of directions to the Member States of the European Union, requiring such states to implement certain requirements in their own national laws. The result of this is that while the laws of each Member State are required to be consistent with the directive, they will often differ from each other in certain, potentially significant ways. This is important because entitles in control of operations involving the processing of personal data (also called "controllers") must comply with the data protection laws of the country in which they are established, as well as the laws of the particular Member State(s) in which they process personal data.[58]

Basic Principles Applicable to Data Processing

The directive addresses the protection of personal data from a number of different perspectives. At its most basic level, the directive establishes certain conditions that must be met to process personal data. The directive specifies that there are only six situations pursuant to which entities can process personal data:

1. the individual has provided his or her unambiguous consent to such processing;[59]
2. the individual has entered into a contract that provides for, or anticipates, the processing of the data;[60]
3. the processing is necessary to fulfill a legal obligation of the individual;[61]
4. the processing is necessary to protect the individual's "vital interests";[62]

5. the processing is in the public interest or is being done at the behest of an official authority;[63] or

6. the processing is necessary to pursue the legitimate interests of the party collecting or using the data, except to the extent that those interests are overridden by the rights of the individual to the privacy of the information about himself or herself.[64]

In addition to these general preconditions, which are applicable to all kinds of personal data, the directive places heightened restrictions on the collection and use of "special categories" of personal data, which consist of "personal data revealing racial or ethnic origin, political opinions, religious or philosophical beliefs, trade union membership, and . . . data concerning health or sex life."[65] These special categories of data may only be processed if

1. the individual has provided his or her consent, provided that the laws of the particular Member States recognize it;[66]

2. the party collecting or using the information is doing so in fulfillment of its legal obligations relating to employment law;[67]

3. the individual is unable to give consent, and his or her vital interests are at stake;[68]

4. the party collecting or using the information is a nonprofit organization with a political, philosophical, religious, or trade union aim of which the individual is a member or is regularly associated;[69]

5. the information is the subject of legal claims or has otherwise been made public;[70]

6. the information concerns health care, provided it is collected or used by a professional under a legal or professional obligation of confidentiality;[71] or

7. such use or collection of data is in the interest of substantial public interest, in accordance with national law.[72]

Notice Requirements

The Data Protection Directive also has significant notice requirements. Under the terms of the directive, entities processing personal data must report their actions to the data protection supervisory authority[73] of the Member State in which they are operating.[74] The supervisory authorities of each Member State tend to have their own procedural and notice requirements. However, generally, the notice that is made to the supervisory authorities must indicate

1. the name and address of the controller and of his or her representative(s);[75]

2. the purpose(s) of processing;[76]

3. a description of the category or categories of the data subject and of the data or categories of data relating to him or her;[77]

4. the recipients or categories of recipient to whom the data might be disclosed;

5. proposed transfers of data to third countries;[78] and

6. a general description allowing a preliminary assessment to be made of the appropriateness of the measures taken pursuant to Article 17 to ensure the security of personal data processing.[79]

In many countries, failing to act in accordance with the notice requirements can leave the controller subject to serious penalties. The notice requirements play an important role in the overall scheme of personal data protection. The intent of the comprehensive notice requirements appears to be to ensure that the individual who is the subject of data-processing operations can effectively monitor the movement of his or her personal data between different data processors and data controllers.

The Rights of the Data Subject

The directive provides individuals who are data subjects with significant rights to ensure that the entity controlling the processing of their data is not processing more personal data than is necessary and is processing the correct data. Specifically, pursuant to the terms of the directive, data subjects have the right to obtain the following information from the data controller:[80]

1. whether the controller has any data about the individual;

2. the purpose for which the data are being used, if any;

3. the categories of data that have been obtained;

4. the recipients or categories of recipients of the data;

5. the actual data undergoing processing, in a readable form;

6. the source of the data, if known; and

7. to the extent the data are being used in any "automated decision making" capacity, the logic by which such decisions are being made.

The directive requires that such information be provided to the data subject "without constraint" and "without excessive delay or expense."[81] Such rights of access and rectification, not generally available in the

United States, appear to be an important part of ensuring that personal data are used properly and in compliance with applicable law. If access and rectification rights are truly available and are actually used by data subjects, the likelihood that incorrect data will linger in organizations' systems diminishes substantially.

Data Security

The directive also requires data controllers and processors to implement appropriate security measures to protect personal data. This obligation to ensure that personal data are afforded adequate security is a requirement that is appearing in an increasing number of laws and regulations both in the United States and abroad. When analyzed, the requirement is highly logical. In reality, entities' promises concerning the limitations on the use and transfer of personal data that they collect are only as useful as the security measures that they implement to protect such data.

The Data Protection Directive establishes a relatively broad and general rule concerning the security of personal data. The directive provides that "Member States shall provide that the controller must implement appropriate technical and organizational measures to protect personal data against accidental or unlawful destruction or accidental loss, alteration, unauthorized disclosure or access, in particular where the processing involves the transmission of data over a network and against all other unlawful forms of processing."[82]

Further, in determining what security measures would be appropriate, data controllers are called upon to consider the state of the art, the cost of the implementation of the security measures, the risks represented by the processing, and the nature of the data to be protected.[83]

The result of the use of such general language in the directive is that there are considerable differences in the security requirements—and the penalties for violating those requirements—from country to country. Many Member States have implemented stringent requirements that may vary somewhat based on the kind of processing that is being undertaken. Spain, for instance, requires entities to implement high security measures for processing operations involving personal data revealing racial or ethnic origin, political opinions, religious or philosophical beliefs, trade union membership, or data concerning health or sex life, and data for police purposes, whenever there is no consent of the data subjects.[84] Entities that fail to implement such high-level security requirements when processing these types of data may face fines from €60,100 to €601,000.

It is also notable that the European approach to data security seeks to hold the controller accountable for the security measures implemented by any third-party data processors involved with processing the personal data. Under the terms of the directive, controllers are not able to simply delegate their security obligations to the processing entities. Instead, the directive compels controllers that rely on data processors to "choose a processor providing sufficient guarantees in respect of the technical security measures and organizational measures governing the processing to be carried out."[85] Furthermore, the directive requires the controller and processor to enter into an agreement that binds the processor to the controller and stipulates that the processor may act only on the instructions of the controller and that the processor must act in compliance with the security requirements of the directive as they are implemented in the laws of the relevant Member State(s).[86]

Data Transfer Provisions

Background

One of the most notable aspects of the Data Protection Directive is the section concerning transfers of personal data to countries outside of the European Economic Area. Article 25 of the directive prohibits the transfer of personal data to third countries that do not provide adequate protection to personal data unless one of several limited exceptions apply.

Determining Adequacy

Article 25(2) of the directive sets forth a list of factors to be taken into account when judging the adequacy of protection in third countries. In determining whether a particular jurisdiction provides adequate protection to personal data, European authorities are required to assess not only the actual privacy laws of the country at issue but also the efficacy of those laws.

Significant in relation to making adequacy assessments is the working party that was established pursuant to Article 29 of the Data Protection Directive (the "Working Party") and is composed of data protection commissioners from each EU Member State, along with European Commission officials. The Working Party has produced useful guidance documents on the approaches that are to be taken when evaluating whether the level of protection provided in a third country is adequate. The approach put forth by the Working Party focuses on a set of principles. The first principle is the purpose limitation principle. According to this principle, personal data should be processed for a specific purpose and subsequently used or further communicated only insofar as this process is compatible with the purpose of the transfer.

The second principle is the data quality and proportionality principle. According to this principle, data should be accurate and, where necessary, kept up to date. Furthermore, personal data should be adequate, relevant, and not excessive in relation to the purposes for which they are transferred or further processed.

The third is the transparency principle. In accordance with this principle, individuals should be provided with information about the purpose of the processing and the identity of the data controller in the third country, and other information insofar as this information is necessary to ensure fairness.

Next is the security principle. Pursuant to this principle, technical and organizational security measures should be taken that are appropriate to the risks presented by the processing. Any person acting under the authority of the data controller must not process data except on instructions from the data controller.

The individual's rights to access, rectification, and opposition must also be considered. According to this principle, the data subject should have a right to obtain a copy of all processed data relating to him or her and a right to rectification of those data where they are shown to be inaccurate. In certain situations, he or she should also be able to object to the processing of the data relating to him or her.

Finally, restrictions on onward transfers must also be considered. Generally, transfers of personal data from the recipient to another third party should not be permitted, unless a means is found of contractually binding the third party in question, thereby providing the same data protection guarantees to the data subjects. This principle is important in relation to the European regulators' intent to prohibit the use of countries with "adequate" protection as intermediaries for exporting data to the actual destination country where that country does not provide adequate protection to personal data.

Principles for Determining Adequacy of Privacy Protection in Third Countries

Purpose limitation principle

Data quality and proportionality principle

Transparency

Security

Individual rights to access, rectification, and opposition

Restrictions on onward transfers

To date, only a handful of countries have been approved by the European Commission as providing adequate protection to personal data. Currently, only Argentina, Hungary,[87] Switzerland,[88] and Canada[89] are considered to provide adequate protection to personal data. Notably, the entities participating in the Safe Harbor program that was negotiated between officials of the European Union and the U.S. Department of Commerce are also considered as providing adequate protection to personal data.[90]

Concerns about the possibility of a "trade war" resulting from the data transfer provisions in the Data Protection Directive led to negotiations between American and European representatives that eventually resulted in the Safe Harbor program. Entities that desire to participate in the program must certify that they comply with the seven major principles of the initiative, which are notice, choice, onward transfer, access, security, data integrity, and enforcement. These principles are summarized hereafter.[91]

While Safe Harbor may not be the perfect solution for the differences in data protection requirements found in the European Union and the United States, the program does offer a number of advantages for entities that process personal data. For instance, entities engaging in frequent transfers of data between the European Union and the United States are likely to appreciate the predictability and continuity offered by the Safe Harbor program. Instead of having to analyze each and every proposed transfer of data to determine whether it complies with one of the exceptions contained in the Data Protection Directive, entities participating in Safe Harbor will simply have to comply with the program's principles and the certifications made to the U.S. Department of Commerce. In addition, the Safe Harbor program provides for a comparative flexible approach that many small and medium enterprises are likely to welcome.

Although the negotiation of the Safe Harbor initiative is something that was long anticipated, there has not been a large response to the program. At the time of this writing, only 390 entities had signed on to participate in the initiative.[92] There are a number of possible reasons for this lackluster response. One is that many entities are simply not aware of the requirements of the Data Protection Directive and the possibility

Safe Harbor Principles

Notice. An organization must inform individuals about the purposes for which it collects and uses information about them, how to contact the organization with any inquiries or complaints, the types of third parties to which it discloses the information, and the choices and means the organization offers individuals for limiting its use and disclosure. This notice must be provided in clear and conspicuous language when individuals are first asked to provide personal information to the organization or as soon thereafter as is practicable, but in any event before the organization uses such information for a purpose other than that for which it was originally collected or processed by the transferring organization or discloses it for the first time to a third party.

Choice. An organization must offer individuals the opportunity to choose (opt out) whether their personal information is (1) to be disclosed to a third party or (2) to be used for a purpose that is incompatible with the purpose(s) for which it was originally collected or subsequently authorized by the individual. Individuals must be provided with clear and conspicuous, readily available, and affordable mechanisms to exercise choice.

For sensitive information (i.e., personal information specifying medical or health conditions, racial or ethnic origin, political opinions, religious or philosophical beliefs, trade union membership, or information specifying the sex life of the individual), they must be given affirmative or explicit (opt in) choice if the information is to be disclosed to a third party or used for a purpose other than that for which it was originally collected or subsequently authorized by the individual through the exercise of opt-in choice. In any case, an organization should treat as sensitive any information received from a third party where the third party treats and identifies it as sensitive.

Onward transfer. To disclose information to a third party, organizations must apply the notice and choice principles. Where an organization wishes to transfer information to a third party that is acting as an agent, it may do so if it first either ascertains that the third party subscribes to the principles or is subject to the directive or another adequacy finding or enters into a written agreement with such third party requiring that the third party provide at least the same level of privacy protection as is required by the relevant principles. If the organization complies with these requirements, it will not be held responsible (unless the organization agrees otherwise) when a third party to which it transfers such information processes it in a way contrary to any restrictions or representations, unless the organization knew or should have known that the third party would process it in such a contrary way and the organization has not taken reasonable steps to prevent or stop such processing.

Security. Organizations creating, maintaining, using, and disseminating personal information must take reasonable precautions to protect it from loss, misuse, and unauthorized access, disclosure, alteration, and destruction.

Data integrity. Consistent with the principles, personal information must be relevant for the purposes for which it is to be used. An organization may not process personal information in a way that is incompatible with the purposes for which it has been collected or subsequently authorized by the individual. To the extent necessary for those purposes, an organization should take reasonable steps to ensure that the data are reliable for their intended use, accurate, complete, and current.

Access. Individuals must have access to personal information about them that an organization holds and must be able to correct, amend, or delete that information where it is inaccurate, except where the burden or expense of providing access would be disproportionate to the risks to the individual's privacy in the case in question, or where the rights of persons other than the individual would be violated.

Enforcement. Effective privacy protection must include mechanisms for ensuring compliance with the principles, recourse for individuals to whom the data relate affected by noncompliance with the principles, and consequences for the organization when the principles are not followed. At a minimum, such mechanisms must include (1) readily available and affordable independent recourse mechanisms by which each individual's complaints and disputes are investigated and resolved by reference to the principles, with damages awarded where the applicable law or private sector initiatives so provide; (2) follow-up procedures for verifying that the attestations and assertions businesses make about their privacy practices are true and that privacy practices have been implemented as presented; and (3) obligations to remedy problems arising out of failure to comply with the principles by organizations announcing their adherence to them and consequences for such organizations. Sanctions must be sufficiently rigorous to ensure compliance by organizations.

of enrolling in Safe Harbor as a means for achieving compliance. Other companies, while aware of the issue, may not believe that achieving compliance with the requirements of the Data Protection Directive and the relevant implementing legislation is worth the time and expense or the assumption of additional legal liabilities in the United States. Still other companies may have determined that other compliance solutions better fit their needs and business models. It will be interesting to monitor this situation and analyze whether any increase in enforcement actions on the part of the Europeans leads to increased enrollment in Safe Harbor in the United States.

Exemption on Prohibitions of Transfers

In considering the transfer of personal data to third countries, attention should be directed toward the exemptions that are included in the Data

Protection Directive. Article 26(1) of the directive provides certain exemptions from the requirement for adequate protection. The first exemption concerns situations in which the data subject provides his or her unambiguous consent to the proposed transfer. While it is likely that many enterprises will attempt to rely on this exemption when making transfers of personal data to third countries, it is important that the particular facts of the proposed transfers, as well as the specific requirements of relevant national laws, be reviewed carefully before relying on this exemption. Generally, to be valid, consent must be freely given, specific, and informed. However, the national laws of the Member States implementing the directive may contain different nuances concerning the interpretation of consent. Accordingly, when attempting to implement a mechanism for obtaining user consent for a data transfer, it will be necessary to examine specific national interpretations of the meaning of consent in this context.

The second and third exemptions are somewhat related in that they both concern the performance of a contract. Article 26(2)(b) of the directive provides that a transfer of personal data can proceed to a third country, regardless of whether there has been a finding of adequacy in that country, if "the transfer is necessary for the performance of a contract between the data subject and the controller or the implementation of pre-contractual measures taken in response to the data subject's request." There are a number of scenarios that might fit under this exemption. For instance, if an individual in Denmark contracts with a Danish travel company to arrange for a trip to New York, the travel agency would likely be permitted to transfer the personal data of the Danish resident to the tour company in the United States in order to make the requested travel arrangements.

Similarly, Article 26(2)(c) provides that such transfers may proceed where "necessary for the conclusion of performance of a contract concluded in the interest of the data subject between the controller and a third party." While these exemptions are relatively broad, it is once again necessary to caution against taking the exemptions at face value. Instead, national law must be examined to understand the precise interpretation of the exemption at issue under the law of the Member States(s) from which one is attempting to transfer personal data.

The next exemption provides that transfers of data may proceed where "necessary or legally required on important public interest grounds, or for the establishment, exercise or defense of legal claims."[93] This category of exemption might be used where personal data are being transferred between various public administrations, such as between the *douane* of France and the customs agents of the United States. It may also be relied on within the context of international litigation.

The fifth exemption under Article 26 of the directive applies when the "transfer is necessary in order to protect the vital interests of the data subject." When analyzing the potential use of this exemption, it is necessary also to consider Recital 31 of the directive, which defines "vital interest" narrowly as interests "essential for the data subject's life."[94] Based on such a definition, this exemption appears to be limited to situations such as those in which the transfer of data would be necessary to provide urgent medical care to an individual.

The final exemption is somewhat of a catchall, providing that transfers of data may proceed if the "transfer is made from a register which according to laws or regulations is intended to provide information to the public and which is open to consultation either by the public in general or by any person who can demonstrate legitimate interest, to the extent that the conditions laid down in law for consultation are fulfilled in the particular case."[95]

On the face of it, this list of derogations from the requirements of Article 25 of the directive does appear rather broad. However, the actual utility of any of the foregoing options will depend to a great extent on how they are actually interpreted and implemented under the relevant national law.

Summary of Derogations from Article 25 of the Data Protection Directive

Unambiguous consent of the data subject

Necessary for the performance of a contract between the data subject and the controller or the implementation of precontractual measures

Necessary for the conclusion or performance of a contract concluded in the interest of the data subject between the controller and a third party

Important public interest grounds; establishment, exercise, or defense of legal claims

Necessary to protect the vital interests of the data subject

Made from a public register

Contractual Solutions

While one or more of the derogations listed may be useful with respect to certain transfers of data, it may not always be possible to rely on one of the aforementioned categories. One method that may be used to transfer personal data when such a transfer would not otherwise be authorized in accordance with one of the exceptions is through the use of contracts. Article 26(3) of the directive provides that Member States may authorize transfers of personal data to countries that do not provide adequate protection to personal data where the controller "adduces adequate safeguards with respect to the protection of the privacy and fundamental rights and freedoms of individuals."[96] This section goes on to indicate that the "adequate safeguards" may result from the use of appropriate contractual clauses. Relying on this approach is probably one of the most palatable options for the business community, which is well accustomed to using contracts for a number of purposes, including the achievement of regulatory compliance. However, some level of caution is once again necessary. In practice, European regulators may desire and expect much more burdensome contractual clauses than many American companies receiving data would be willing to accept.

Self-Regulation

Another potential option for ensuring the continued free flow of data from Europe to third countries such as the United States is through the development and implementation of various self-regulatory initiatives. Thus far, the opinions issued by the Working Party appear to have left open the option for the use of industry self-regulation as a means of ensuring adequacy of data protection. The approval of specific self-regulatory initiatives at the European Community level would be particular attractive to American companies, which are accustomed to working within the confines of self-regulatory initiatives in a number of different areas, including, notably, the advertising sector. At the same time, however, while self-regulation remains at least a theoretical possibility, it may be difficult to convince European regulators that a self-regulatory plan would actually offer effective data protection.

Summary of the European Approach

It is evident from the foregoing that the European Union takes a drastically different view of privacy than the United States. In Europe, protection of individual privacy is viewed as a fundamental human right, and violations of that right are taken very seriously. Europe's history and treatment of privacy appears to have contributed to the region's early involvement in encouraging the application of principles of privacy to new technologies, and such early involvement appears to have given the

Europeans somewhat of a head start with respect to Internet privacy issues.

CANADA

Enactment of Personal Information Protection and Electronic Documents Act

On January 1, 2001, the first phase of the Personal Information Protection and Electronic Documents Act (the Canadian Act) entered into force in Canada.[97] The Canadian Act is comprehensive legislation that is intended to "govern the collection, use and disclosure of personal information to protect the privacy of individuals"[98] while recognizing "the need of organizations to collect, use or disclose personal information for purposes that a reasonable person would consider appropriate in the circumstances."[99]

The Canadian Act has been implemented in three phases. The first phase, which became effective on January 1, 2001, applies to certain data collected in connection with the operation of a "federal work, undertaking or business," as well as to organizations that, in the course of commercial activity, disclose the personal information outside the province in exchange for consideration. During the second phase, which commenced in 2002, the health care sector was required to comply with the terms of the act. Finally, the third phase, commencing in 2004, broadens the reach of the law to regulate all personal information collected, used, or disclosed in the course of all commercial activity. A significant aspect of the Canadian Act is that it has no grandfather clause. Personal information collected prior to the effective date of the act cannot be used or disclosed following the effective date unless such information was collected in accordance with the act.

General Requirements

The Canadian Act incorporates[100] the Canadian Standards Association Model Code for the Protection of Personal Information, a model code that was adopted by the National Standard of Canada in 1996. Although these principles are described in the act as recommendations, an entity's failure to comply with such recommendations can constitute grounds for a complaint. The code and the act are based on ten principles: (1) accountability; (2) identifying purposes; (3) knowledge and consent; (4) limiting collection; (5) limiting use, disclosure, and retention; (6) accuracy;

(7) safeguards; (8) openness; (9) individual access; and (10) challenging compliance.

1. *Accountability.* Pursuant to this principle, an organization is responsible for personal information under its control and most designate one or more individuals to be responsible.

2. *Identifying purposes.* In accordance with this second principle, the purpose for which the personal information will be used must be identified by the organization either before or at the time that the information is collected, and such purposes must be documented.

3. *Knowledge and consent.* This principle provides that, except in certain cases, the knowledge and consent of an individual are required for the collection, use, or disclosure of personal information.

4. *Limiting collection.* According to this principle, both the amount and type of personal information collected must be limited to that which is necessary for the purposes disclosed to the individual.

5. *Limiting use, disclosure, and retention.* This principle requires that personal information may be used or disclosed only for the purposes for which it was collected, unless the individual provides consent for such other use, or disclosure or law requires the use or disclosure of the information.

6. *Accuracy.* According to this principle, personal information must be accurate, current, and complete as needed for the purposes for which the information will be used.

7. *Safeguards.* This principle provides that an organization must use appropriate security safeguards to protect the personal information that it processes.

8. *Openness.* Pursuant to this principle, an organization's policies and practices relating to the management of personal information must be available for scrutiny without unreasonable effort and in a form that is generally understandable.

9. *Individual access.* Upon request, an individual must be informed about the existence, use, and disclosure of his or her personal information. Additionally, he or she must have the ability to challenge the accuracy, currency, and completeness of the personal information.

10. *Challenging Compliance.* According to this principle, an individual must be able to challenge an organization's compliance with the principles set forth in the act. Further, the organization must have procedures in place to receive and respond to complaints.

The act places two key categories of obligations on entities: (1) obligations concerning the processing of personal information, and (2) various administrative obligations. In terms of the substantive obligations concerning the processing of personal information, entities are required to identify and document the limited purposes for which the personal data they collect will be processed. They also must ensure that they have the data subject's consent for the processing of their data for that specific identified purpose.

The act applies to personal data collected in Canada. Accordingly, it may not be possible to escape the requirements of the act by only using data collected from Canada while outside the Canadian territorial jurisdiction. Even entities that are not doing any business in Canada but are receiving data from entities in Canada will be impacted by the act. If a Canadian company transfers personal information to a subsidiary, affiliate, or third party in the United States, the act compels the Canadian company to "use contractual or other means to provide a comparable level of protection while the information is being processed." Thus an American company that wishes to receive personal information from a Canadian firm, affiliate, or subsidiary will likely be required to execute a contract that commits the company to following Canada's privacy law.

On the administrative side, companies are required to designate an individual in charge of the personal data, adopt policies to give effect to the act, maintain the accuracy of the personal information, retain personal information for only as long as is necessary for the purpose of its processing, adopt security safeguards to protect personal information, provide access and rectification procedures to data subjects, and adopt procedures to respond to inquiries and complaints concerning compliance with the act.

Exceptions

The act specifies exceptions to the requirement that an organization acquire consent before collecting, using, or disclosing personal information. It also provides for exceptions to the access requirements. The following excerpts are not exhaustive but reflect some of the situations where information may be collected, used, or disclosed without the subject's knowledge and consent and situations where access may be denied or limited. The act stipulates that consent is not required when (1) collection of information clearly benefits the individual (which is not defined) and consent cannot be obtained in a timely way; (2) it is reasonable to expect that the collection would compromise the availability or accuracy of the information and the collection is reasonable for purposes related to investigating a breach of an agreement or a contravention of the laws of Canada or a province; (3) the collection is solely for journalistic, artistic, or literary purposes; and (4) the information is publicly available and is specified by the regulations.[101]

The act also stipulates that knowledge and consent are not required when, in addition to the foregoing exceptions, the information is used (1) because the organization reasonably believes the information would be useful, and is used, to investigate an ongoing, past, or proposed contravention of the laws of Canada, a province, or a foreign jurisdiction; (2) in connection with an emergency that threatens the life, health, or security of an individual; or (3) in connection with statistical, or scholarly study or research, for purposes that cannot be achieved without using the information, provided that the information is used in a manner that will ensure its confidentiality, it is impracticable to obtain consent, and the organization informs the commissioner of the use before the information is used.

The act stipulates that knowledge and consent are not required when the information is disclosed for a number of reasons. Those reasons include disclosures (1) made for the purposes of collecting a debt owed by the individual to the organization; or (2) additional purposes that echo those set forth in the foregoing paragraphs and include disclosure made in connection with interests of national security and the conservation of historical records.

The act sets forth various exceptions to the requirement that organizations provide access to an individual's personal information. A number of them concern access to information provided to a government institution in connection with subpoena, law enforcement investigations, or matters of national security. The act also provides that access may be refused where (1) the information is protected by solicitor-client privilege, or (2) to do so would reveal confidential commercial information (and the confidential information is not severable from the requested information).[102]

Enforcement Mechanisms

Complaints can be initiated by anyone, including customers, suppliers, and competitors. The privacy commissioner is empowered to investigate all complaints under the act and to attempt to resolve them by a number of methods, including mediation or conciliation. The privacy commissioner has broad investigative powers. Provided that the commissioner is satisfied that there are reasonable grounds to proceed with the pursuit of a complaint, the privacy commissioner can search and investigate entities' premises, administer oaths, and conduct interviews. Notwithstanding the powers of the privacy commissioner, individuals who contend that their rights under the act have been violated still have recourse to the courts. Entities who violate the act are subject to a range of penalties, including public disclosure of the information practices, fines (for which company directors, officers, and employees may be personally liable), and court-ordered damages.

SOUTH AMERICA

A number of South American countries have begun to follow the lead of countries in Europe and North America and have started to enact comprehensive privacy legislation. This action appears to be based at least in part on the restrictions that that European Data Protection Directive places on the transfer of personal data to countries outside the EU that are considered as failing to provide adequate protection to personal data. In 1999 Chile became the first country in South America to enact legislation pertaining to the protection of personal information. The Law for the Protection of Private Life came in force on October 28 of that year.[103] The legislation covers the processing and use of personal data in the public and private sector. In addition to setting forth guidelines pertaining to the collection, use, and disclosure of personal information, the Chilean act provides individuals with the right to access and correct their personal information and includes fines and damages for the unlawful denial of such access and correction rights.

Argentina also recently enacted the Privacy Data Protection Law.[104] This is a comprehensive law that addresses a number of different aspects of privacy rights. A review of this legislation suggests that it is intended to follow the European Data Protection Directive. In fact, the European Commission recently ruled that Argentina's law provides "adequate" protection to personal data for the purposes of the Data Protection Directive.

Other countries in this region have data protection laws that date back even further. In Brazil, for example, the 1990 Code of Consumer Protection and Defense provides consumers with the right to access information concerning them that is stored in files, archives, and registries, as well as the right to amend incorrect data.[105] This law also requires all consumer data files to be objective, clear, true, and written in a manner that is easily understood. Also significant in Brazil, the Informatics Law of 1984 provides certain protections to the confidentiality of stored, processed, and disclosed data.[106] This law also provides individuals with the right to access and correct their personal information held in private or public databases.

A number of other Latin American countries are considering proposals for data protection legislation that could affect companies outside Latin America that receive personal data from within Latin America. These developments highlight the growing importance of the regulation of privacy and serve as a reminder of the importance of remaining vigilant about local national regulatory developments when operating a Web site that is accessible throughout the world.

ASIA

A number of Asian countries have also implemented comprehensive data privacy laws. Notable among such countries is Hong Kong, which has rather stringent data protection legislation. Hong Kong's main data protection law dates back to 1995, the same year that the European Data Protection Directive was passed. The Personal Data (Privacy) Ordinance establishes six principles to regulate the collection, accuracy, use, and security of personal data.[107] It also requires data users to inform data subjects about their data processing and grants data subjects the right to be provided a copy of their personal data and to demand corrections to such data. It also imposes additional restrictions on certain uses of personal data, including data matching and cross-border transfers of personal data.

Also similar to the European Data Protection Directive, which establishes data protection supervisory authorities in each of the European Union Member States, the Hong Kong ordinance establishes the Office of the Privacy Commissioner.[108] In Hong Kong, the mandate of the privacy commissioner is to promote and enforce compliance with the relevant statutory requirements. Similar to the situation in the United Kingdom, the privacy commissioner of Hong Kong has broad enforcement power and may initiate investigations of suspected violations of the statutory requirements.

A number of other Asian countries are in various stages of developing and implementing specific privacy laws. The continued rollout of privacy legislation in Asia and elsewhere will only increase the compliance obligations of entities engaging in electronic commerce of a global basis.

RESPONDING TO INCREASED PRIVACY LEGISLATION

Developing a Privacy Program

As has been demonstrated, companies engaging in cross-border electronic commerce have a plethora of legal requirements with which to comply. Notwithstanding these diverse requirements, there is one basic rule when it comes to privacy on the Internet: Do what you say. In recent years, the debate over the privacy of personal information on the Internet has become more intense and more complicated through the passage of a slew of legislation both here and abroad. While it is true that privacy laws contain a number of different requirements, if one makes adequate disclosures about the kinds of personal data that will be collected, how such personal data will be used, whether they will be transferred and to whom, *and* if one acts in a manner consistent with those disclosures, it is likely that many of the requirements of the applicable privacy laws will have been met.

Developing and implementing an effective privacy plan is not only important to ensure compliance with law; it truly is part of an effective e-commerce business plan. Research has repeatedly shown that many consumers are reluctant to engage in electronic transactions because of concerns about the privacy of their personal data.[109] Privacy policies and accurate public statements outlining such policies are a vital step toward encouraging openness and trust in electric commerce among visitors to Web sites. They can help visitors to make informed choices about entrusting an entity with personal data and doing business with it.

Key Tips in Privacy Policy Development

Web site privacy policies come in all shapes and sizes. While such policies should set forth information about the Web site operator's compliance with its various legal requirements, they should also provide specific information about the entity's endeavors and its policies with regard to the collection, use, and transfer of personal information. Accordingly, it not advisable to simply post a model privacy policy on one's Web site. That being said, however, there are a number of features that should be included in all privacy policies. At a basic level, a privacy policy should disclose the following information:

- What personal data are collected
- The name and contact information for the organization that is collecting the personal data
- How the personal data collected through the Web site will be used
- Whether the personal data collected through the Web site will be transferred or made available to any third parties and, if so, to whom and for what purpose

- What choices the individual has concerning the use of his or her personal data
- What kinds of security measures have been implemented to protect the personal data that are provided
- How individuals may find out what personal data are held by the organization and how such information may be corrected or deleted

Set forth hereafter is a sample privacy policy for a relatively simple Web site through which a relatively small amount of personal data is collected. This sample privacy policy is included to serve as an example of some of the issues that one may wish to address when developing a privacy policy. It is not intended to represent form policy capable of being posted on any Web site. Most lawyers will advise against copying and using forms in all areas of practice. Such a rule is particularly important within the context of privacy policies. The whole purpose of a privacy policy is to explain what an entity will and will not do with the personal data that it collects. Using a policy developed by someone else for their own service will not help to accomplish this objective.

Once the privacy policy is developed, it will be essential to evaluate the policy. The Web site operator should ensure that the privacy policy accurately reflects the entity's policies and practices with regard to the collection, use, and disclosure of personal data. Additionally, the draft policy should be analyzed to ensure that it complies with any national, regional, and international laws or self-regulatory programs that will be applicable to the organizations. Finally, the operator should ensure that the policy reads smoothly and is error free.

Privacy Policies On-Line and Off

When developing and implementing privacy policies, the Web site operator must determine whether such policies will apply to on-line and off-line activities alike. Many operators have developed and implemented Web site privacy policies under the assumption that such policies would apply only to personal data collected on-line through their Web site.[110] However, relatively recent comments from the FTC make clear that the commission takes a broader view of the application of privacy policies and consider that on-line privacy policies will apply off-line unless otherwise stated.[111] Furthermore, if an entity is participating in the Safe Harbor program, it will be required to indicate whether its certification applies to off-line data. Accordingly, when developing a privacy policy, it will be essential to determine whether the policy should apply to both

Sample Annotated Privacy Policy

This Privacy Policy was last updated on [_____].

> [*Commentary*: *If the Web site privacy policy will be revised from time to time, it will be important to state the date of the last revision.*]

Welcome

Welcome to Web site ("the Site") of ABC Co. Inc. ("ABC"). The Site is owned by ABC and has been created to provide information about our company and our services (the "ABC Services"). This Privacy Policy sets forth ABC's policy with respect to information that is collected from individuals who access and use the Site ("you" or "users")

> [*Commentary*: *The introductory section can be used to set forth the identity of the Web site operator and establish the definition for key terms used in the policy.*]

What Information Do We Collect?

Personal Data. We collect personally identifiable information ("Personal Data") from you when you voluntarily choose to provide such information, such as when you contact us with inquiries or register for certain ABC Services. When you contact ABC, we may keep a record of that correspondence and may occasionally ask you to complete surveys for research purposes. Wherever ABC collects Personal Data, we make an effort to provide a link to this Privacy Policy. By voluntarily providing us with your Personal Data, you are consenting to our use of it in accordance with this Privacy Policy. If you provide Personal Data to this Site, you acknowledge and agree that such Personal Data may be transferred from your current location to the offices and servers of ABC and the authorized third parties referred to herein located in the United States and in other countries.

> [*Commentary*: *This section can be used to describe all of the personal data collected from users. It will be important to describe all collections of data. The precise description of the data collected will depend on the nature of the Web site and its information collection practices.*]

Nonidentifiable Data. When you interact with ABC through the Site, we receive and store certain personally nonidentifiable information. Such information, which is collected passively using various technologies, cannot presently be used to specifically identify you. ABC may store such information itself, or the information may be included in databases owned and maintained by ABC affiliates, agents, or service providers. This Site may use such information and pool it with other information to track, for example, the total number of visitors to our Site, the number of visitors to each page of our Site, and the domain names of our visitors' Internet service providers. It is important to note that no Personal Data is available or used in this process.

In operating this Site, we may use a technology called "cookies." A cookie is a piece of information that the computer that hosts our Site gives to your browser when you access a Web site. Our cookies help provide additional functionality to the Site and help us analyze Site usage more accurately. For instance, our Site may set a cookie on your browser that keeps you from needing to remember a password and then enter it more than once during a visit to the Site. In all cases in which we use cookies, we will not collect Personal Data except with your permission. On most Web browsers, you will find a "help" section on the toolbar. Please refer to this section for information on how to receive notification when you are receiving a new cookie and how to turn cookies off. We recommend that you leave cookies turned on because they allow you to take advantage of some of the Site's features.

[*Commentary*: *It is recommended that the Web site privacy policy disclose whether cookies are used on the Web site and, if so, what kind of information is collected through the cookies.*]

Aggregated Personal Data. In an ongoing effort to better understand and serve the users of the ABC Services, ABC often conducts research on its customer demographics, interests, and behavior based on the Personal Data and other information provided to us. This research may be compiled and analyzed on an aggregate basis, and ABC may share this aggregate data with its affiliates, agents, and business partners. This aggregate information does not identify you personally. ABC may also disclose aggregated user statistics in order to describe our services to current and prospective business partners, and to other third parties for other lawful purposes.

[*Commentary*: *It is advisable that the Web site privacy policy also explain any collection and use of nonidentifiable information, including statistical information, nonidentifiable data collected via cookies and other similar means, and aggregated personal data.*]

What Are Your Choices?

You can always use the publicly accessible areas of this Site without providing your Personal Data. However, it will be necessary to provide some Personal Data in order to utilize certain ABC Services. For instance, if you would like to order a product from our Site, it will be necessary to provide information such as name, address, and billing information.

[*Commentary*: *It will be important to describe the choices that the individual has when deciding whether to provide personal data to the Web site. The explanation should also include a description of any consequences for not providing personal data to the site.*]

How Do We Use Your Personal Data and Other Information?

ABC uses the Personal Data you provide in a manner that is consistent with this Privacy Policy. If you provide Personal Data for a certain reason, we may use the Personal Data in connection with the reason for which it was provided. For in stance, if you contact us by e-mail, will we use the Personal Data you provide to answer your question or resolve your problem. ABC and its affiliates may also use your Personal Data and other personally nonidentifiable information collected through the Site to help us improve the content and functionality of the Site, to better understand our users, and to improve our products and services. ABC and its affiliates may use this information to contact you in the future to tell you about services we believe will be of interest to you. If we do so, each communication we send you will contain instructions permitting you to "opt out" of receiving future communications. In addition, at any time you wish not to receive any future communications or to have your name deleted from our mailing lists, please contact us as indicated below. If ABC intends to use any Personal Data in any manner that is not consistent with this Privacy Policy, you will be informed of such anticipated use prior to, or at the time at which, the Personal Data is collected.

[*Commentary*: *A significant part of the privacy policy will involve describing all the possible uses of the personal data provided through the Web site. In doing so, the challenge is to be sufficiently broad so as not to limit the business goals of the Web site operator and sufficiently narrow to provide the individual user with a description of the use of his or her personal data.*]

Do We Share the Information That We Receive?

ABC is not in the business of selling your information. We consider this information to be a vital part of our relationship with you. There are, however, certain circumstances in which we may share your Personal Data with certain third parties without further notice to you, as set forth below.

[*Commentary*: *It is very important to indicate the entities to which personal data may be transferred. While it is important to limit disclosures, it will be essential to clearly and accurately list all the circumstances under which transfers of personal data may be made.*]

Business Transfers. As we develop our business, we might sell or buy businesses or assets. In the event of a corporate sale, merger, reorganization, dissolution, or similar event, Personal Data may be part of the transferred assets.

[*Commentary*: *If it is contemplated that personal data would be a part of any merger, acquisition, or other business transfer, this should be disclosed in the privacy policy.*]

Agents, Consultants, and Related Third Parties. ABC, like many businesses, sometimes hires other companies to perform certain business-related functions. Examples include mailing information, maintaining databases, and processing payments. When we employ another company to perform a function of this nature, we provide them only with the information that they need to perform their specific function.

[*Commentary*: *Most Web site operators rely on third-party service providers to perform various functions that involve the disclosure of personal data to such service providers. If personal data might be disclosed to any such third parties, it should be disclosed in the privacy policy.*]

Legal Requirements. ABC may disclose your Personal Data if required to do so by law or in the good-faith belief that such action is necessary to (1) comply with a legal obligation, (2) protect and defend the rights or property of ABC, (3) act in urgent circumstances to protect the personal safety of users of the Site or the public, or (4) protect against legal liability.

[*Commentary*: *Web site operators may be required to disclose personal data in a variety of circumstances, such as when required by a legal obligation or compelled by governmental authority. The possibility of such disclosures should be disclosed in the privacy policy.*]

Exclusions

This Privacy Policy does not apply to any Personal Data collected by ABC other than Personal Data collected through the Site.

[*Commentary*: *It is important to clearly specify any exclusions from the privacy policy. Some Web site operators choose to exclude personal data contained in unsolicited communications, such as e-mails concerning new product ideas, and so forth, from the application of the privacy policy. Furthermore, if it is determined that the Web site privacy policy should apply only to the collection of personal data through the Web site (and not through other means such as phone conversations and letters in paper form), this should be stated explicitly.*]

Children

ABC does not knowingly collect Personal Data from children under the age of 13. If you are under age 13, please do not submit any Personal Data through the Site. If you are under 13 years of age and would like to register for access to the Subscription Service, please inform your parent or guardian, who may register you for access to the Site. We encourage parents and legal guardians to monitor their children's Internet usage and to help enforce our Privacy Policy by instructing their children never to provide Personal Data on this Site without their permission. If you have reason to believe that a child under the age of 13 has provided Personal Data to ABC through this Site, please contact us, and we will endeavor to delete that information from our databases.

[*Commentary*: *Because of concerns about COPPA, personal data from children under the age of 13 will not be collected through the Web site, and the privacy policy should clearly state this. On the other hand, if personal data are indeed collected from children under the age of 13 through the site, the site operator must ensure that the privacy policy that is posted on the Web site complies with the requirements of COPPA.*]

Links to Other Web Sites

This Privacy Policy applies only to the Site. This Site may frame or contain references or links to other Web sites not operated or controlled by ABC (the "Third Party Sites"). The policies and procedures we have described here do not apply to the Third Party Sites. The links from this Site do not imply ABC's review or endorsement of the Third Party Sites. We suggest contacting those sites directly for information on their privacy policies.

> [*Commentary*: *The privacy policy should make clear that the policy applies only to the Web site on which it is posted and not to any other sites that may be accessible via links from the site on which the privacy policy is posted.*]

Security

ABC takes reasonable steps to protect the Personal Data provided via the Site from loss, misuse, and unauthorized access, disclosure, alteration, or destruction. However, no Internet or e-mail transmission is ever fully secure or error free. In particular, e-mail sent to or from this Site may not be secure. You should therefore take special care in deciding what information you send to us via e-mail. Please keep this in mind when disclosing any Personal Data to ABC via the Internet. Moreover, where you use passwords to access the Subscription Service, it is your responsibility to safeguard them.

> [*Commentary*: *It will be important for the Web site operator to explain what technical and organizational security measures are utilized to protect the personal data provided to the Web site by users. Operators of Web sites that collect highly sensitive personal data may wish to provide much more detailed information about the specific security measures that have been implemented. At the same time, however, it is essential that Web site operators avoid making any security guarantees that are not entirely accurate.*]

Other Terms and Conditions

Your access, to and use of, this Site are subject to the Terms of Use.

> [*Commentary*: *If the Web site also has a Terms of Use agreement that sets forth the conditions under which a user may use the site, the Terms of Use agreement can be referenced in the Privacy Policy.*]

Changes to ABC's Privacy Policy

The Site and our business may change from time to time. As a result, at times it may be necessary for ABC to make changes to this Privacy Policy. ABC reserves the right to update or modify this Privacy Policy at any time and from time to time without prior notice. Please review this policy periodically, and especially before you provide any Personal Data. This Privacy Policy was last updated on [*date*]. Your continued use of the Site after any changes or revisions to this Privacy Policy will indicate your agreement with the terms of such revised Privacy Policy.

[*Commentary*: *Many Web site operators will have to alter their privacy policies from time to time. Before doing so, operators should have a procedure in place for implementing changes and providing users with notice of changes. Many site operators take the view that changes to the privacy policy will be enforceable upon posting and will apply to personal data collected prior to the change. However, if such a tactic is employed, users may be able to successfully argue that they did not have notice of the revised privacy policy and that they did not consent to it. Accordingly, the process for implementing changes and providing users with notice thereof should be given considerable thought.*]

Access to Information

We will take reasonable steps to update or correct Personal Data in our possession that you have previously submitted via this Site. To request access to your Personal Data and to request an update, correction, or deletion of such information, please contact us as specified below.

[*Commentary*: *The Web site operator should provide individuals with the right to know what information the operator holds concerning the individual, as well as how to request a correction or deletion of such information.*]

Contacting ABC

Please also feel free to contact us if you have any questions about ABC's Privacy Policy or the information practices of this Site. You may contact us as follows:

[*Commentary*: *It is important to provide contact information so that individuals can contact the Web site operator with comments or questions.*]

on-line and off-line activities. If the policy not is intended to apply to off-line collection of data, this must be clearly stated.

Taking Steps to Avoid Privacy Litigation

While the specific strategies necessary to avoid governmental enforcement actions and private privacy lawsuits will depend on the precise facts involved in an entity's collection, use, and transfer of personal data, several key steps should be considered when attempting to avoid such enforcement actions and lawsuits. First and foremost, it will be necessary to be cognizant of existing legal requirements while also remaining vigilant about changes to the privacy requirements. The realty is that entities engaging in e-commerce must navigate a complex and treacherous legal and regulatory environment. As demonstrated in this chapter, there is a large body of laws and regulations that require entities to comply with certain privacy requirements when collecting, using, and transferring personally identifiable information. Significantly, there also continue to be a great number of legislative proposals both in the United States and abroad. Accordingly, there is every reason to believe that there will continue to be new legislation.

Second, it is essential to act only in a manner that is consistent with the privacy policy. Entities may face complications, including governmental enforcement actions and private lawsuits, if they attempt to collect, use, or transfer personally identifiable information in a manner that is inconsistent with their stated privacy policy. For example, a large number of Web site privacy policies include a blanket statement informing individuals that the information that they provide through the Web site will *never* be transferred, sold, or disclosed to third parties for any reason. While such a statement may bolster individual confidence when disclosing personal data to the Web site, many companies may not be in a position to make such a statement accurately. For instance, there are many occasions in which an entity may desire or be required to transfer personal data to third parties. Unless such potential transfers are disclosed in the privacy policy, the entity may be prohibited from doing so.

There have been a number of cases that clearly demonstrate the importance of acting in accordance with the stated privacy policy. In July 2000, for example, the FTC commenced an enforcement action against bankrupt e-tailer Toysmart.com, LLC, and Toysmart.com, Inc. (collectively, "Toysmart"). The FTC was alerted when, in conjunction with its dissolution, Toysmart attempted to sell personal data collected via the Internet, even though the privacy policy posted at the time the personal data were collected assured customers that the information would never be shared with third parties. Specifically, the privacy policy contained a provision that stated that "Personal Information, voluntarily submitted by visitors to our site, such as name, address, billing information and shopping preferences, is never shared with a third party." The policy continued, "When you register with toysmart.com, you can rest assured that your information will never be shared with a third party."

On May 22, 2000, Toysmart announced that it was closing its operations and selling its assets. Despite the assurances in Toysmart's privacy policy, Toysmart offered personal data collected via its Web site as part of the assets it was selling.

As a result of Toysmart's actions, the FTC initiated an enforcement action against the company, charging that it had violated Section 5 of the FTC Act by misrepresenting to customers that personal data would never be shared with third parties and then disclosing, selling, and offering for sale that personal data in violation of the company's stated privacy policy.

This action eventually ended in a settlement whereby Toysmart was prohibited from selling its customer list as a stand-alone asset.[112] The settlement permitted Toysmart to sell such customer lists containing personal data only (1) as part of a package which included the entire Web site, (2) to an entity that was in a related market, and (3) to an entity that expressly agreed to be Toysmart's successor-in-interest as to the personal data. Under the terms of the settlement, the buyer of Toysmart's assets would have to agree to abide by Toysmart's privacy policy and to obtain the affirmative consent (opt-in) of the data subjects before using their personal data in any manner that was inconsistent with Toysmart's original privacy policy.[113]

Toysmart's difficulties with the FTC clearly illustrate the hazards of posting a privacy policy that is not completely accurate. For Toysmart, as well as many other companies of a similar nature, personal data are a major asset. By drafting a privacy policy in a very restrictive manner, Toysmart effectively limited its business plan and was not able to use one of its primary assets as it had intended. When the company attempted to transfer the personal data it had collected in contravention of its privacy policy, the FTC prevented Toysmart from doing so.

Next, it is also essential to ensure that the technical and organizational security measures that have been undertaken to protect the personal data are sufficient and will enable the organization to avoid inadvertent disclosures of personal data. The importance of this principle is clearly demonstrated by a recent case involving pharmaceutical giant Eli Lilly. This company became the subject of an enforcement action brought by the FTC after the company inadvertently disclosed personal data collected through its Web site.

Eli Lilly manufactures a number of pharmaceutical products, including the antidepressant Prozac. In marketing Prozac, Lilly operates a Prozac Web site, through which it collects various personal data from visitors to the site. From March 2000 to June 2001, Eli Lilly offered a service called "Medi-Messenger" through its Prozac Web site. The Medi-Messenger service enabled registered users to receive individualized e-mail reminders from Lilly concerning their Prozac medication or other matters. On June 27, 2001, Lilly sent a form e-mail message to subscribers to the service. The message included, in the "To" entry line, the e-mail addresses of every individual subscriber.

The FTC commenced an action against Eli Lilly, alleging that it had made false or misleading representations in the privacy policy for the Medi-Messenger service.[114] The privacy policy that was posted on the Web site at the time the information was collected stated that Eli Lilly employed measures appropriate under the circumstances to maintain and protect the privacy and confidentiality of personal data obtained from or about consumers through the Prozac site. The FTC alleged that Lilly had not employed such measures or taken such steps. Further, it contended that Lilly had failed to provide appropriate training for its employees regarding consumer privacy and information security; failed to provide appropriate oversight and assistance for the employee who sent out the e-mail, an individual who had no prior experience in creating, testing, or implementing the computer program used; and failed to implement appropriate checks and controls on the process, such as reviewing the computer program with experienced personnel and testing the program internally before broadcasting the e-mail.

Eli Lilly eventually settled the matter with the FTC and signed a consent order containing provisions intended to prevent the company from engaging in similar acts and practices in the future.[115] The consent order applies broadly to the collection of personal data from or about consumers in connection with the advertising, marketing, offering for sale, or sale of any pharmaceutical, medical, or other health-related product or service by Eli Lilly.[116] It consists of six parts, but the most significant to the current discussion are the first two. The first part of the consent order prohibits misrepresentations regarding the extent to which Lilly maintains and protects the privacy or confidentiality of any personal data collected from or about consumers. The second part of the order requires Eli Lilly to implement a four-stage information security program designed to protect the confidentiality and security of consumers' personal data, and to protect it against unauthorized access, use, or disclosure. The four stages require Lilly to

- designate appropriate personnel to coordinate and oversee the program;
- identify foreseeable risks to the security, confidentiality, and integrity of personal data, and to address these risks in each relevant area of its operations;

- conduct an annual written review by a qualified body that monitors and documents compliance with the program, evaluates its effectiveness, and recommends changes to it; and

- adjust the program in light of any findings and recommendations resulting from reviews or ongoing monitoring.

The FTC action against Eli Lilly should serve as a wake-up call to all companies. In response to the unfortunate incident, the FTC took the opportunity to offer Lilly (and, in fact, all other companies) a lesson about the elements a proper personal data privacy and security plan should contain. The FTC's emphasis on the designation of a supervisory authority, the identification and rectification of reasonably foreseeable internal and external risks to personal data, and the administration of an annual written review of personal data security policies and procedures should serve as a reminder for all companies that collect personal data.

Next, all entities should be cautious when collecting any personal data from children. As discussed earlier in this chapter, COPPA places strict requirements on operators of Web sites that are directed at, or knowingly collect personal data from, children under the age of 13. The FTC has already brought a number of cases against Web site operators for their alleged violation of the COPPA requirements, and all indications are that the FTC will continue to enforce COPPA in a rigorous manner.

Finally, Web site operators must consider potentially applicable foreign law when developing and implementing their privacy policies. As reviewed in this chapter, a number of jurisdictions, including, notably, the European Union, have data privacy laws that are much more stringent than those in the United States. Such laws can become relevant to American companies in a number of instances, for example, when such companies attempt to transfer personal data collected in foreign jurisdictions to locations in the United States.

CONCLUSION

Privacy is and will continue to be a significant part of electronic commerce.[117] Companies collecting personal data on-line will continue to struggle to make consumers feel comfortable when disclosing their personal data on-line. At the same time, companies will also face the increasingly vexing challenge of ensuring that their privacy policies and practices are in compliance with a large and growing body of international law and regulation. In the midst of all this complexity, however, there really is one simple rule that should always be included when developing privacy compliance programs: Be open and honest about data collection practices. While it may sometimes be tempting to make certain promises and assurances about privacy collection practices, making any promises or assurances that are not fully accurate can lead to a legal liability and (perhaps even more important) a deterioration of consumer trust and confidence.

In the next chapter, the focus shifts to a discussion of issues related to advertising and marketing. Entities participating in e-commerce will often engage in various marketing and advertising initiatives. While extremely important to the growth and development of enterprises, marketing and advertising on the Internet have also become considerably regulated. Chapter 5 explores some of the current regulations applicable to advertising and marketing on-line and offers suggestions about how entities can tailor their on-line activities to comply with these legal requirements. The next chapter also explores key issues related to the various advertising and marketing agreements.

Chapter 5

ON-LINE ADVERTISING AND MARKETING

This chapter explores several key issues that are raised by advertising and marketing on the Internet. While the Internet has created incredible sales and marketing opportunities for businesses, today's companies need to be aware of the large body of laws that regulate the way in which they market their products and services on-line. There are laws that govern the transmission of unsolicited commercial e-mail, the use of comparative advertising, and the use of certain languages when making marketing messages, among other activities related to on-line marketing. Of course, many jurisdictions also regulate the use of deceptive advertising and prohibit fraudulent activity on-line.

Just as businesses need to be concerned about the amount of legislation and regulation impacting their on-line marketing and advertising, so consumers must be concerned about new risks raised by the Internet. The advent of the Internet and its increased usage for business has helped to raise new concerns about consumer protection. Indeed, many consumers remain concerned about engaging in transactions on-line because of uncertainties about issues such as Web site security and potential fraud. Although the fraudulent and deceptive activities that are being carried out on the Internet closely mirror the kinds of activities that are being carried out through other media, the virtual anonymity and sheer size of the Internet has helped to compound the risks of deceptive practices arising out of the use of the Internet. Moreover, the Internet is particularly conducive to certain types of fraudulent and deceptive practices, such as chain letters and pyramid schemes.

Finally, this chapter also examines key issues related to on-line marketing agreements, with a particular focus on co-branding arrangements. Agreements concerning on-line marketing raise a number of significant issues, including those related to performance concerns, privacy, liability, and, of course, revenues. This chapter will present key tips on negotiating such agreements to ensure that one will reap their benefits.

UNSOLICITED COMMERCIAL E-MAIL

The use of e-mail as a marketing tool has accompanied the development and growth of the Internet. Clearly, there are a number of advantages to using e-mail, as opposed to other media, when attempting to distribute marketing messages. For instance, the distribution of large amounts of e-mail is much less costly than other types of media, such as ordinary mail or telephone calls. Furthermore, with e-mail, marketers are better able to reach a large group of individuals in diverse locations. In addition, entities distributing unsolicited commercial e-mail may be better able to target their marketing message to individuals who have demonstrated some level of interest in the products or services that are being marketed.

While valued by some marketers, the transmission of unsolicited commercial e-mail, or "spam," raises a number of important issues. Many people object to the unwelcome intrusion of spam. While receiving one or two pieces of unsolicited e-mail per day might not be objectionable to some people, many users find themselves virtually inundated by spam. This can be particularly problematic when spam is sent to the e-mail accounts that individuals use in connection with their employment. Parsing through and deleting spam can occupy considerable amounts of employee time and result in wasted business resources. As such, spam can constitute more than a personal annoyance. It can actually be something that affects businesses quite negatively.

The U.S. Approach

Statutory Response

In addition to being objectionable to many users, spam is prohibited by most Internet service providers and many state laws.[1] In addition, there have also been several proposals for federal legislation that would place certain limitations on the use of spam. Furthermore, a number of groups are attempting to take action against spam, including by lobbying for legislation that would prohibit or at least further regulate the use of spam. Notable among such entities are Junkbusters and the Coalition against Unsolicited Commercial Email (CAUCE). Entities such as these have helped to bring the issue of spam to the attention of the public and have led significant lobbying efforts. However, such efforts have not yet resulted in enacted federal legislation.

Although no federal legislation prohibits the transmission of unsolicited commercial e-mail, there are a number of state laws concerning this method of marketing. Currently, 19 states regulate spam in some way.[2] In 1998 Washington became the first state to regulate spam. Since then, a number of other states have followed suit. Of the more than 30 states that regulate spam in some capacity, very few actually prohibit the transmission of unsolicited commercial e-mail. Instead, the vast majority of laws seek to prevent marketers from sending fraudulent or misleading e-mail messages. In addition to such truth-in-labeling requirements, a large number of state laws also require e-mail marketers to provide the individual with a mechanism for opting out of receiving additional unsolicited commercial e-mail from the entity.

While there are a number of similarities between the different state laws concerning spam, such laws are sufficiently different to cause some level of concern and confusion about entities that wish to engage in the legitimate distribution of commercial e-mail. Accordingly, although federal legislation regulating spam may still be a way off, a unified federal approach is likely the best way for dealing with concerns about disparate state-based rules concerning the transmission of unsolicited commercial e-mail. Still, it is unclear whether there will be federal legislation prohibiting spam any time soon. One thing that does appear certain, however, is that efforts in this area are likely to continue. Each year there are numerous proposals for federal legislation concerning spam.

Other Action against Spam

As mentioned in the previous section, Internet service providers (ISPs) have also been playing a significant role in attempts to control spam. The user agreements of the vast majority of ISPs contain prohibitions against spam, and many state laws permit ISPs to bring legal actions against spammers that violate an ISP's user agreements. For example, California has made it unlawful to utilize the system of an "electronic mail service provider" in a manner that violates that ISP's policies restricting or prohibiting the sending of unsolicited commercial e-mail.[3] In addition, some laws enable ISPs the right to seek damages equal to at least $10 per message sent to each individual customer of the ISP or for each individual message sent through the ISP's network.

To date there have been a number of instances in which ISPs have brought actions against spammers.[4] In many of these early cases, the ISPs have proceeded against the alleged spammers on the basis of breach of contract (for violating the terms of the service agreement) or under tort law such as nuisance, trespass, or conversion. In *CompuServe, Inc., v. Cyber Promotions, Inc.,*[5] for example, the defendant was enjoined from sending e-mail advertisements through CompuServe's computer facilities under a theory of trespass-to-chattels.[6] The applications of the theory of trespass-to-chattels have been followed by other courts in other cases, including *American Online, Inc., v. IMS.*[7]

The European Approach

As with most of the other subjects discussed in this book, the European approach to the regulation of spam is somewhat different from the approach taken in the United States. European legislators have demonstrated concern regarding spam for considerable time now, and the regulation of spam within the European Union recently became even more stringent. After intense debate and much objection from certain business and direct marketing groups, European legislators recently agreed to include in a new directive a requirement that unsolicited commercial e-mail be sent only to those subscribers who have given their prior consent. This same standard would apply for commercial messages transmitted by automated calling systems and fax.

The Directive concerning the Processing of Personal Data and the Protection of Privacy in the Electronic Communications Sector (hereafter the "Electronic Communications Directive") is comprehensive legislation that concerns a number of different issues relating to the privacy of electronic communications.[8] European Union Member States have until October 31, 2003, to implement the new directive in their national laws. The directive contains requirements regarding various issues relevant to electronic communications, including data retention, the use of cookies, and the use of mobile phone location data. Regarding spam, the directive generally restricts the transmission of spam to individuals who have opted in to the receipt of such commercial messages. The final rule, as incorporated in the directive, is as follows: "The use of automated calling systems without human intervention (automatic calling machines), facsimile machines (fax), or electronic mail for the purposes of direct marketing may only be allowed in respect to subscribers who have given their prior consent."[9]

Still, the directive does contain certain exceptions to this general rule. Specifically, the legislation provides:

> Notwithstanding paragraph 1, where a natural or legal person obtains from its customers their electronic contact details for electronic mail, in the context of a sale of a product or service, in connection with Directive 95/46/EC, the same natural or legal person may use these electronic contact details for the marketing of its own *similar* products or services provided that customers clearly and distinctly are given the opportunity to object, free of charge and in an easy manner to such use of electronic contact details when they are collected and on the occasion of each message in case the customer has not initially refused such use.[10]

One of the main potential problems with this exception is its focus on "similar" products and services. Many businesses, especially large enterprises, will have a wide range of products and services, many of which might be considered as being similar to one another. Unless more specific guidance is provided at the national level, complying with the requirements of the directive might therefore require businesses to attempt to understand how end users might perceive their marketing messages. In many cases, this will prove to be difficult because of the subjectivity that is involved. For example, while one consumer might view a laptop computer and a personal digital assistant to be similar products, another consumer might consider these products to be quite different. Even prior to the passage of the Electronic Communications Directive, many EU Member States had enacted legislation placing certain restrictions on unsolicited commercial e-mail. In Denmark, for instance, the transmission of unsolicited commercial e-mail has been largely banned by the Danish Marketing Practices Act.[11] Section 6a(1) of this act states:

> Where a supplier sells goods, immovable or movable property or work or services to customers, he shall not be allowed to make calls to anybody using electronic mail, automated calling systems (automatic calling machines) or facsimile machines (fax) for the purposes of such selling unless the particular customer has made a prior request for such calls.[12]

Although many European Union Member States did already have antispam legislation in place before the enactment of the directive, it should play an important role in the future regulation of spam. By providing a comprehensive, unified, and strict approach for regulating spam, the directive will be an important weapon against spam.

Other Jurisdictions

Other jurisdictions have adopted more hands-on approaches for attempting to counter spam. In South Korea, for instance, the government has recently launched a comprehensive initiative designed to block unsolicited commercial e-mail and to prevent foreign companies from using Korea as a launching pad for spam distribution campaigns. In accordance with this initiative, the Ministry of Information and Communication recently conducted a massive inspection of computer systems at various companies. The campaign appears to be working, as the Korean Ministry of Information and Communication has reported a dramatic decrease in the quantity of complaints from overseas regarding spam relayed through Korea.[13]

Japan has also been taking actions against spam. Legislation that requires senders of unsolicited commercial e-mail to attach messages telling receivers that the e-mail is unsolicited advertising and informing them how to reject any future transmissions of unsolicited commercial e-mail went into effect in July 2002.[14] In addition to the foregoing restrictions, this new legislation also prohibits entities that transmit unsolicited commercial e-mail from mailing such e-mails again once they have been rejected. Furthermore, it prohibits sending a large amount of e-mail to random addresses.

Entities that violate Japan's spam legislation may face orders from authorities to improve or suspend business. However, if an entity continues violating the requirements of this legislation, the individuals responsible may be given prison terms of up to two years or fined up to ¥3 million. In addition, companies that are responsible for the violations may face a fine of up to ¥300 million.[15]

In many other nations, spam is not regulated. In some countries, such as Canada, Australia, and the United States, ISPs play an important role in controlling spam. Even where spam is regulated by law, businesses must often rely on a combination of technical solutions, ISP policies, and legislation in their attempts to control the effects of spam.

Practice Pointers

Ensuring That Commercial E-Mail Is Not Viewed as Spam

Although many individuals view spam in a highly unfavorable light, many enterprises find the transmission of commercial e-mail to be a useful business tool. The key is thus to ensure that commercial e-mail campaigns are carried out in compliance with existing law. The problem with this, of course, is that the Internet is a global medium, and there are many different national laws concerning spam. Moreover, in the United States alone, due to some states' regulation of spam, there are more than 30 different regulatory requirements applicable to spam. In addition, in the United States, many states without specific spam legislation have begun to use existing consumer protection laws in their attempts to control spam. Accordingly, it will be necessary to consider the specific legislation in the jurisdiction(s) that will be targeted.

While it will be necessary to consider the specific requirements in applicable law, there are several key tips that should be taken into consideration in all jurisdictions. First, it will be important to ensure that the subject line of the e-mail message accurately reflects its content. It will also be essential to use valid and confirmed e-mail addresses to send all messages and to provide end users with a simple, user-friendly way for opting out of future communications. Following recommendations such as these may enable an enterprise to still use commercial e-mail while reducing consumer concerns regarding spam.

Protecting Your Company from Spam

In addition to ensuring that the e-mails sent by a company do not constitute unsolicited commercial e-mail, companies will also need to take steps to protect their own system from spam-related losses. "Spam in e-mail systems can now cause costly problems for any company."[16] When received in large quantities, spam can overload companies' computer servers. Clearly, this is a greater risk for smaller companies, but it can impact larger ones, as well. Further, spam has a number of costs in terms of lost productivity and time. According to a recent study conducted in the European Union, the total cost to Internet users of spam worldwide is approximately $9.4 billion annually.[17] Significantly, the problem does not show any real indications of abating. Indeed, a recent report suggested that by the end of 2002, spam would constitute the majority of all e-mail messages sent via the Internet.[18]

A number of different technical measures can be employed when attempting to protect a company's computer systems from the intrusion of spam. While none of these solutions will eliminate spam in its entirety, they can lead to reductions in the quantity of spam and the frequency with which it is distributed. Accordingly, such measures should be considered in connection with one's overall efforts to combat the negative effects of spam.

Conclusions on Spam

Unsolicited commercial e-mail is likely to continue to be a significant issue in the future. Thus far, neither technical measures nor legal regulations have succeeded in eliminating spam. At the same time, many enterprises remain committed to the benefits that they believe are garnered through the use of unsolicited commercial e-mail. Clearly, additional efforts need to be directed toward striking a better balance among the diverse interests of electronic direct marketers, ISPs, and individual consumers.

DECEPTIVE AND FRAUDULENT PRACTICES

One of the problems associated with the increased use of the Internet for business purposes is the rise in deceptive marketing practices. At least one estimate has suggested that as much as 10 percent of on-line commerce may involve consumer fraud.[19] In addition, some statistics suggest that consumers lose approximately $3.2 million per year as a result of Internet fraud.[20]

At present, a wide variety of fraudulent conduct is occurring on-line. One of the most common fraudulent activities being perpetrated is the marketing of false business opportunity. The Internet is being used by a large number of companies and individuals to promote various business opportunities that are not exactly as they appear to be. To this date, U.S. authorities have brought a number of actions against companies for having presented bogus business opportunities on-line. For instance, authorities have brought actions against work-at-home schemes,[21] businesses designed to locate people who are owed money by a government agency,[22] credit repair schemes,[23] various franchises,[24] and other on-line shopping programs.[25]

Another common type of on-line fraud concerns the use of pyramid schemes. Although pyramid schemes clearly existed prior to the Internet, it has been connected to a proliferation in this type of fraud. Pyramid schemes conducted on-line work in much the same way as those conducted off-line. Usually the promoter of the pyramid scheme will collect payment from consumers for the right to recruit new participants and to collect money for doing do. The FTC has brought a number of law enforcement actions against perpetrators of Internet-based pyramid schemes.[26]

Most of this troublesome activity is readily identifiable as such, and reputable companies are not likely to engage in such behaviors. Accordingly, this chapter will not discuss at length the legal remedies that can be used against entities that engage in such conduct. On the other hand, there is a considerable likelihood that entities can face legal difficulties as a result of having had engaged in misleading conduct on-line. The fact that misleading content is not as easily distinguishable is complicated by the fact that many jurisdictions have different standards for what constitutes misleading conduct. Such issues will be explored in greater detail in the following sections.

In addition to leaving businesses exposed to a variety of civil and criminal penalties, the cumulative effect of questionable on-line practices by certain companies could discourage individuals from concluding transactions on-line.[27] For all of the foregoing reasons, businesses have a strong interest in avoiding deceptive marketing practices and other questionable on-line activities. Accordingly, most enterprises will not require advice on how to avoid deceptive marketing practices. Most will already be attempting to avoid such practices on their own. Instead, most companies will need to focus on implementing appropriate procedures to avoid the transmission of misleading advertising messages and ensure the compliance with all other applicable advertising requirements. While such tasks will be challenging for most enterprises, they are likely to be even more vexing for entities that engage in cross-border commerce and thus must consider the potential application of foreign laws.

REGULATION OF ADVERTISEMENTS AND ON-LINE MARKETING

The General U.S. Approach

In the United States, the FTC plays an important role in protecting consumers. In connection with its mandate to provide for consumer protection, the FTC serves as a watchdog over the way in which companies market their products and services to consumers. While the FTC's duties originated with traditional media, the rise of the Internet has resulted in the FTC also regulating activities occurring on-line.

The FTC plays an important role in ensuring that advertisements and other promotional materials delivered via the Internet are truthful and not misleading. The role of the FTC in this area can be traced back to Section 5 of the Federal Trade Commission Act,[28] which prohibits parties from engaging in unfair and deceptive acts or practices. Such prohibition on unfair and deceptive trade practices applies to all media, including the Internet. In addition, the FTC has issued a number of rules and guides applicable to specific industries and practices. Such rules and guides are often applicable regardless of the type of medium that is being used.[29] Furthermore, the FTC has assumed an active role in advising on various Internet-specific issues, such as controlling the use of unsolicited commercial e-mail and preventing on-line fraud.

While it is necessary to consider the particular facts of one's own business and proposed marketing plans, certain guidelines apply to all advertisements. Specifically, the following should be considered:

- *Truth.* The claims contained in the advertisement must be truthful and not directly or indirectly misleading.[30]
- *Substantiation.* Advertisers must be able to substantiate their claims with facts.
- *Fairness.* Advertisements cannot be "unfair."[31]

In addition to considering such general recommendations, it is essential to note any specific requirements that are applicable to the particular industry in which one is operating and the particular products or services that one is distributing via the Internet. Specific disclosures may be necessary in a number of instances, including the following: franchises and business opportunity ventures; foreign language materials; endorsement and testimonials; negative option plans; environmental marketing claims; use of the word "free"; comparative advertising; and the provision of warranties and guarantees.

Furthermore, the FTC has also issued rules relating to certain industries, including the following:

- automobiles and used automobile parts
- fur, textile, and wool
- household furniture
- jewelry, precious metals, and pewter
- pay-per-call services
- tires
- smokeless tobacco
- home appliances
- leather and imitation leather products
- retail food
- private vocational and distance education schools
- home insulation
- law books

- nursery industry
- amplifiers used in home entertainment products

In some cases, the rules require that certain disclosures be made to consumers.[32] Where disclosures are required, they must be placed in a "clear and conspicuous" manner. A number of factors should be considered when analyzing whether a particular disclosure is "clear and conspicuous." First of these is the placement and proximity of the disclosures. Generally, disclosures should be placed near the particular advertisement or claim to which they apply. The disclosure should be located in a place that will increase the likelihood that an individual viewing the claim contained in the advertisement will actually view the disclosure and associate it with the claim.

In evaluating whether a disclosure is sufficiently "clear and conspicuous," one should also examine the prominence of the particular disclosure. When considering prominence, the following points should be addressed:

- *Size.* Disclosures should be at least as large as the ad copy.
- *Color.* Disclosures should be in a color that contrasts with the background.
- *Graphics.* Graphics can make a disclosure more noticeable.

Advertisers should also consider the potential of distractions. The FTC has recommended that other parts of the advertisement should not distract the consumer from the applicable disclosure. One should view the particular advertisement in its entirety to analyze whether any of its components might distract the consumer from any necessary disclosures that are included within or near the advertisement.

Important disclosures should also be repeated, as repetition may increase the likelihood that a consumer will actually view the disclosure. Specifically, advertisers should consider the following recommendations:

- *Repeat disclosures on lengthy Web sites.* Because consumers can enter a Web site through the home page, in the middle, or anywhere else without necessarily navigating through the whole site, advertisers should evaluate whether consumers who view only a portion of a site will miss important disclosures. Because of such risks, Web site operators should consider including important disclaimers on all relevant pages of the Web site.
- *Repeat disclosures with repeated claims.* Where a disclosure is tied closely to a claim, the disclosure may need to always accompany that

claim. Advertisers can use repeated hyperlinks to accomplish this
objective.

- *Audio disclosures.* Where a claim is in audio form, the disclosure should
  air at a sufficient volume and cadence. Because some consumers lack
  the technology to receive audio information, the disclosure should also
  be visual.

- *Visual disclosures.* Visual disclosures should appear for a sufficient du-
  ration. Fleeting disclosures tend to be ineffective.

Finally, attention must also be directed toward the language that is
used in drafting the disclaimer. Disclosures should be written in clear
language and syntax and should avoid legalese or technical language.

The FTC and other law enforcement agencies monitor the Internet for
compliance with the FTC rules. Failing to comply with the FTC rules
can result in enforcement actions and civil lawsuits. Entities under the
jurisdiction of the FTC can face orders to cease and desist, fines of up
to $11,000 per violation, and injunctions by federal district courts.[33] In
addition, in some instances, entities may also be obliged to pay consumers actual damages as a result of civil lawsuits.

Specific Advertising Regulations in Other Jurisdictions

In Europe alone there is great diversity between national laws that
regulate the transmission of advertisements and promotional materials.
This fact was highlighted particularly well in a European Commission
Green Paper that cataloged the laws pertaining to misleading marketing
practices in the 15 Member States of the European Union.[34] The Green
Paper illustrates quite clearly the divergences between the EU Member
States with respect to many types of advertising, including the rules on
comparative advertising, rules pertaining to direct advertising, the regulation of competitions and sweepstakes, the regulation of advertisements
directed toward children, and price advertising.

European legislators have attempted to harmonize certain areas of the
law related to advertising and consumer protection. For instance, the
European Commission has enacted a directive that provides baseline
rules governing comparative advertising within the EU (the Comparative
Advertising Directive).[35] The Comparative Advertising Directive was an
amendment of previously existing legislation concerning misleading advertising (the Misleading Advertising Directive).[36] Member States were
required to have transposed the Comparative Advertising Directive into
their own national laws by April 23, 2000.

The aims of the Misleading Advertising Directive were to control misleading advertising in the interests of consumers, competitors, and the general public. In examining whether particular advertisements were misleading, Member States were called upon to consider the characteristics of the goods or services; the price; the conditions governing the supply of the goods or the provision of services; and the nature, qualities, and rights of the advertiser. To control misleading advertising, the directive required Member States to ensure that persons or organizations with a legitimate interest were able to bring a court action against misleading advertising or bring the advertising before a competent administrative body to rule on the complaints or to institute the appropriate legal proceedings.

The Comparative Advertising Directive introduced the concept of comparative advertising, which is defined as "any advertising which explicitly or by implication identifies a competitor or goods or services offered by a competitor." The Comparative Advertising Directive permits the use of comparative advertising if the following conditions are met:

- the advertising is not misleading;
- it compares goods or services meeting the same needs or intended for the same purpose;
- it objectively compares one or more material, relevant, verifiable, and representative features of those goods or services, which may include price;
- it does not create confusion in the marketplace between the advertiser and a competitor;
- it does not discredit or denigrate the trademarks, trade names, or other distinguishing signs of a competitor;
- for products with designation of origin, it relates to products with the same designation;
- it does not take unfair advantage of the trademark or other distinguishing sign of a competitor; and
- it does not present goods or services as imitations or replicas of goods or services bearing a protected trademark or trade name.

Significantly, the Comparative Advertising Directive provides for the establishment of a system for dealing with cross-border complaints regarding comparative advertising.

Despite the enactment of the two directives and continued work geared toward harmonizing the advertising legislation within the EU,[37] key differences among the Member States remain and can present a potential trap for the unwary Internet marketer.[38] Consider, as one example, the restrictions that are placed on entities that provide promotional gifts in conjunction with their advertising campaigns. In Germany there are strict prohibitions on the use of promotional gifts. In other jurisdictions, such as the Netherlands, promotions are allowed, but with restrictions. Certain countries have specific requirements applicable to the use of promotional gifts. In Italy, for instance, the Ministry of Finance must approve all promotions.[39] Denmark also has clearly defined rules applicable to the distribution of promotional gifts:

> Where a person carrying on a trade or business sells goods or real property to consumers or performs work or provides services for consumers, he shall not provide any collateral gift or similar inducement, unless such gift or inducement is of negligible value. The advertising of any such gift or inducement shall similarly be prohibited.[40]

There are also disparate rules relating to the kinds of advertising permissible. European legislators have attempted to harmonize some of the rules concerning advertising in certain industries, as well as the rules relating to certain business practices, by enacting a number of directives, including ones concerning foodstuffs,[41] cosmetics,[42] textile names,[43] medicinal products for human use,[44] package travel,[45] contracts negotiated away from business premises,[46] consumer credit,[47] distance selling contracts,[48] measuring instruments,[49] and time-shares.[50] Nonetheless, despite such directives, the rules applicable to certain products and services vary considerably from country to country. For instance, regulations applicable to the advertising of products for children,[51] good products,[52] pharmaceuticals,[53] and financial services vary widely.[54]

Local Language Requirements

Entities advertising on the Internet will also be required to pay attention to specific local requirements, such as rules mandating the conclusion to certain disclosures and use of specific languages. The requirement of using a specific national language is likely to be an issue in many Francophone countries.

In France, for instance, the Toubon Law imposes the compulsory but nonexclusive use of the French language in specific fields. Specifically, the Toubon Law requires that all documents used to inform the user or the consumer (such as labeling, instructions, leaflets, catalogs, brochures, etc.) be made available in French. Significantly, operating procedures integrated in computer and game software and containing screen displays or sound messages are considered as instructions. Consequently, operating procedures for software applications and operating system software must be established in French, whether they are on paper or integrated into the software. The Toubon Law also applies to all advertisements concerning goods, products, and commercialized services, whether such ads are written, spoken, or in audiovisual form. The precise application of the Toubon Laws to Internet Web sites remains subject to debate. A few years back, Georgia Tech Lorraine, an affiliate of the Georgia Institute of Technology, was brought to court because the home page for its Web site was offered only in English—despite the fact that the courses that the institute offered were only provided in English.[55] This case eventually concluded in Georgia Tech's favor. However, there continues to be a risk that actions will be brought against companies that do not comply with France's language requirements.

Similar requirements exist in other jurisdictions, including, notably, Quebec.[56] Of particular concern is Article 52 of the French Language Charter, which requires that catalogs, brochures, leaflets, commercial directories, and all other publications of a similar nature must be in French.

The application of Quebec's French language law to the Internet has been the subject of considerable controversy. With the rise of the Internet, there have been an increasing number of cases in which Quebec Web site operators have received demands from the Office de la Langue Francaise (OLF) to either translate or take down Web sites presented only in the English language.[57] In some cases, operators have been fined for failing to comply with the OLF's demands.

Many of the cases concerning French language requirements and Web sites have been dealt with out of court or are still pending before the courts. There has been one interesting case that has been reviewed by the Supreme Court of Canada. In 1999 the OLF asked the operator of a Web site located at http://www.hyperinfo.ca to translate the English Web site into French. The operator attempted to comply with the request and translated portions of the site. This did not prove to be sufficient for the OLF, which reiterated its request for HyperInfo Canada to translate its site. When the Web site operator again refused the OLF brought the matter to the court.[58]

Simon Sunatori, the owner and CEO of HyperInfo, represented himself and, in doing so, raised several interesting arguments against the application of Quebec's French language laws to his company's Web site. First, he contended that since his Web site was geared mainly toward customers in the United States, he should qualify for an exemption applicable to companies whose products are not widely available in Quebec. The court rejected this argument, maintaining that the exemption applied to labeling requirements and not to commercial publicity concerning a product, such as the publicity being made available by HyperInfo through its Web site.

Mr. Sunatori then contended that his company should be entitled to rely on technical and legal measures designed to limit the availability of the Web site to residents of Quebec. Specifically, the HyperInfo Web site included a disclaimer that indicated that "the products and services on this Web site are not available to residents of Quebec due to 'la Charte de a Langue Francaise.'"[59] In addition, HyperInfo implemented technical measures so that users from ".qc" addresses would not be permitted to access the site. Again, the court dismissed Mr. Sunatori's arguments, contending that the technological measures were imperfect and that Web site operators could not rely on Web site disclaimers as a means for avoiding compliance with Quebec's language requirements.

Finally, Mr. Sunatori also argued against the very application of the language laws to the Internet. He contended that because the Internet was a borderless medium, it was unfair for the government of Quebec to oblige companies operating Web sites from Quebec to comply with language requirements that were not imposed on companies operating Web sites from outside the province.

The court also rejected Mr. Sunatori's final argument. Although the court acknowledged that content posted on Web sites generally passes freely between different jurisdictions, the court maintained that this fact alone was not sufficient to impact the sovereign rights of the government to regulate on-line activity, especially where such activity is commenced from within the jurisdiction of such government.

The rationale for the actions of language authorities in jurisdictions such as France and Quebec can be understood when one considers that worldwide, approximately 86 percent of Web sites are in English and only 2 percent are in French.[60] Nonetheless many Web site operators have found such measures extremely intrusive and objectionable. For example, one Web site operator that was forced to translate its site into French ended up removing many portions of the site and including the following notice on its site: "Thanks to l'office de la Langue Francaise for closing off some sections of the homepage. For comments and complaints, please contact them at: scom@olf.gouv.ca."

The HyperInfo case emphasizes the importance of local requirements when engaging in on-line cross-border commerce. Still, the requirement to comply with language rules represents only one of the many local requirements that can impact one's e-business initiatives.

MARKETING AGREEMENTS

Introduction

This section examines key issues related to on-line marketing agreements. Marketing is an extremely important part of e-commerce, and entities engaging in e-commerce via the Internet often participate in a diverse selection of advertising and marketing activities, ranging from posting ordinary advertisements to participating in complex co-branding promotional arrangements. Whether an entity is participating in the marketing of its own products or services or performing marketing services on behalf of another company, it will be necessary to understand the key elements of advertising agreements.

Co-branding Agreements

Purposes and Advantages of Co-branding Agreements

There are a number of different types of on-line advertising agreements. One type of commonly viewed marketing arrangement is the co-branding agreement. This kind of agreement is often used because it can be quite beneficial to both parties in the arrangement—the party that is providing the Web site and the content available there ("the provider") and the party that will be adding its branding to such services ("the brander").

From the provider's perspective, a co-branding arrangement permits the provider to distribute its content and services through a number of different channels. In so doing, the provider may have the opportunity to reach new groups of potential customers and also increase revenues. From the brander's perspective, a co-branding relationship may allow it to offer its customers a range of products and services that is broader than what the brander would be able to deliver on its own. For both parties, participating in a co-branding arrangement may increase user traffic to their own Web site because users of the co-branded service will usually be able to link from the co-branded page to each party's home page with relative ease. This might help to expose each of the parties to a broader class of potential users. Consider, for instance, if a bank and a travel company join together to develop a co-branded Web site on which a foreign currency converter is made available. The currency converter might be attractive to a number of individuals who are neither clients of the bank nor clients of the travel company. Once such individuals use the foreign currency converter, however, they would be able to link to the Web site of the bank to actually purchase foreign currency and to the Web site of the travel company to continue making travel arrangements.

Promotional Efforts

Co-branding arrangements have a number of distinctive features. A key feature of this type of relationship is the promotion of the co-branded Web pages. There are a number of ways in which the parties may work to promote the co-branded Web pages. Promotional efforts can range from the relatively simple, such as providing links to the co-branded pages in the navigation bars of the parties' Web sites, to using co-registration boxes on the co-branded Web pages. Sponsorship efforts may also involve the provision of editorial and other content and can involve the use of actual advertising and sponsorship. For instance, the parties may be able to promote the co-branded Web pages by including references to the co-branded pages in the e-mails, newsletters, and other correspondence that it sends to the registered users of its own site. The parties may also decide to promote the co-branded pages through contests, sweepstakes, and other promotions.

The precise language that is used when describing the parties' rights and obligations with respect to the promotion of the co-branded Web pages will depend on the parties' business arrangement. Box 5.1 presents a sample of general promotional language. This language foresees a structure pursuant to which the brander's marketing obligations would be specified in greater detail on an attached exhibit.

Referral Tracking

Another important element of co-branding arrangements is the ability of the brander, or even both parties, to track the number of individuals referred to their respective Web sites from the co-branded Web pages. The ability to obtain an accurate calculation of referrals is important because the number of referrals can impact significant issues such as the calculation of revenues and the parties' abilities to use the personal data provided by the referrals.

There are a few primary mechanisms through which the parties can track referrals to the co-brand Web pages. For instance, the parties can establish a unique URL that will be used to identify the co-branded Web pages. If the parties use this method, they will be able to establish clear rules regarding the calculation of referrals to the co-branded pages.

The parties may also wish to consider implementing a system that

---

Box 5.1
Sample Promotional Activities Language

Promotional Activities

(a) The parties shall each publicize and promote the Co-branded Web Pages at their sole expense in accordance with the promotional activities plan set forth on Exhibit A (the "Promotional Plan"). Brander shall obtain Provider's prior written consent to all additional promotional plans relating to the Provider Web Site.

(b) Brander and Provider will cooperate with each other to prepare and issue a joint press release regarding the launch of the Co-Branded Web Pages.

---

would require referrals to register at the co-branded Web site. Thereafter, the referrals can be tracked continually by a number of different methods, including requiring subsequent log-ins at the co-branded pages and the use of cookies. While such a method might facilitate the computation of referrals, the parties in a co-branding relationship might be somewhat reluctant to take this approach because of concerns that users may have a negative view of registration requirements.

In addition, the parties may also opt to place a cookie in the user's cookie file without causing the user to actually register. While the use of cookies may be somewhat more palatable to the user because he or she will not actually be required to take positive action to register with the site, the use of cookies is not without its problems. For instance, individuals may refuse the cookies or subsequently delete the cookie.

Furthermore, the parties will be able to track referrals by recording the URL that the users were last visiting before visiting their site. If the user was visiting the URL of the co-branded pages just prior to visiting the home pages of the parties' Web sites, it may be possible to count such individuals as being referred from the co-branded Web pages.

Depending on the type of system that is actually implemented for tracking referrals, it may be appropriate to include an audit right, pursuant to which the provider would be able to confirm whether the figures claimed by the brander are actually correct. Box 5.2 presents a sample audit clause that might be used in such circumstances.

Exclusivity

Exclusivity is an important element of some co-branding arrangements. In certain arrangements, such as where the provider desires to obtain maximum promotion from the brander, the provider will require the brander to grant some form of exclusivity. Still, even when exclu-

---

Box 5.2
Sample Audit Language

Reports and Records

(a) Within thirty (30) days after the end of each calendar month during the term of this Agreement, Brander shall forward to Company a report specifying for such calendar month the number of page impressions attributable to the Provider Web Site on the Brander Web Site and any other information as reasonably requested by Provider.

(b) Throughout the Term and for a period of two (2) years thereafter, Brander shall maintain complete and accurate records that are sufficiently detailed to enable Provider to verify the number of page impressions and other requested information, and Brander shall make available such documentation available to Provider, upon written request from Provider.

---

sivity is agreed upon, the exclusive relationship can be played out in a number of ways. For instance, the exclusive aspect of the relationship may be limited to a list of identified competitors. In this kind of agreement, a party would be able to develop a list of companies with whom the other party cannot enter into specified types of relationships. This approach has certain advantages, the most significant of which is the fact that the parties' obligations will be clear and well defined. The main disadvantage is that the approach is not flexible and may not accommodate the addition or deletion of other competitors.

Of course, exclusivity can also be based on categories so that one or more of the parties would be restricted from entering into specified types of relationships with companies that are involved in certain industries. For example, a co-branding agreement might prohibit the brander from entering into similar agreements with other banks. The difficulty with having an exclusive relationship that focuses on categories is that categories of companies are not always clearly defined. In the foregoing example, for instance, would the restriction on establishing relationships with banks include foreign-based banks or U.S. subsidiaries of foreign banks? Would it include Internet-only banks? Would it include only banks in existence as of the effective date of the co-branding agreement, or would it also include banks that come into existence subsequently? To avoid potential disputes, the agreement must define categories as specifically as possible.

As is the case with many other terms of the co-branding agreement, the precise wording of the exclusivity clause will depend on the business arrangement that had been agreed to by the parties. Box 5.3 presents a

---

Box 5.3
Sample Exclusivity Clause

Exclusivity. During the Term, Brander will not create, host, or maintain co-branded Web pages featuring Brander's Brands or Services on Web sites whose primary function, focus, and content are to enable individuals to provide travel information and services to individuals.

---

sample exclusivity clause that is intended merely to provide an idea of the kinds of issues that are generally raised in connection with the inclusion of an exclusivity clause in agreements of this type.

The sample language presented in box 5.3 contains a rather broad restriction. It would be in the Brander's interests to make the restrictions contained in this clause narrower. For example, the Brander might wish to include geographic limitations on the exclusivity clause. On the other hand, in this scenario, the Provider is likely to want to leave the restriction as broad as possible to prohibit the Brander from engaging in similar relationships with the largest class of potential competitors possible.

Personal Data Exchange and Privacy

The parties that participate in a co-branding arrangement are often quite eager to obtain new customers and, accordingly, will be interested in obtaining the personally identifiable data (personal data) that users provide through the other party's Web site. Having such personal data may enable the party desiring the information to contact the individual in order to offer products or services and to inform the individual regarding special offers and promotions.

While personal data are often viewed as a valuable commodity, consumers are becoming increasingly protective in safeguarding the privacy of their personal data. In addition, as was discussed in chapter 4, personal data are also afforded considerable protection by law. Accordingly, when entering into a co-branding agreement, it is essential to clearly specify the parties' respective rights and obligations concerning personal data that is collected through the co-branded Web pages. Box 5.4 contains sample data privacy language.

Payments and Fees

The parties entering into a co-branding arrangement will be required to include in the agreement that will govern such arrangement a clear description of all fees that are to be paid under the agreement. Generally,

---

Box 5.4
Sample Personal Data and Privacy Clause

Personal Data and Privacy
(a) Brander shall obtain Provider's prior written consent before collecting any personally identifiable data ("Personal Data") from visitors to the Co-branded Web Pages. All Personal Data that End Users provide through the Co-branded Web Pages shall be the Confidential Information of Provider.

(b) During the term of this Agreement, both parties agree to implement, display, and comply with an on-line privacy policy that clearly explains such party's use of data collected from visitors to their respective Web sites.

---

in most co-branding arrangements, four different types of payments may be at issue. The first of these are the development fees. In creating the co-branding pages, one or both of the parties will incur certain developmental costs. The co-branding agreement should clearly specify the parties' respective obligations for the various developmental costs that will be involved in establishing the co-branding relationship.

Second, some arrangements might also involve the payment of exclusivity fees. If one party is agreeing to particularly stringent exclusivity restrictions, the other party may pay the party who is being subjected to the restrictions a fee to compensate for such exclusivity. The amount and payment frequency of the exclusivity payments will depend on the particular facts and circumstances of the business relationship.

Placement fees are another type of fee involved in co-branding arrangements. Such fees are often used to compensate a party for actual or guaranteed promotions on the co-branded Web pages. Such fees are often regarded as accruing once the actual placements are delivered.

In co-branding agreements, fees may also be based on user activity. Click-through fees are one type of fee based on user activity. In some arrangements, the provider will pay the brander based on the number of users who "click through" from the brander's Web site to the co-branded Web pages. Bounties are another type of variable fee based on actual user activity. In certain arrangements, the provider will pay the brander based on the number of individuals who actually sign up for the provider's services or purchase the provider's products through the co-branded Web pages. Such payments are often referred to as bounties.

Finally, many arrangements also include the obligation to pay fees based on advertising sales. If the parties agree to include advertising on the co-branded Web pages, it will be necessary to agree about which parties can include advertisements on the pages, as well how the parties will split any advertising revenues generated.

The co-branding arrangement might also involve transaction fees. In many such arrangements, the provider will desire to sell products or services via the co-branded Web pages. Often, the distribution and sale of such products and services will involve various costs, and the co-branding agreement should specify which party will bear the burden of paying the transaction costs.

Proprietary Rights

Co-branding agreements, like many other agreements through which parties' intellectual property rights are commingled, should specify clearly which rights belong to which party. When defining the parties' intellectual property rights, attention should be directed not only to the copyrighted materials and trademarks of the parties but also to the user information that is collected through the Web pages. If a license will be granted to either of the parties' intellectual property rights, any restrictions, such as any geographic limitations on the scope of the license, should also be set forth clearly in the agreement.

Service Levels

In many co-branding arrangements, one party will demand certain service level commitments from the party that is operating the Web site. There are a number of issues that are often included in service level commitments. One is uptime. This refers to the percentage of time that the co-branded Web pages are actually available to individuals. In a perfect world, Web services would be available 24 hours a day, seven days a week, without interruption. However, the parties may agree on reduced percentages of uptime, especially if high percentages are guaranteed during key hours.

In some agreements, the parties will also agree on the minimum server speed and on the minimum size of the data pipeline. Furthermore, in many arrangements, the parties may agree on procedures and time frames for the correction of errors in the software that is used in connection with the operation of the co-branded Web pages. The parties may also wish to specify the minimum security measures to be implemented in order to protect the security of the co-branded Web pages.

Conclusions about Co-branding Agreements

Co-branding arrangements are an important part of marketing products and services that are made available through the Internet. While such agreements are valuable and are frequently used, they are also somewhat complicated, covering a wide range of different issues. To maximize the benefits of such arrangements, it is important to have an understanding of all the issues and the parties' respective business positions. If a co-branding agreement is concluded without a full understanding of the issues involved, both parties are likely to be disappointed by the results of the arrangement. On the other hand, if the agreement is concluded after sufficient reflection, discussion, and negotiation, the parties are likely to enjoy a productive, mutually beneficial relationship.

CONCLUSION

This chapter has examined a number of legal issues related to on-line advertising and marketing. Launching a successful e-business initiative usually involves the distribution of advertising materials via the Internet and participation in various on-line marketing efforts. While advertising and promotional campaigns can help to increase business, if such campaigns are not carried out in compliance with applicable law, they can also lead to liability. Accordingly, this chapter has endeavored to present recommendations for carrying out promotional activities in a manner that is consistent with law.

The next chapter will explore specific techniques to consider when attempting to protect one's property on-line. Engaging in e-commerce by operating an Internet Web site often involves the distribution of various materials and information protected by intellectual property laws. As such, when engaging in e-commerce, it is essential to ensure that one's own intellectual property rights are properly protected and that steps are taken to ensure that participation in various e-commerce initiatives will not infringe the intellectual property rights of others.

Chapter 6

PROTECTING PROPERTY
ON-LINE

Intellectual property assets (IP assets) are a significant part of all companies' e-commerce initiatives. Most companies engaging in e-commerce rely on their own IP assets as well as the IP assets of third parties for the successful launch, implementation, and operation of their commercial endeavors. Accordingly, e-business strategies must include a significant focus on protecting and enhancing the value of IP assets.

While IP assets will be of great value to all e-commerce initiatives, engaging in e-commerce also raises the risks that one's IP assets will be infringed. Operating an e-commerce Web site will usually necessitate making various IP assets, including copyrighted materials, trademarks, trade secrets, and patented processes, available through a large, borderless medium. Accordingly, what follows in this chapter is a briefing on some of the fundamental strategies for protecting one's own IP assets while also minimizing the risks of infringing the IP assets of third parties.

PROTECTING IP ASSETS

Overview

When operating an e-business Web site, most companies will make a substantial portion of their IP assets available through the Internet. There are, of course, certain risks associated with this. The following sections will examine specific steps that can be taken to minimize such risks.

Identifying IP Assets

The first crucial step in minimizing the risks and maximizing the value of e-business is to identify and categorize all relevant IP assets that will be utilized in the company's e-business endeavors. The precise steps to be included in an IP asset audit will depend on the particular facts and circumstances, including the size of the company and the amount of IP assets owned or used by the particular entity. For certain large enterprises with voluminous libraries of IP assets, it may be most appropriate to use a third-party auditing firm to examine and document all IP assets.

The investigation into IP assets should distinguish third-party IP assets from the company's own IP assets and note the terms and conditions that govern the use of all third-party IP assets. Once the actual IP assets have been identified and inventoried, it will be necessary to take action to protect and maximize the value of such assets.

Protecting Copyrighted Materials

When operating an e-business Web site, most companies will make a substantial amount of copyrighted material available via the Internet. Copyright protects the original expression of ideas fixed in any tangible medium of expression.[1] Examples of copyrighted material commonly made available through Web sites include articles, stories, the computer code for the Web site, and the Web site itself. Many Web sites also use databases, and the selection and organization of such databases can be protected by copyright if the content of such databases is selected and organized in a sufficiently creative manner.[2]

In the United States, particular attention is paid to the registration of copyrights. While registration is not necessary to have copyright protection, registration does provide certain statutorily prescribed benefits, including, notably, the rebuttable presumption that the registrant is the copyright owner and the possibility of obtaining attorneys' fees and treble damages in an infringement suit. Therefore companies should consider pursuing registration rapidly upon the work's creation. With respect to a Web site, registrations should be filed for each copyrighted work on the site, such as articles or databases, as well as for the site as a whole. Furthermore, since copyrighted content made available via the Internet will be accessible worldwide, the rights holder should also consider any steps needed to protect the copyrighted information abroad, especially in jurisdictions in which the company engages in substantial commerce.

In addition to filing copyright registrations, companies should consider including appropriate copyright notices on all copyrighted materials, including each page of the Web site. Under the Copyright Act, a proper copyright notice consists of three elements: (1) the copyright symbol (Copyright, Copr., or ©; (2) the year of first publication or completion; and (3) the name of the copyright owner. There are, however, two important issues to note. First, under the Universal Copyright Convention, only the symbol "©" is used. Additionally, under the Buenos Aires Convention, the use of the words "all rights reserved" is also required. An example of a copyright notice that takes all of these factors into account is "© 2002 ABC Co., Inc. All rights reserved."

Notice of copyright should be affixed to copies of the work in such a way as to give "reasonable notice" of the claim of copyright. For Web sites, it is advisable to include the copyright notice in a prominent position on the home page, in close proximity to other notices of significance such as Web site Terms of Use agreements, as well as on every page thereafter. Furthermore, appropriate notices should also be placed on each discretely registered work, such as images, artwork, and articles.

Protecting New Business Methods

An important part of leveraging IP assets will be protecting all patentable inventions, including, notably, new methods of doing business. Before 1998, methods of doing business were generally not thought to be patentable in the United States. In recent years, however, the U.S. Patent and Trademark Office has patented a number of business methods. The system underwent notable changes in 1998 when in *State Street & Trust Co. v. Signature Financial Group, Inc.,*[3] the Federal Circuit held that a business method could be patented provided that statutory condition for patentability have been met. Since the *State Street* case, the United States Patent and Trademark Office (USPTO) has issued a great number of e-business method patents. Furthermore, all indications are that Internet-related patents will be a key area of the future work of the USPTO. In March 2000 the USPTO announced an action plan for business method patents. The plan includes greater training for examiners, revised examination guidelines for computer-related inventions, and expanded search activities.[4]

Internet-related patents are likely to have an important effect on the future of e-commerce and can play an important role in the development of one's business. The protection provided by patents is strong, and patent holders are able to control the use of their technology. Indeed, a patent on a particular business method would prevent another entity from using such method. Accordingly, business method patents can help a company to obtain important commercial advantages, and if licensed to other companies, such patents may prove to be a major source of revenue.

For all of the foregoing reasons, it is important to have patent counsel involved in reviewing a company's e-business initiatives to determine whether any patentable business methods are being used. Today many methods commonly used in e-commerce, such as payment methods and ordering methods, are being patented. Because the Internet is a global medium and patents are country specific, it will also be important to protect such patentable methods in countries other than the United States.

Protecting Trade Secrets

Trade secrets are extremely important to many companies—both on-line and off. Trade secrets can generally be understood as commercially valuable secret information. The classic example of a trade secret is the formula for Coca-Cola. Trade secrets are protected by state tort law. Such laws protect against the misappropriation of proprietary information by all third parties, including the competitors of the trade secret holder.[5]

The increasing use of the Internet by businesses also raises concerns about the protection of trade secrets. Companies engaging in e-commerce need to protect trade secrets just as other companies do. Because of the damaging consequences of disclosures of trade secrets on the Internet, companies must implement strategies to reduce the likelihood of such disclosures, as well as mitigate any resulting damages.

Preventing the unauthorized disclosure of trade secrets on the Internet should begin with the organization's internal policies. Entities concerned about the potential disclosure of their trade secrets through the Internet should create and enforce written guidelines indicating what kinds of information may and may not be posted on the Internet or sent by e-mail. Having such policies in place should help reduce the incidence of "innocent" disclosures by employees who might have been unaware of the consequences of their actions and also eliminate the likelihood that an employee could claim that he or she was not made aware of the company's policy in this regard.

It is also recommended that companies concerned about the potential disclosure of valuable trade secrets monitor Web sites that are likely to contain information about their company, such as news groups about the company or its products and services. In the event that information pertaining to trade secrets is spotted on such a Web site, the company should ensure that such information is removed. In addition, it is a good idea to replace the removed information with a statement indicating that the posting was removed because it had been made without the company's permission and may have contained information misappropriated from the company.

Various technical mechanisms should be employed to prevent the disclosure of trade secrets on the Internet. For example, companies may wish to utilize a document-tracking device to determine if any specific documents have been viewed or downloaded. It may also be in a company's interest to hire outside investigators to monitor certain Web sites or to perform random searches to ascertain whether any trade secrets are being posted to the Internet.

Box 6.1 presents a summary of key strategies for protecting trade secrets on the Internet. While the precise methods that are used will depend on a number of factors, including the industry of the company, the type of trade secrets, and so forth, the strategies listed in the box constitute a general recommendation to consider in conjunction with any program designed to protect IP assets.

Protecting Rights in Trademarks

Trademarks are words, symbols, and other designations that are used to distinguish one entity's goods and services from those of another. Accordingly, trademarks are often an important part of a company's commercial success. For these reasons, when operating an e-commerce Web site, it will also be necessary to take steps to protect all trademarks. There

---

Box 6.1
Strategies for Protecting Trade Secrets on the Internet

- Implement and enforce written guidelines concerning what may and may not be disclosed on the Internet and via e-mail.
- Monitor Web sites on which trade secrets and other valuable company information may appear, such as company or industry-related news groups. Execute appropriate nondisclosure agreements with third-party consultants and contractors.
- Mark confidential information as "confidential."
- Conduct a trade secret audit.
- Implement various technical measures to protect trade secrets.

are a number of reasons why the development of e-business is increasing the risks of trademark infringement. The growth and development of the Internet as a tool of commerce has been accompanied by an exponential increase in trademark infringement as well as counterfeiting.[6]

In addition, the law applicable to trademarks developed at a time in which goods and services were sold in markets separated by physical distances. The rise of the Internet leads to the possibility that previously geographically remote trademark owners using their marks on the Internet will result in a likelihood of confusion over the parties' respective marks. The importance of conducting thorough trademark searches and filing for registration of all trademarks has thus assumed a new sense of urgency. It is significant to note that in the United States, trademark rights arise even if the relevant mark is not registered with either the state or federal governmental authorities. However, federal registration does offer certain procedural advantages. Namely, registration of a trademark on the Principal Register of the PTO is prima facie evidence of the exclusive right to use the applicable mark nationwide in connection with the identified products and services.

Once the PTO issues a certificate of registration for the applicable mark, efforts should be exerted to ensure that the federal trademark registration symbol "®" appears after the federally registered mark when it is used to identify the goods or services recited in the registration. Until such time as a federal registration is issued, the symbols "™" or "SM" can be used to indicate a claim of rights to a trademark or service mark.

It is also important to monitor the use of one's own trademarks by third parties, including any licensees, on the Internet. There are a number of different contractual relationships pursuant to which a trademark license may be granted. One of the most common examples is the co-branding agreement discussed in chapter 5. It will be important to enforce the restrictions on trademark usage contained in such agreements, as well as to ensure that no unlicensed third parties are using trademarks in an unauthorized manner.

Scouring the Internet for Infringement

When implementing a program intended to protect IP assets on-line, a proactive approach will likely generate the most positive results. To best protect IP assets, companies should scour the Internet for infringement of their rights. There are a number of software tools that permit companies to go through the Internet and identify sites that infringe IP assets. Once infringements are detected, they should be investigated and addressed. In many instances, the early detection and termination of the unauthorized use of IP assets may help to mitigate any possible damages.

MINIMIZING THE RISKS OF LIABILITY FOR THE INFRINGEMENT OF THIRD-PARTY INTELLECTUAL PROPERTY RIGHTS

Overview

In addition to protecting one's own IP assets, it will also be necessary to avoid infringing third-party IP assets in connection with the operation of e-commerce initiatives. While most companies will not intend to use third-party IP assets in an unauthorized manner, some common business practices can lead to potential liability.

Linking and Framing

Overview of Concerns about Linking

When considering intellectual property and the Internet, the potential risks surrounding the practices of linking and framing must be addressed. Hypertext links are used on many Web sites. In fact, some would argue that links are one of the most important characteristics of the Internet. Through links, Web site users are able to jump from one Web page to another.

Clearly, the use of hyperlinks is a fundamental part of the Internet. However, in some cases this common practice can give rise to liability, including, notably, through trademark infringement. Generally, the use of simple hyperlinks to the home page of a third-party Web site will not be problematic. However, it is still recommended that all companies review the linking policies of the Web sites to which hyperlinks will be established and, to the extent necessary, obtain the prior written consent of the operator of the Web site to which the link will be made.

In some cases, the establishment of links to third-party Web sites may lead to intellectual property claims by implying an association between the initial Web site and the linked Web site. A number of cases, both in the United States and abroad, have examined various intellectual property claims that arise through linking. While the law concerning linking is not fully settled, a review of such cases will provide some guidance concerning the kinds of circumstances under which linking may be viewed as problematic.

Copyright Infringement

There have been a few cases where linking has led to claims of copyright infringement. One of the most interesting in the United States is *Intellectual Reserve, Inc., v. Utah Lighthouse Ministry, Inc.*[7] In this case, the defendant had originally posted substantial portions of the plaintiff's copyrighted "Church Handbook of Instructions" on the defendant's Web site and had provided links to other Web pages on which the handbook was made available. As a result, the plaintiff brought an action for direct and contributory copyright infringement.

The defendant subsequently removed the posting and the links upon order of the court. However, the defendant then placed a notice on its Web site that the handbook was available on-line, provided three domain names of Web sites containing the handbook, and posted e-mails on its Web site that encouraged browsing those Web sites and printing and forwarding the handbook.

The court granted the plaintiff's motion for a preliminary injunction against the posting of the domain names of other Web sites on which the plaintiff's handbook was made available. The court reasoned that the defendant could be liable for contributory copyright infringement because the defendant had encouraged browsing of the infringing materials. The court contended that since browsing causes a copy of the materials to be made in the computer's RAM, it is a direct copyright infringement in which the defendant knowingly participated. The defendant appealed the court's injunction, but on November 29, 2000, the parties announced that they had settled the case.[8]

There have also been a number of interesting cases overseas. In *Church of Scientology v. Spaink,*[9] a court in the Netherlands held that a service provider that hyperlinks to copyrighted materials without consent of the copyright owners and with notice of the infringement has infringed the copyrights. Also, in the case of *SNC Havas Numerique v. SA Kelijob,*[10] a French court ruled against a defendant that had provided deep links to the plaintiff's Web site without authorization. In drafting the injunction, the court made a distinction between surface linking, which the court appeared to find acceptable, and deep linking, which the court viewed as requiring authorization.

The Special Case of Deep Linking

As was noted in the French case of *SNC Havas Numerique v. SA Kelijob,* deep linking raises more concerns because it enables end users to enter a given Web site through means other than the site's home page.

By entering the site through deep links, end users are able to bypass the site's home page, thereby also bypassing important legal notices and revenue-producing advertising that are displayed solely on the home page. The risks of various intellectual property claims are likely to increase if the links are made not to the home page but to internal pages within the site to which the links are made, through a process referred to as deep linking. Accordingly, it is strongly recommended that companies avoid any deep linking without the prior written permission of the operator of the linked site.

One of the most frequently cited cases concerning deep linking is *Ticketmaster Corp. v. Microsoft Corp.* (discussed in chapter 3).[11] This case arose after Microsoft created a link from its Web site to Ticketmaster's on-line ticketing service. The link enabled users to proceed directly to Ticketmaster's ticketing services, thereby bypassing Ticketmaster's home page and other pages with substantial advertising. Ticketmaster brought an action for trademark dilution and unfair competition. As in many other cases involving claims arising out of linking and framing, the parties eventually settled the dispute.

Another significant case concerning deep linking originated in Scotland. This case, *Shetland Times Ltd. v. Wills,*[12] arose when the *Shetland Times* brought an action for copyright infringement against *Shetland News* after *Shetland News* posted on its Web site verbatim headlines from the *Shetland Times* that deep linked to the corresponding articles on the *Shetland Times* Web site. The *Shetland Times* complained that the actions of *Shetland News* created the false impression that *Shetland News* had published the articles that were actually taken from the *Shetland Times.*

In his short opinion, the presiding judge Lord Hamilton noted that the plaintiff had a prima facie case that its Web site constituted a cable program service under the United Kingdom's Copyright Act of 1988. Lord Hamilton held that the defendant was infringing the 1988 act both in relation to "copying"[13] and in the inclusion in a cable program service.[14] The judge considered that it was fundamental to the plaintiff that users were only allowed to access the information *directly* from their Web site (as opposed to being able to bypass the front page). Although the violation by the defendant did not lead to actual loss, the plaintiffs were likely to lose potential advertising revenue in the future.

This opinion was based on a short interim hearing. It was certainly not clear whether the judge held that there was a prima facie case that the hypertext links themselves (as opposed to the copying of the headlines) amounted to infringement. The long-awaited final decision on this case, however, never materialized, as the parties settled the matter out of court. In conjunction with the settlement, the *Shetland Times* agreed to permit *Shetland News* to link to *Shetland Times* articles, provided that (1) the *Shetland Times* was acknowledged under each applicable headline, (2) the *Shetland Times* logo was adjacent to each applicable headline, and (3) the logo was a hypertext link to the *Shetland Times* "on-line headline page."

Framing

Even more controversial than deep linking is framing, which is really a subset of linking that allows a Web site operator to divide the browser window into multiple parts and to place elements from different Web sites into each part. For reasons similar to those examined in the discussion of deep linking, the use of framing technology should also be avoided unless specific permission is obtained in advance.

One of the most notable cases concerning framing is *Washington Post Co. v. Total News, Inc.*[15] This case commenced when six large American media companies, (including the *Wall Street Journal,* the *Washington Post,* the *Los Angeles Times,* and CNN) filed a lawsuit against Total-NEWS, a small Web news aggregator site that was creating links to news content on the Web but placing that content within a frame of TotalNEWS.

At the time the lawsuit was commenced, the Web site of TotalNEWS contained three small frames and one large frame. The three small frames contained, respectively, (1) "hot buttons" that provided links to major news sites, (2) a "back button" bearing the TotalNEWS logo that sent the user back to the page of news links that he or she had last viewed, and (3) a rotating banner advertisement for a third-party product or service for which TotalNEWS could theoretically receive advertising revenues. The large frame would contain the news Web site that had been chosen by the user from the displayed list of links.

The TotalNEWS Web site was organized in such a way that when the user selected one of the possible links, he or she would not actually leave the TotalNEWS site (i.e., the TotalNEWS URL remained in the browser's location indicator). Rather, the large TotalNEWS frame acted as a window to the linked-to site. The Web site of TotalNEWS contained a disclaimer page that explained the workings of the site and instructed users as to how they could disable the frame format. The disclaimer of TotalNEWS also indicated that TotalNEWS had no affiliation with the sites to which it provided links and attributed ownership of trademarks.

Despite the efforts of TotalNEWS in including disclaimers, the news companies whose sites were being framed found the practices objectionable and filed suit. The complaint that the publishing companies filed against TotalNEWS was based on a number of allegations, including misappropriation, trademark dilution and infringement, willful copyright violations, and other tortious acts.[16]

The first count of the complaint was misappropriation. This count was based on the allegation that by usurping the content of the plaintiffs' Web sites and causing each of the plaintiffs' Web sites to appear within a window on the defendant's site, the defendant unfairly misappropriated valuable commercial property belonging to the plaintiffs.[17] The plaintiffs alleged that the defendant's conduct constituted misappropriation and unfair competition because it took the entire commercial value of the news reported at each of the plaintiffs' sites and literally sold it to others for the defendant's own profit.

The second count of the complaint was based on allegations of federal trademark dilution. Here the plaintiffs alleged that the acts of the defendant diluted and detracted from the distinctiveness of the plaintiffs' famous trademarks.[18] This, in turn, was alleged to have caused damage to the plaintiffs and the business and goodwill symbolized by those trademarks. The plaintiffs also argued that unless restrained, the acts of the defendant would cause further, irreparable harm to their interests.

The third count of the complaint was based on allegations of trademark infringement.[19] Specifically, the plaintiffs alleged that the defendant's unauthorized use of the plaintiffs' trademarks in connection with the defendant's advertisements, which had not been approved by the plaintiffs, was likely to cause confusion. It was the plaintiffs' further contention that the defendant's use of the plaintiffs' trademarks in such a manner could lead to mistakes and could deceive customers about the source or origin of the content depicted at the defendant's Web site. In this regard, the plaintiffs argued that the defendant's acts of trademark infringement caused great and irreparable injury to the plaintiffs, to their respective trademarks, and to the business and goodwill represented by such trademarks.

The fourth count of the complaint was based on allegations of false designation of origin. Specifically, the plaintiffs argued that by framing their news in such a way, the defendant made false, deceptive, and misleading statements that constituted false representation and false advertising.[20] The plaintiffs further alleged that such actions caused irreparable injury to the plaintiffs' goodwill and reputation.[21]

The fifth count of the complaint was based on allegations of trademark infringement and unfair competition under state law.[22] The allegations made under this count were similar to those made pursuant to federal law under the third count of the complaint, except that under the fifth count, the alleged violations were claimed to have been committed under state law.[23]

The sixth count of the complaint was based on allegations of trademark dilution under state law.[24] The allegations made under this count were similar to those made under the second count with respect to federal law, except that under the sixth count, the alleged violations were claimed to have been committed under state law.[25]

The seventh count of the complaint was based on allegations of deceptive acts and practices. This was another claim based on state law.[26]

The eighth count of the complaint was based on allegations of copyright infringement. The plaintiffs alleged that in order for the defendant to provide its news service, the defendant caused the plaintiffs' sites to appear within a window displayed as part of "totalnews.com," surrounded and partially obscured by material totally unrelated to the original content of the plaintiffs' sites. The plaintiffs further alleged that the defendant's conduct had been in willful violation of the plaintiffs' repeated warnings to the defendant that the plaintiffs did not want their sites and content depicted in such a way.

The ninth count was based on a claim of tortious interference. The plaintiffs alleged that the defendant had designed its site to display third-party advertising simultaneously and in competition with material placed by the plaintiffs on their own sites, including material from the plaintiffs' advertisers. It was the plaintiffs' contention that by running other advertising material in the totalnews.com frame adjacent to the content of the plaintiffs' sites, and by partially obscuring the plaintiffs' sites with their frames, the defendant made the plaintiffs' performance of their advertising contracts more burdensome. Moreover, it was further alleged that the defendant's actions interfered with the benefits that the plaintiffs' advertisers had bargained for when they purchased space on the plaintiffs' sites. As such, it was alleged that the defendant's conduct constituted intentional and improper interference with the plaintiffs' performance of their advertising contracts.

As a result of the foregoing allegations, the plaintiffs requested an order that would compel the defendant to discontinue its actions immediately and account to the plaintiff for any profits received by the defendant and any damages sustained by the plaintiffs arising from the acts of misappropriation, copyright infringement, and unfair competition. The plaintiffs further requested actual and statutory damages, attorneys' fees, and costs.

In the summer of 1997, TotalNEWS settled the lawsuit brought by the *Wall Street Journal,* the *Washington Post,* the *Los Angeles Times,* CNN, and others.[27] Many in the legal realm were disappointed by the settlement, as most wanted to receive a clear answer from the court concerning the legality of framing. However, the defendant in this case was a small company and apparently did not have the resources necessary to endure a lengthy legal battle.

As part of the settlement, TotalNEWS agreed to permanently cease to cause any of the plaintiffs' Web sites to appear on any user's computer screen with any material supplied by, or associated with, the defendants or any third party acting in privity with the defendant or under the defendant's direct or indirect control. Specifically, the defendant agreed to cease the practice of framing the plaintiffs' Web sites.

In connection with the settlement, the plaintiffs also agreed that the defendants could link from the TotalNEWS Web site or any other Web site to any plaintiffs' Web site, provided that

1. defendants may only link to plaintiffs' Web sites via hyperlinks consisting of the names of the linked sites in plain text;
2. defendants may not use any of plaintiffs' proprietary logos or other distinctive material as a hyperlink or in any other way; and
3. defendants may not otherwise link in any manner reasonably likely to (a) imply affiliation with, or endorsement or sponsorship by, any plaintiff; (b) cause confusion, mistake, or deception; (c) dilute plaintiffs' marks; or (d) otherwise violate state or federal law.

The settlement agreement was significant because it can be understood as implicitly supporting the legality of link licenses. It should be emphasized, however, that while the outcome of this case did support the existence of implied link licenses, the settlement agreement did not actually establish the legality of link licenses. Even though the dispute between TotalNEWS and the American media giants was resolved through a settlement, the case did not fully resolve the controversy over the use of framing. Subsequent to the dispute with the American companies, TotalNEWS was still receiving complaints from Japanese and other media companies whose publications were being framed by TotalNEWS. Moreover, other companies that have engaged in framing have faced similar issues.

Another interesting framing case arose in September 1997 when Futuredonics, the owner of a Web site containing a dental referral service, filed a complaint against a defendant who was framing material from the

Futuredonics Web site.[28] The frame that was enclosing Futuredonics material contained the defendant's own logo and customer service information. In pursuing its case, the plaintiff argued that the framing constituted "derivative work."[29] In response, the defendant countered with the "reference" argument, contending that the frame should only be viewed as a "lens" through which users could view the information that Futuredonics had itself placed on the Web. The court denied the defendant's motion to dismiss; however, it also denied the plaintiff's motion for a preliminary injunction, ruling that Futuredonics had failed to establish a probability of success that would allow for such a preliminary injunction.

As demonstrated through a review of the *TotalNEWS* case, framing a site can cause trademark dilution problems. The case of *Playboy Enterprises v. Frena* further emphasizes this point.[30] In this case, a federal court ruled that when a dial-up computer bulletin board service (BBS) uploaded computer images that displayed the trademark of Playboy, then removed the trademarks and added the name of the BBS to the photographs, the BBS service infringed Playboy's copyright.[31] In this case, the court determined that the frame surrounding a target site that displays the logo of the framing site can be considered an obscuring of the trademark and thus an infringement.

Recommendations for Linking and Framing

The discussion of linking and framing will conclude with some practical advice. One effective way to manage the potential risks of linking and framing is to refrain from such practices until an agreement is reached with the operator of the Web site to which the links will be established. Some Web site operators post their own linking policies and form linking agreements on their Web sites. In other circumstances, however, it may be necessary to develop one's own linking agreement. In either scenario, there are several key issues that should be addressed by the linking agreement. Many of the issues are similar to those that also arise in connection with co-branding agreements, as discussed in chapter 5.

When entering into a linking agreement, it will be useful to include a description of the link that will be permitted. It is necessary to describe the link fully, focusing on issues such as the size of the link, whether it will be text or an icon, how large the link will be, where it will appear on the Web site, and so forth. In most cases, it will be useful to attach an image of the link so as to reduce the likelihood of future disputes.

It will also be necessary to include a license grant with restrictions that are appropriate to the circumstances. A sample license grant is contained in box 6.2.

Many linking arrangements will be without fees; some linking agreements will involve monetary consideration in the form of a flat fee, a percentage of transaction or membership fees, or a split of advertising revenues. The determination of the appropriate fees and the frequency of payments will be worked out between the parties based on their respective business needs.

More elaborate linking arrangements will usually also address issues such as service levels, maintenance of the Web site, collection of information, and privacy. However, simple linking arrangements will focus on describing permissible and prohibited linking practices, clarifying the parties' respective intellectual property rights, setting forth the parties' respective termination rights and the effects of termination, and establishing any indemnification obligations.

While the most effective way to mitigate the risks associated with linking is to refrain from engaging in such practices except pursuant to a written agreement, many entities decide to proceed with establishing links to third-party sites without first obtaining the prior written approval of the Web site to which the link will be made. Even if the decision is made to provide links to third-party sites, certain issues should be taken into consideration before linking. First, the Terms of Use agreements for each site to which links will be established should be reviewed. Some Web site operators prohibit linking altogether or establish restrictions on linking. Other Web sites encourage other site operators to link to their sites. It will be extremely important to ensure that any linking that is actually done is in compliance with the linking policies posted on the applicable Web site.

Box 6.2
Sample License Grant Language

Subject to the terms and conditions of this Agreement, Company hereby grants Linking Party a nonexclusive, nontransferable, nonsublicensable, limited, revocable license to use the Company Site Link for the sole purpose of promoting the Company Site on the Linking Site. Linking Party acknowledges and agrees that this license may be revoked at any time for any reason or no reason at Company's discretion and without cause upon notice by Company to Linking Party. All rights not expressly granted to Linking Party herein shall be retained by Company.

Secondly, any linking practice that might be viewed by the operator of the linked Web site as a threat to revenue or as a source of confusion to the end user may be viewed as objectionable by the operator of the linked site. Accordingly, such practices should not be attempted without obtaining the prior written consent of the applicable Web site operator.

Third, because of the increased likelihood of user confusion, as well as the fact that home pages that may contain important legal notices and revenue-generating advertising will be bypassed, companies should avoid establishing deep links into the subpages of Web sites. For similar reasons, the use of frames should also be avoided unless specifically authorized by the operator of the linked Web site.

Fourth, it is also important to closely review the content of the Web site to which links will be established. This review should ensure that the target Web site does not contain any infringing, defamatory, or otherwise questionable content. In all instances, but especially where there are concerns about the content of the linked site, it will be necessary to ensure that the links do not create an appearance of ownership, relationship, sponsorship, or endorsement that does not exist. In fact, it is important to make clear to the end user that the Web site operator does not control and is not responsible for any third-party Web sites that are accessed through links on the primary Web site.

Heretofore, the discussion has focused on mitigating the potential risks associated with establishing links to third-party Web sites. Of course, all Web site operators will also need to protect themselves and their Web sites from unwelcome and unauthorized linking. Just as linking agreements are recommended for operators of sites that will be providing links, they will also be useful for operators of Web sites that may be linked to by third parties. Through the use of linking agreements, it will be possible to establish clear terms and conditions pursuant to which linking will be permitted. It will also be important to clearly post the linking policies on all Web sites and to enforce such policies consistently.

In addition, operators of Web sites to which links may be established should also consider including important legal notices, or at least links thereto, on each page of the applicable Web site. This way, even if individuals are able to enter the site through deep links established by a third party, they will not simply miss such legal notices. The same holds true for advertising. If advertisements are a major source of revenue and the use of deep linking is a big concern, it may be useful to include advertisements on some of the key internal pages of the Web site. As such, individuals who access such key pages directly through the use of deep links will also be viewing the advertisements.

As a means of summary, table 6.1 contains a list of some of the key considerations for Web site operators that establish links to third-party Web sites and for operators of Web sites to which links may be established.

The Digital Millennium Copyright Act's Safe Harbor

The Digital Millennium Copyright Act (DMCA) is important federal legislation designed to accomplish a number of objectives.[32] Among such objectives is the provision of limited immunity for the temporary storage of infringing materials. The "safe harbor" provided pursuant to the DMCA applies to service providers engaging in certain categories of conduct. It is significant that under the DMCA, a service provider is defined broadly as "a provider of on-line services or network access, or the operator of facilities therefor."[33] Accordingly, many Web site operators may fall under the definition.

If a Web site operator wishes to obtain a safe harbor for such "caching," it must (1) adopt and implement a policy of terminating the accounts or subscriptions of repeat infringers; (2) inform subscribers and account holders of the policy; and (3) accommodate and not interfere

Table 6.1
Summary of Key Considerations for Linking

Key Considerations for Operators of Web Sites That Establish Links	Key Considerations for Operators of Linked Sites
Consider the use of a linking agreement.	Consider the use of a linking agreement.
Review the Terms and Conditions for the Web site to which links will be established, including any linking policy and comply with the requirements thereof.	Establish clear linking policies and take steps to ensure that such policies will be enforceable against Web site users.
Avoid linking likely to contribute to end user confusion.	Include key legal notices, or at least links thereto, on every page of the Web site.
Avoid linking likely to lead to revenue losses for the operator of the linked Web site.	Consider putting adverisements in the subpages as well as the home page.
Review the sites' content before linking to ensure that such sites do not contain infringing, defamatory or otherwise objectionable content.	Attempt to keep authorized linkers apprised of major changes in content.
Avoid deep linking without specific permission.	Employ technology to keep undesired links or frames off the site.
Refrain from using frames without authorization.	

with "standard technical measures."[34] In addition, the Web site operator must designate an agent to receive notification of claimed acts of infringement and furnish contact information about the agent on its Web site and in a filing with the U.S. Copyright Office.[35]

In practice, Web site operators may be able to escape liability for such infringing materials posted on their sites if the proper DMCA procedures are followed and provided that the site operator

1. does not have actual knowledge that the material at issue is infringing;

2. is not aware of the facts or circumstances from which infringing activity is apparent;

3. does not receive a financial benefit directly attributable to any infringing activity that it has the right and ability to control; and

4. if properly notified of the infringing activity or otherwise obtaining knowledge or awareness of the infringement, responds expeditiously to remove or disable access to the infringing material.[36]

Furthermore, it will be necessary to ensure that one's Web site contains information regarding the contact information of the agent, as well as the company's procedures for responding to claims of copyright infringement. Box 6.3 presents sample language that Web site operators may wish to incorporate into their Web site Terms of Use agreements or otherwise include on their Web sites.

From an international perspective, it is also important to note that the European Community's E-Commerce Directive contains provisions that are somewhat similar to the safe harbor provisions found in the DMCA.[37] Specifically, Article 13 of the directive states:

1. Where an information society service is provided that consists of the transmission in a communication network of information provided by a recipient of the service, Member States shall ensure that the service provider is not liable for the automatic, intermediate, temporary storage of that information, performed for the sole purpose of making more efficient the information's onward transmission to other recipients of the service upon their request, on condition that:

    (a) the provider does not modify the information;

    (b) the provider complies with conditions on access to the information

    (c) the provider complies with rules regarding the updating of the information, specified in a manner widely recognized and used by industry;

Box 6.3
Sample DMCA Language for Web Site Posting

Procedures for Claims of Copyright Infringement
If you believe, in good faith, that any materials on the Site infringe your copyrights, you should send a notice of claimed copyright infringement, pursuant to Title 17, United States Code, Section 512(c)(2) (a portion of the "Digital Millennium Copyright Act"), to our designated agent at the address set forth below.

Service provider(s):

Designated agent:

Address:

Telephone number:

Facsimile number:

E-mail address:

In order to be effective, the notification must include the following:

- a physical or electronic signature of a person authorized to act on behalf of the owner of an exclusive right that is allegedly infringed;
- identification of the copyrighted work claimed to have been infringed, or if multiple copyrighted works at a single on-line site are covered by a single notification, a representative list of such works at that site;
- identification of the material that is claimed to be infringing or to be the subject of infringing activity and that is to be removed or access to which is to be disabled, and information reasonably sufficient to permit the service provider to locate the material;
- information reasonably sufficient to permit the service provider to contact the complaining party, such as an address, telephone number, and, if available, an electronic mail address at which the complaining party may be contacted;
- a statement that the complaining party has a good-faith belief that use of the material in the manner complained of is not authorized by the copyright owner, its agent, or the law; and
- a statement that the information in the notification is accurate and, under penalty of perjury, that the complaining party is authorized to act on behalf of the owner of an exclusive right that is allegedly infringed.

Upon receipt of the written notification containing all required information as outlined above, we will

- remove or disable access to the material that is alleged to be infringing;
- forward the written notification to such alleged infringer; and
- take reasonable steps to promptly notify the subscriber that it has removed or disabled access to the material.

(d) the provider does not interfere with the lawful use of technology, widely recognized and used by industry, to obtain data on the use of the information; and

(e) the provider acts expeditiously to remove or to disable access to the information it has stored upon obtaining actual knowledge of the fact that the information at the initial source of transmission has been removed from the network, or access to it has been disabled, or that a court of an administrative authority has ordered such removal or disablement.[38]

These provisions appear to have originated out of concerns that there were considerable differences in the ways in which the different EU Member States addressed the issue of service provider liability.[39] In constructing the provision, European legislators were seeking to "strike a balance between the different interests at stake and establish . . . principles upon which industry agreements and standards can be based."[40]

Member States were required to have transposed this provision and, of course, all of the other requirements of the E-Commerce Directive into their national laws by January 17, 2002.[41]

It is clear from a review of the directive's language that there are a number of similarities between the U.S. approach, as set forth in the DMCA, and the EU approach, as set forth in the E-Commerce Directive. Still, while such similarities exist, there are also certain differences that are worth noting. For instance, unlike the DMCA, the E-Commerce Directive does not have a notice and takedown procedure. In addition, a more significant distinction is that the DMCA applies only to liability for copyright, whereas the liability limitation contained in the E-Commerce Directive is of more general application.

Use of Third-Party Trademarks

In running an e-commerce Web site, an operator may find it necessary or desirable to display other companies' trademarks on the operator's own site. For example, if one's Web site provides links to third-party sites, the operator of the site providing the links may wish to use the third party's trademark to indicate the link. To avoid potential claims of trademark misappropriation, it is extremely important that all use of third-party trademarks be in accordance with the terms of any license agreement or trademark use guidelines provided by the trademark owner. Complying with the terms of the license agreements will, of course, also be essential when making copyrighted content or patented processes licensed from third parties available through a company's own Web site.

Avoiding Claims of Patent Infringement

As discussed earlier in the chapter, the U.S. Patent and Trademark Office has recently issued a wide range of patents related to e-commerce. Many of these patents affect numerous different aspects of the distribution of products and services via the Internet. Accordingly, when developing a new Web site, it will be important to conduct a thorough search to ensure that the business methods used on the site are not already covered by existing patents.

COMPUTER CRIME AND ABUSE

The Problem

Another very important part of protecting one's IP assets on-line will be ensuring that the Web site and its content are safe from intrusion. In recent years there has been a considerable rise in on-line security breaches and lapses. While much of the recent media focus has been on the risks of cyberterrorism, many companies remain vulnerable to more mundane breaches such as those committed by employees and juvenile hackers.

Companies that have suffered a data security breach, whether through hacking, identity theft, denial of service, virus, or some other means, have a variety of options for responding to the breach. A number of civil and criminal laws pertaining to data security breaches exist at both national and state levels. The best method of responding to a breach will depend on the particular facts and circumstances of the case, as well as the applicable entity's expectations. Many organizations that suffer breaches decide not to pursue legal remedies against the breach because of concerns about negative publicity and fears that informing law enforcement officials will lead to a loss of control over the investigation and may expose the company to an intrusive investigation of its own policies and practices. There really is no easy answer to these concerns. Clearly, the best course of action is to prevent the breach in the first place. In the event a breach does occur, the various means of responding should be considered and evaluated based on the particular facts and circumstances.

Due to the considerable frequency with which computer crimes occur in the United States and the important role that computerized networks have come to hold in modern America, there have been a number of legislative responses to this issue. The next section examines some of the federal criminal and civil statutes that might be relied on in the event of a data security breach. This section is not intended to present an all-inclusive view of the various laws and measure that can be used against those who commit computer crime. Rather, it is intended to give an overview of some of the main laws and regulations that are likely to come into play regarding criminal behavior using computers.

U.S. Federal Criminal Laws

The Computer Fraud and Abuse Act of 1984 (CFAA) was the first federal statute to address the issue of computer crime.[42] It is important to note that, despite its name, the CFAA did not create a comprehensive regime intended to address all instances of computer crime. Rather, the legislation addresses certain aspects of computer crimes that have an impact on federal interests. The CFAA was substantially rewritten and expanded in 1996. Furthermore, it was recently amended and expanded further pursuant to the U.S.A. Patriots Act of 2001.

The CFAA regulates the activities of offenders, who are defined as individuals who knowingly and without authority, or beyond the scope of their authority, intentionally access a protected computer[43] and commit various violations, including the following:

1. intentionally obtaining information from a protected computer;
2. knowingly, and with the intent to defraud, obtaining access to a protected computer and thereby furthering the fraud and obtaining something of value;
3. knowingly causing the transmission of computer code that intentionally causes damage to a protected computer;
4. intentionally gaining access to a protected computer and thereby causing damage;[44]
5. trafficking in a password or other access device;
6. extorting money or property by means of a threat to damage a personal computer; and
7. attempting to do any of the foregoing.

The CFAA provides for considerable penalties. The legislation provides three levels of punishment to a maximum of 10 years' imprisonment. Additionally, repeat offenders can have their maximum penalties doubled.

Also significant is the Identity Theft and Assumption Deterrence Act.[45] This legislation penalizes a variety of activities involved in the manufacture, sale, and unlawful obtaining of "means of identification."[46] Obtaining and transferring computer-based identification information, passwords, and other means of identifying individuals are made criminal by the act.

The Economic Espionage Act provides that illegally obtaining, transferring, or receiving trade secrets in interstate commerce may be grounds for federal prosecution.[47] It is important to note that penalties for violating this act can be quite stiff and can be imposed on domestic and foreign actors alike.

The Electronic Communications Privacy Act (ECPA) is also significant when discussing computer and information security.[48] This act criminalizes the unauthorized access into an electronic communications service, such as an ISP. It also criminalizes any activity by which an unauthorized person prevents access to stored electronic communications. A denial-of-service attack is an example of the kind of activity that might be considered as preventing access to stored electronic communications. The possible penalties that are available under ECPA depend on a number of factors, including the purpose of the unauthorized access and whether it was the perpetrator's first or second offense.

State Laws

It is beyond the scope of this chapter to explore the myriad of state laws concerning computer crime. However, it is important to note that there is a large and growing body of state laws that address various aspects of computer and data security, including matters such as theft of computer services, unauthorized access to computer services, and identity theft.[49] Accordingly, entities that experience security breaches or other forms of computer crime should also consider the various remedies that may be available to them under state law.

International Issues

One of the biggest problems with responding to computer crime results from jurisdictional issues. Criminal activity involving computerized networks often traverses national boundaries. In many cases, entities that are victimized by computer crime will find that there is some international element to the violation that has been perpetrated. For instance, the individual who committed the breach may have done so from a foreign location, or the data that has been acquired through the breach may have been sold or otherwise made available to a foreign entity or individual.

The fact that many breaches of computer security involve an international element has been recognized by legislators. As noted in the previous sections, many U.S. federal laws criminalizing various aspects of computer crime attempt to include, at least to a certain extent, computer crimes committed by foreign actors. Furthermore, due to the current perception that U.S. companies are under considerable risk of foreign cyberterrorism, it is likely that we will continue to see new laws and modifications to existing laws that are designed to target foreign perpetrators of computer crime.

It is also significant to note that there are a number of initiatives under way that are intended to increase cross-border cooperation in preventing, detecting, and responding to computer crime. While there have been a number of initiatives to reduce international cybercrimes, one of the most promising appears to be the Council of Europe's Draft Convention on Cybercrime[50] (the "Cybercrime Convention"), which was adopted by the foreign ministers of the Council of Europe on November 8, 2001, and opened for signature on November 23, 2001. At the opening ceremony, the convention was signed by 26 of the 43 member states of the Council of Europe, along with Canada, Japan, South Africa, and the United States, who participated in the drafting of the convention but are not member states of the Council of Europe. The Cybercrime Convention may be opened for signature by additional non–member states in the future.

The Cybercrime Convention is a lengthy endeavor, the main aim of which is to pursue "a common criminal policy aimed at the protection of society against cybercrime, inter alia by adopting appropriate legislation and fostering international co-operation."[51] The convention seeks to do this by establishing international agreement on the kinds of offenses that will be considered as cybercrimes, harmonizing various procedures for detecting and responding to international cybercrime, and setting forth rules concerning mutual assistance in the detection, investigation, and prosecution of cybercrime.

The Cybercrime Convention calls on participating states to consider specific acts involving computers as crimes.[52] These acts are divided into four main categories:

- offenses against the confidentiality, integrity, and availability of computer data and systems,[53] including illegal access, illegal interception, data interference, system interference, data interference, system interference, and misuse of devices;

- computer-related offenses, including forgery and computer fraud;[54]
- content-related offenses, including production, dissemination, and possession of child pornography;[55] and
- offenses related to infringement of copyright and related rights, including the wide-scale distribution of pirated works.[56]

The Cybercrime Convention does not call on participating states to classify the violation of data protection rules or other violations of privacy protections as criminal behavior.

The convention also seeks to harmonize certain procedural measures related to cybercrime.[57] Specifically, it requires parties to ensure that the following measures are available under their national law: expedited preservation of stored data; expedited preservation and disclosure of traffic data; the ability to order a person to provide computer data under his or her control and to order a service provider to provide subscriber information under its control; search and seizure of stored computer data; and real-time collection of traffic data and interception of content data. Currently such procedures are extremely important in detecting, investigating, and prosecuting international cybercrime, and their significance is only likely to grow in the future.

Of all the provisions, those pertaining to international cooperation are particularly notable.[58] The obligations pertaining to mutual assistance contained in the Cybercrime Convention are broad and cover many areas, including extradition, spontaneous information, preservation of computer data and traffic data, disclosure of or and access to computer and traffic data, transborder access to stored data, and real-time collection of traffic data and interception of communications. The Cybercrime Convention also allows parties to make requests for mutual assistance by expedited means, such as fax or e-mail.

The convention provides that participating nations must establish jurisdiction for offenses committed in their territory, on ships flying their national flag, on aircraft that they have registered, and by their nationals (unless another nation has territorial jurisdiction for such crimes).[59] It further provides that when one party claims jurisdiction over an alleged offense established in accordance with the convention, the parties shall, where appropriate, consult with each other in an effort to determine the most appropriate jurisdiction for the prosecution.

In addition to considering multinational efforts to respond to computer-related crime, it is also useful to note the unilateral efforts that are under way in this area.

In Europe, many of the data protection and privacy statutes discussed in chapter 4 also contain important data security provision. However, most of these focus on the duties of the entity that is in control of data-processing operations to protect the security of the data in its possession. With respect to criminal laws, applicable to cybercrime, considerable differences continue to exist from nation to nation. As a result, a number of initiatives have been proposed to harmonize such legislation. Prominent among them is the European Commission's proposal for a Council Framework Decision on Attacks on Information Systems (the "Framework Decision").[60]

The stated objective of the Framework Decision is to "improve co-operation between judicial and other competent authorities, including the police and other specialized law enforcement services of the Member States, through approximating rules on criminal law in the Member States in the area of attacks against information systems."[61] The Framework Decision would require Member States to ensure that illegally accessing information systems[62] and illegally interfering with information systems are punishable as criminal offenses.[63] The Framework Decision also contains provisions relating to the liability of legal persons,[64] sanctions for legal persons,[65] the determination of jurisdiction[66] and information exchange,[67] as well as other significant provisions.

At the same time as there have been new multilateral efforts, many foreign countries have been enacting new computer crime laws and strengthening existing legislation. Such enhanced efforts at cross-border cooperation, along with the strengthening of national laws concerning computer crime, may prove useful to U.S.-based companies that face the threat of computer crimes perpetrated from abroad.

CONCLUSION

This chapter has examined the numerous risks related to IP assets that may arise in connection with the operation of an e-business Web site. While protecting IP assets has long been important to many companies, the increased use of the Internet for all kinds of commercial activities has made protecting IP assets even more important. Operating an e-business Web site increases the likelihood that protected works such as copyrighted materials, patented processes, trademarks, and trade secrets will be made available to a large, geographically diverse population of users. At the same time, the use of the Internet for commerce may also increase the risk that one's own commercial activities may lead to the infringement of third-party intellectual property rights.

Accordingly, it is essential for companies to closely monitor the use of their copyrighted materials, trademarks, patents, and trade secrets via the Internet, as well as to examine how e-business efforts incorporate the IP assets of third parties. An appropriate way to accomplish both of these objectives is to make a comprehensive audit of IP assets associated with the e-business initiatives. Once there is a clear understanding regarding the IP assets that are being made available via the Internet, as well as how third-party IP assets are being used in connection with e-business initiatives, it will be possible to adopt some of the strategies outlined here to maximize the value of the IP assets and also minimize the associated risks.

This chapter has also analyzed some of the legal mechanisms that companies will have for responding to an area of increasing concern for many companies, that is, computer security. Due to the large and increasing number of computer security breaches, as well as concerns about cyberterrorism, there will be continuing momentum toward strengthening existing computer security laws and enacting new laws in this area.

By summarizing the various legal issues explored throughout this book, the next and final chapter will present a kind of road map for conducting a legal review of a commercial Web site. While chapter 7 does not focus on all of the legal issues that can possibly arise through the operation of a Web site, it does seek to call attention to prominent legal concerns.

Chapter 7

CONCLUSION

This book has presented information about some of the main legal issues that companies will encounter when developing and operating an e-commerce Web site. As a summary and conclusion, this chapter presents an annotated checklist of the issues that should be considered when conducting a legal review of one's own e-commerce Web site.

WEB SITE DEVELOPMENT

Does the Company Have All Necessary Web Site Agreements in Place?

The precise agreements that an entity will require for the setup and continued operation of its Web site will depend on a number of factors, including the functionality of the Web site and the extent to which third parties will provide services related to the operation of the site. For most Web sites, the agreements discussed hereafter will play a significant role in the site's development and operation. Since the development and launch of a Web site play such a key role its eventual success, such agreements will be key to many sites.

Web Site Development Agreements

Development agreements, which were discussed in chapter 2, play a significant role in how the Web site will operate and the level of control that the site operator will be able to exercise over the site. Specifically, such agreements will usually govern key issues such as the ownership of what is developed by the developer, the time frame during which the site will be developed, and the site's functionality. Clearly, such agreements will be instrumental in the initial development of a company's Web site. However, their importance also extends beyond development and into everyday operation. In many cases, such agreements can play a significant role in the ultimate success or failure of a Web site.

Software Licenses

Software licenses are also necessary for the launch and continued operation of the Web site. Even if the Web site operator is able to successfully negotiate for ownership of the software that is developed by the site developer pursuant to the development agreement, it is very likely that certain third-party software will also be involved in the site's operation. Licenses to various software programs may be necessary to ensure the portability of the Web site and for the site and its affiliates to legally use all software on and in support of the site.

Consulting Agreements

Many Web site operators engage consultants in developing the site. Such consultants often play a critical role in the development of various aspects of the Web site, including its "look and feel." Proper review and negotiation of consulting agreements will be necessary to ensure that consultants are bound to comport with the Web site's interests, including assigning intellectual property developed in the course of their services.

Web Site Hosting Agreements

While many entities choose to host their own Web sites, many others contract with third-party hosts for the provision of such services. When using a third-party host, particular attention will have to be directed to the hosting agreement. Such agreements will be essential to maintaining a functional Web site. They should contain important provisions, including the performance warranties of the host. They should also clearly set forth the remedies available to the Web site operator in the event that the host fails to provide the hosting services as specified in the agreement.

Have the Necessary Web Agreements Been Reviewed, Both for Content and for Interoperability?

Before launching an e-commerce Web site, it is necessary to review the agreements that are instrumental to the functioning of the site. The review should focus on determining whether the Web site operator has all the rights necessary to operate the site as intended. For example, as discussed in chapter 2, whenever a third-party contractor such as a Web site developer creates something for the site operator, the agreement governing that relationship should clearly indicate that the company for which the development work is being undertaken will own the site. Even if the Web site operator has paid the developer for the development work, the site operator may not own what has been developed unless there is written agreement that the work is being performed as a "work made for hire" and that the site operator will own the resulting deliverables. Without a written conveyance of ownership, or at least a very broad (and, ideally, exclusive) license, the company for whom the Web site has been developed may not have the necessary level of control over the site.

Reviewing the key agreements also entails ensuring that they are interoperable. For instance, the development agreement or consulting agreement might require developers or consultants to access certain software. If such software is not proprietary to the Web site operator but is instead owned by a third party, it is necessary to review the applicable license agreements to ensure that the third-party developers or consultants will be permitted to access the software as foreseen.

These are just two examples of the numerous issues that can arise in connection with Web site agreements. Conducting a thorough review of such agreements before the launch of the Web site may help to reduce the likelihood of difficulties arising during the course of the continued expansion of the company's e-business efforts.

INTELLECTUAL PROPERTY ISSUES

Overview

Intellectual property rights are extremely important for most businesses. Such rights are likely to be even more important for companies with a significant on-line presence. In fact, for such companies, intellectual property is likely to be among the primary assets. Operating an e-business Web site will necessitate making various intellectual property assets available via the Internet. In the vast majority of cases, it will also lead to the use of the intellectual property of others. Accordingly, it is important to ensure that the intellectual property that is made available via the Internet is protected and that business operations will not lead to the infringement of the intellectual property rights of third parties.

The first step in protecting one's intellectual property rights while also reducing the risk that third parties' rights will be infringed is to conduct a thorough audit of all intellectual property assets. Before being able to analyze whether such intellectual property rights are being adequately protected and whether any license grants are being breached, it will be necessary to conduct a full inventory of all intellectual property rights. Once this information has been obtained, it will be possible to proceed to analyzing specific issues relative to different types of intellectual property rights.

Copyrights

Have Copyrights Been Registered?

As discussed in chapter 6, in the United States it is not necessary to register one's copyrights in copyrighted works. However, because of the benefits that accompany registration (including, notably, the shifting of the burden of proof and the ability to obtain treble damages and attorneys' fees), the registration of copyrighted works is recommended.

Have Proper Copyright Notices Been Affixed to Copyrighted Works?

A copyright notice in the form of "© Date, Author, All Rights Reserved" should be affixed to all copyrighted works, including each page of the Web site. Such notices should also be placed on distinct works such as images and artwork. Embedding the copyright notice in the image may make it more difficult for someone to remove the copyright notice and copy the image.

Does the Web Site Terms of Use Agreement Include Appropriate Restrictions on the Use of Copyrighted Materials?

As discussed in chapter 3, a Terms of Use agreement is an important component of risk management for many Web sites. With respect to the protection of copyrighted materials, the Terms of Use should specify the authorized uses of all copyrighted materials that are displayed on the Web site. Specially, the agreement should specify whether and to what extent end users are permitted to copy, use, transmit, and modify the copyrighted materials.

Have All Necessary Licenses and Clearances Been Obtained?

In addition to protecting one's own copyrighted materials, it will also be necessary to minimize the risks that the copyrighted materials of others will be infringed. Companies can be held directly liable for copyright infringement for posting the copyrighted materials of third parties without the proper authorization. It is thus essential to obtain licenses for all materials that are owned by third parties. Even items that appear to be made freely available via the Internet, such as clip art and some types of computer code, usually require a license.

Are the Terms and Conditions of All Third-Party Licenses Being Complied With?

Of course, it is not enough to simply ensure that license agreements have been executed. The terms and conditions of such agreements also need to be complied with. Accordingly, when launching a new Web site or reviewing an existing Web site, the use of all third-party materials should be reviewed against the their license agreements.

Have Steps Been Taken to Obtain "Safe Harbor" Protection Pursuant to the Digital Millennium Copyright Act?

Provided that certain conditions are met, section 512 of the Digital Millennium Copyright Act (DMCA) provides limitations on the liability of service providers for transmitting, routing, providing connections for, and providing intermediate storage of materials that infringe a copyright. To qualify for the safe harbor protections made available pursuant to the DMCA, a service provider must implement procedures for terminating the access of individuals who repeatedly violate the copyrights of others. Furthermore, the provider must not have knowledge of the infringement and must not obtain financial benefit from the infringement. In addition, service providers must post information regarding procedures for reporting copyright infringement and must also remove infringing materials once notice thereof is obtained.

Trademarks

Have Proper Searches Been Ordered, and Has the Prosecution of the Mark Been Commenced?

A search should be strongly considered for each trademark selected to reduce the risk of liability for infringement. If there does not appear to be any infringement, then consideration should be given to attempting to register the applicable trademarks.

Are Trademark Symbols Being Used Correctly?

The federal trademark registration symbol ® should appear immediately after all federally registered marks when used to identify the goods or services covered by the registration. Until federal registration issues, the symbol ™ can be used to designate a claim of rights to a trademark.

Has the Company Obtained All Necessary Clearances to Use Trademarks Owned by Third Parties?

In some instances it will be desirable to include third-party trademarks on one's own Web site. However, this should not be done without the specific written agreement of the trademark owner. Furthermore, use of such third-party trademarks must be in conformance with any requirements established by the trademark owner and agreed to pursuant to the trademark license agreement.

Have Desired Domain Names Been Registered?

Has the domain name that has been selected for the Web site been registered across available top-level domains? If not, consideration should be given as to whether the risk of a competitor's using the same domain name in a different top-level domain poses a significant competitive risk. This risk also bolsters the need for prosecution of the trademark contained in the domain name.

Does the Company Have a Cause of Action Pursuant to the Anticybersquatting Consumer Protection Act?

A common question is what one should do if a desired domain name is already taken. If the domain name has been secured in bad faith, then there are available remedies under the International Corporation for Assigned Names and Numbers Uniform Dispute Resolution Policy and under the Anticybersquatting Consumer Protection Act.

Trade Secrets

Does the Company Have a Clearly Defined and Systematic Policy for Protecting Trade Secrets?

Trade secrets are a critical component of many businesses' operations. At the same time, the advent of the Internet has led to increased risks that a company's trade secrets will be disclosed. While ensuring adequate protection of trade secrets has long been an important part of sound commercial practice, it has taken on a new sense of urgency and significance in the Internet age.

Have Appropriate Agreements Been Executed with Employees and Third-Party Consultants and Contractors?

A significant part of protecting trade secrets consists in ensuring that all parties that have access to such information—both inside and outside the company—are bound to maintain the confidentiality of such information.

Have Confidential Documents and Materials Been Labeled as Such?

It is recommended that everything that contains confidential information be clearly labeled "CONFIDENTIAL."

Does the Company Regularly Review Web sites on Which Company Trade Secrets and Other Proprietary Information May Be Disclosed?

Companies should consider developing a policy to review the Internet for disclosures of company information. Often disclosures of trade secrets and other proprietary information are made via the Internet and can be posted on Web sites that relate to the company or the industry in which it operates. Early detection of improper disclosures may help to better position the company to respond to such leaks.

Has the Company Developed and Implemented Procedures for Conducting Regular Trade Secret Audits?

Companies should consider submitting to external audits of trade secret practices on a periodic basis. The depth and frequency of such audits will depend on the nature of the company as well as the type and quantity of confidential information in its possession. Generally, such audits should involve an assessment of the integrity of trade secrets, the destruction of unnecessary copies of information, and the analysis of security measures that have been implemented to protect confidential information.

Patents

Does the Web Site Use Any Business Methods That Are Covered by Patents Held by Others?

The United States Patent and Trademark Office has been granted a number of business method patents in recent years. Patents have been issued for some methods commonly used in e-commerce. Accordingly, it is important to review business methods used in connection with one's Web site in light of existing patents.

Are Any of the Methods Used in Connection with the Company's E-business Initiatives Capable of Being Patented?

Inventions created in connection with e-business initiatives should be reviewed by patent counsel to determine whether such inventions might be patentable. E-commerce business method patents provide the patent holder with significant rights for a considerably long period of time and can thus lead to important sources of revenue for the patent holder.

Is the Pursuit of International Protection of Patents Advisable?

This will depend on the jurisdictions in which business is being conducted and the nature of the invention. The advantages and procedures for seeking patent protection in foreign jurisdictions should be reviewed carefully with patent counsel.

THIRD-PARTY CONTENT

Licensed Content

Has Permission Been Obtained for the Inclusion of All Third-Party Content?

Operating an e-commerce Web site often involves making the proprietary materials of third parties available through one's Web site. To avoid potential claims of infringement, it will be necessary to ensure that proper permission, usually in the form of a license agreement, is obtained before displaying such content.

Is Third-Party Content Being Displayed in Accordance with the Requirements of the Applicable License Agreement?

In the event that third-party content is licensed, it is extremely important to ensure that the use and display of such content complies fully with the terms and conditions of the applicable license agreement.

Is Third-Party Content Properly Attributed to Its Owner?

Web site operators also need to ensure that content that is licensed from third parties is properly attributed to them. Often the applicable license agreement will contain specific information about the kinds of attributions that must be made.

Have Liability and Responsibility for Third-Party Content Been Disclaimed?

It is also recommended that the Web site operator attempt to disclaim liability for third-party content made available through the operator's Web site. It is important that the license agreement with a third party adequately address issues such as limitations on liability and indemnification. At the same time, the Terms of Use agreement for the Web site on which such third-party content is made available should also make clear that the Web site operator is not responsible and will not be liable for any third-party content.

Third-Party Web Sites

If the Web Site Provides Links to or Frames Third-Party Web Sites, Has an Agreement Been Entered Into with the Operator(s) of the Third-Party Sites?

As discussed in chapter 6, unauthorized framing and linking, especially deep linking, can lead to potential liability. As such, it is recommended that framing, deep linking, and other kinds of potentially contentious linking be carried out solely pursuant to an appropriate agreement.

Has the Content of All Third-Party Web Sites to Which Links Have Been Established Been Reviewed to Ensure That It Is Not Illegal, Infringing, or Otherwise Objectionable?

If links will be established to third-party Web sites, such sites should be reviewed before establishing the links in order to ensure that they do not contain illegal, infringing, or otherwise objectionable content.

Have Responsibility and Liability for Third-Party Web Sites Been Disclaimed?

In addition to reviewing the content of third-party Web sites to which links will be established, steps should be taken to ensure that end users receive notice that the Web site operator does not control, is not responsible for, and will not be liable for the content of such third-party Web sites. Web site operators are also advised to consider various technical measures, such as having the linked Web site open into a separate browser window and using pop-up disclaimers to make it extremely clear to end users that clicking on any links to third-party Web sites will result in the user accessing a Web site that is not provided or controlled by the original Web site operator.

WEB SITE TERMS OF USE AGREEMENTS

Have the Content and Functionality of the Web Site Been Reviewed and Considered in Connection with the Development of the Terms of Use Agreement?

When developing a Web site Terms of Use agreement, it will be important to consider the specific attributes, content, and functionality of the applicable Web site. There is not a form Terms of Use agreement that will simply work for all Web sites. Instead, the agreement should be developed in consideration of a number of factors related to the Web site. The following sections examine some of the key considerations to address when developing a Terms of Use agreement.

Is the Web Site Transactional, Brochureware, or Somewhere in Between?

The functionality of the Web site will play an important role in determining the composition of the appropriate Terms of Use agreement.

For example, if the Web site is only brochureware, it may be sufficient to have a relatively brief Terms of Use agreement. On the other hand, if individuals are permitted to engage in transactions, such as purchasing products or subscribing for services through the Web site, a more elaborate Terms of Use agreement will be necessary.

What Kinds of Products and Services Are Made Available on the Web Site?

The appropriate structure and composition of the Terms of Use agreement are also likely to be impacted by the kinds products and services that are made available through the Web site. Clearly, the Terms of Use agreement for an on-line dating service will be quite different from that of a Web-based book retailer.

Are End Users from Other Countries Permitted to Use the Web Site?

When developing the Terms of Use agreement, the site operator should determine whether end users from other countries will be permitted to use the Web site. As has been discussed throughout this book, different countries impose different requirements on the use of the Internet. If end users from particular jurisdictions will be targeted by the company's marketing efforts or even permitted to use the services made available through the Web site, efforts should be directed toward complying with the relevant legal requirements of such jurisdictions.

Have All Recommended Provisions Been Addressed in the Terms of Use Agreement?

As has been discussed, there really is no form Terms of Use agreement that will be effective for all Web sites. Nonetheless there are certain key provisions that Web site operators should consider including in the agreements that govern the use of their Web site. These include

- an identification of the party that is operating the Web site;
- notice to the user that his or her use of the Web site will be subject to the Terms of Use agreement;
- an explanation of how changes to the Terms of Use agreement will be made and a notification of when such changes will become effective;
- a description of any requirements (such as registration or the payment of subscription fees) that will be necessary to access the Web site;

- an explanation of the permitted uses of the Web site and its content;
- a notification of the Web site operator's ownership of the proprietary materials made available through the Web site;
- notification of linking and framing policies;
- notification of policies concerning unsolicited submissions;
- notification of the Web site operator's policies concerning the monitoring of Web site usage;
- a disclaimer of warranty and responsibility for links to third-party Web sites;
- a general disclaimer of warranties;
- a provision limiting the liability of the Web site operator;
- a provision explaining the parties' rights to terminate the agreement and explaining the effects of termination; and
- general provisions, such as choice of law and jurisdiction.

Have Steps Been Taken to Enhance the Enforceability of the Web Site Terms of Use Agreement?

A Web site Terms of Use agreement will only be as useful as it is enforceable. As a result, significant attention must be devoted not only to the contents of the Terms of Use agreement but also to the way in which it is presented on the site. As has been discussed, the law applicable to Web site Terms of Use agreements is still in a state of development. Nonetheless there are certain steps to enhance the enforceability of such agreements that should be considered. The precise steps to take with respect to any given Web site will depend on a number of factors, including the site's contents and functionality.

CONSUMER PROTECTION ISSUES

Have All Necessary Disclosures Been Made?

There are numerous consumer protection requirements that apply to companies' Web-based ventures. Many of these requirements require that certain specific disclosures be made. The content and presentation of the disclosures will depend to a large extent on the kinds of products and services that are being offered as well as the applicable jurisdiction. Many of the disclosure requirements will only be applicable or will have heightened requirements when companies are dealing with consumers. Accordingly, companies that transact with or advertise to consumers are advised to pay special attention to the disclosure requirements.

Do the Form and Content of the Disclosures Comply with Applicable Law?

In some instances where disclosures are required, they will need to contain specific content and be presented in a certain format. Accordingly, if disclosure requirements apply, it is important to review both their form and content in connection with the applicable law.

Have E-Mail Marketing Campaigns Been Reviewed for Compliance with Applicable Laws Concerning Unsolicited Commercial E-Mail?

Many jurisdictions, both in the United States and abroad, have enacted laws and regulations applicable to the transmission of unsolicited commercial e-mail. Accordingly, if there is any intention to use e-mail in connection with marketing and promotional activities, the intended contents of the e-mail and the mode of transmission should be reviewed in light of applicable laws, as well as the policies of any Internet service providers that may be used in connection with the distribution of such e-mail.

Do Any Local Requirements, Including the Obligatory Use of Local Language, Apply to the Web Site?

Certain jurisdictions require that provision of local language translations for certain product information and event advertising materials. Accordingly, it will be important to review the specific requirements of jurisdictions in which company operations are based and in which potential customers will be targeted. Of course, if there is an intention to target individuals in a particular jurisdiction, it may be useful to make important product information and advertising materials available in a language that is understood by that jurisdiction's inhabitants.

Have Procedures and Policies Been Developed to Comply with National Requirements Applicable to Cancellations and Refunds?

A number of jurisdictions mandate specific requirements with respect to cancellations and refunds. In Europe, for instance, Directive 97/7/EC of the European Parliament and of the Council of 20 May 1997 on the Protection of Consumers in respect of Distance Contracts requires the provision of a cooling-off period for certain contracts that are concluded at a distance. When engaging in commerce via the Internet, it is important to ensure that contractual provisions and cancellation policies conform with the applicable legal requirements.

PRIVACY

Does the Entity Collect Individually Identifiable Information through Its Web Site?

If any information, especially personally identifiable data, will be collected through the Web site, the operator should consider the various privacy issues that may be raised through the collection, use, and disclosure of such information. As discussed earlier, the United States has a number of laws that place limitations on the collection, use, and disclosure of certain types and classes of information. Moreover, a number of foreign jurisdictions have enacted strict privacy requirements that apply to the collection, use, and disclosure of all kinds of personally identifiable information.

Does the Web Site Have a Privacy Policy That Describes the Entity's Policies and Practices Related to the Collection, Use, and Disclosure of Individually Identifiable Data?

There are many reasons for developing and posting a privacy policy. In some instances companies will be legally required to post a privacy policy. Often this will depend on factors such as the location of establishment; the types of personally identifiable data that are collected, used, and disclosed; and what, precisely, is done with the data that are collected. In other instances, Web site operators will be required by their membership in various industry organizations to post a privacy policy. Still other companies may be compelled by contractual requirements to post a privacy policy. Furthermore, certain companies may simply decide to post a privacy policy to inform the users of its Web site about the company's policy concerning the collection, use, and disclosure of personally identifiable information.

Has the Entity Adopted and Implemented a Privacy Compliance Program?

Regardless of whether a given entity is subject to specific privacy requirements and regardless of whether a privacy policy has been posted, it will be important to develop and implement a privacy compliance program. The program should be implemented consistently throughout the organization and should be accompanied by the endorsement of the entity's senior management. Furthermore, it will be necessary to provide initial and continued training to all employees. Finally, the compliance program should be reviewed on a regular basis to ensure that it continues to comply with the rapidly evolving law.

Does the Entity Participate in a Privacy Seal Program or Other Self-Regulatory Initiatives?

There are a number of privacy seal programs and other self-regulatory initiatives in which companies may decide to participate. Such programs are not mandatory, but they do offer a clear plan and strategy for providing a certain level of privacy protection to personally identifiable data. The only caveat, however, is that if the decision is made to participate in such a program, the requirements of the applicable program must be complied with closely. Otherwise one might face not only the penalties available under applicable law but also the various remedies that the organization administering the seal program or other self-regulatory initiative has at its disposal.

Is the Entity's Use of Personally Identifiable Data Consistent with Its Privacy Policy, Privacy Compliance Program, and Any Self-Regulatory Initiatives in Which It Participates?

The most important part of a privacy compliance program is ensuring that actual practices comply with stated policies. Several years back, when privacy became an issue in e-commerce, many Web site operators rushed to develop and post privacy policies that strictly limited their rights to collect, use, and disclose personally identifiable data. In many guarantees, such policies proved to be too restrictive to be practical. Accordingly, instead of developing overly restrictive privacy policies, efforts should be directed toward developing accurate privacy policies and ensuring that such policies are followed throughout the organization. Failing to comply with one's own privacy policies can leave an organization exposed to potential legal liability and can damage companies' relationships with their customers.

SECURITY

Have Appropriate Technical, Administrative, and Organizational Measures to Protect Data Security Been Implemented throughout the Company?

As discussed in chapter 6, the importance of maintaining adequate data security has recently assumed new significance. Today's entities are often required by law and contract, not to mention consumer demands, to maintain the security of the data that they process. At the same time, there is an impression that today's commercial entities are facing increasing risks of computer hacking, data theft, and information system sabotage. As a result of the foregoing, the implementation and continued review of technical and organizational security measures must be part of all e-business initiatives.

Do All Agreements with Service Providers Having Access to Company Data Reflect Appropriate Security Requirements?

Many companies will have a certain number of third-party service providers accessing their data. It will be essential to review all agreements with such third-party service providers to ensure that the service providers are required to maintain the security of the data to which they have access.

Have Employees Received Adequate Training on Data Security, and Do They Receive Such Training on an Ongoing Basis?

Protecting data security entails much more than firewalls and other technical measures. One of the most important parts of any data security initiative is the company's employees. All employees having access to company data should receive comprehensive and continuing training about data security.

Do the Privacy Policies and Other Legal Documents Relied On by the Company Reflect Actual Data Security Policies and Practices?

Although all organizations should strive for optimal security, even the most secure system will have certain vulnerabilities. When drafting documents such as privacy policies and security guarantees, efforts should be directed toward ensuring that such documents are an accurate reflection of the actual security practices of the organization.

CONCLUSION

This book has attempted to demonstrate the myriad legal issues that can arise in connection with the development and operation of an e-commerce Web site. While many aspects of commerce are highly regulated, the use of the Internet for commerce is further complicated by the fact that new laws and regulations continue to be passed, and a diverse selection of local, state, and national governments are attempting to regulate the Internet. In addition, such rules and requirements are often accompanied by significant penalties that can be imposed on violators.

As a conclusion to the book, this chapter has sought to identify key issues of concern for companies engaging in e-commerce. This is not an inclusive list of the plethora of legal concerns involved with e-business initiatives. Rather, this summary is merely intended to call attention to significant issues that should be considered in conjunction with any e-business venture.

Appendix 1

COUNTRY TOP-LEVEL DOMAINS

Code	Country	Web Site for Registration Information
.ac	Ascension Island	http://www.nic.ac
.ad	Andorra	http://www.nic.ad
.ae	United Arab Emirates	http://www.emirates.net.ae/
.af	Afghanistan	None listed
.ag	Antigua and Barbuda	http://www.nic.ag
.ai	Anguilla	http://nic.ai
.al	Albania	http://www.inima.al/Domains.html
.am	Armenia	http://www.amnic.net
.an	Netherlands Antilles	http://www.una.net/an_domreg
.ao	Angola	None listed
.aq	Antarctica	None listed
.ar	Argentina	http://www.nic.ar
.as	American Samoa	http://www.nic.as
.at	Austria	http://www.nic.at/
.au	Australia	http://www.aunic.net
.aw	Aruba	None listed
.az	Azerbaijan	None listed
.ba	Boznia and Herzegovina	http://www.utic.net.ba/
.bb	Barbados	None listed
.bd	Bangladesh	None listed

.be	Belgium	http://www.DNS.BE
.bf	Burkina Faso	http://www.onatel.bf/domaine.htm
.bg	Bulgaria	http://www.digsys.bg/bg-nic/
.bh	Bahrain	http://www.inet.com.bh
.bi	Burundi	http://www.nic.cd/
.bj	Benin	None listed
.bm	Bermuda	http://www.bermudanic.bm
.bn	Brunei Darussalam	http://www.brunet.bn/brunet/charges.htm
.bo	Bolivia	http://www.nic.bo
.br	Brazil	http://registro.fapesp.br/
.bs	Bahamas	http://dns.nic.bs
.bt	Bhutan	http://www.nic.bt
.bv	Bouvet Island	http://www.uninett.no/navn/
.bw	Botswana	None listed
.by	Belarus	http://www.tld.by
.bz	Belize	http://www.psg.com/dns/bz/
.ca	Canada	http://www.cira.ca/
.cc	Cocos (Keeling) Islands	http://www.nic.cc/
.cd	Congo, Democratic People's Republic	http://www.nic.cd/
.cf	Central African Republic	None listed
.cg	Congo, Republic of	http://www.nic.cd/
.ch	Switzerland	http://www.nic.ch/
.ci	Côte d'Ivoire	None listed

.et	Ethiopia	http://www.telecom.net.et
.fi	Finland	http://www.thk.fi/
.fj	Fiji	http://www.usp.ac.fj/DomReg
.fk	Falkland Islands (Malvina)	http://www.fidc.org.fk/
.fm	French Micronesia	http://www.fm/
.fo	Faroe Islands	http://www.nic.fo/
.fr	France	http://www.nic.fr/
.ga	Gabon	None listed
.gd	Grenada	None listed
.ge	Georgia	http://georgia.net.ge/domain/
.gf	French Guiana	http://www.nplus.gf/
.gg	Guernsey	http://www.isles.net
.gh	Ghana	http://www.ghana.com/
.gi	Gibraltar	http://www.nic.gi
.gl	Greenland	http://www.nic.gl/
.gm	Gambia	http://www.nic.gm
.gn	Guinea	http://psg.com/dns/gn
.gp	Guadeloupe	http://www.nic.gp/
.gq	Equatorial Guinea	http://www.getesa.gq/
.gr	Greece	http://www.hostmaster.gr
.gs	South Georgia and the South Sandwich Islands	http://www.gs/
.gt	Guatemala	http://www.gt/cir/cir.htm
.gu	Guam	http://gadao.gov.gu

.gw	Guinea-Bissau	None listed
.gy	Guyana	None listed
.hk	Hong Kong	http://www.cuhk.hk
.hm	Heard and McDonald Islands	http://www.registry.hm
.hn	Honduras	http://www.nic.hn
.hr	Croatia (Hrvatska)	http://www.CARNet.hr/DNS
.ht	Haiti	http://www.haitiworld.com/
.hu	Hungary	http://www.nic.hu
.id	Indonesia	http://www.idnic.net.id
.ie	Ireland	http://www.domainregistry.ie
.il	Israel	http://www.isoc.org.il/
.im	Isle of Man	http://www.nic.im
.in	India	http://domain.ncst.ernet.in
.io	British Indian Ocean Territory	http://www.nic.io/
.iq	Iraq	None listed
.ir	Iran	http://aria.nic.ir/forms/domain2.html
.is	Iceland	http://www.isnet.is/nic/
.it	Italy	http://www.nic.it/
.je	Jersey	http://www.isles.net/
.jm	Jamaica	None listed
.jo	Jordan	http://www.nic.gov.jo/dns
.jp	Japan	http://www.nic.ad.jp/

.ke	Kenya	http://www.nbnet.co.ke/index.html
.kg	Kyrgystan	None listed
.kh	Cambodia	http://www.camnet.com.kh/
.ki	Kiribati	None listed
.km	Comoros	None listed
.kn	Saint Kitts and Nevis	None listed
.kp	Korea, Democratic People's Republic	None listed
.kr	Korea, Republic of	http://www.krnic.net/
.kw	Kuwait	None listed
.ky	Cayman Islands	http://www.nic.ky
.kz	Kazakhistan	http://www.nic.kz
.la	Lao People's Democratic Republic	None listed
.lb	Lebanon	http://www.aub.edu.lb/lebanon-online/
.lc	Saint Lucia	http://www.sluonestop.com/
.li	Liechtenstein	http://www.nic.li
.lk	Sri Lanka	http://www.nic.lk/
.lr	Liberia	None listed
.ls	Lesotho	None listed
.lt	Lithuania	http://www.domreg.lt
.lu	Luxembourg	http://www.dns.lu
.lv	Latvia	http://www.nic.lv/DNS/
.ly	Libyan Arab Jamahiriya	http://www.nic.ly/

.ma	Morocco	http://www.anrt.net.ma/nic
.mc	Monaco	http://www.nic.mc/
.md	Moldova, Republic of	http://www.register.md
.mg	Madagascar	None listed
.mh	Marshall Islands	http://www.nic.net.mh/
.mk	Macedonia, Former Yugoslav Republic	http://www.mpt.com.mk/
.ml	Mali	http://www.sotelma.ml
.mm	Myanmar	http://www.nic.mm/
.mn	Mongolia	http://www.mongoliaonline.mn/
.mo	Macau	http://www.umac.mo
.mp	Northern Mariana Islands	http://www.marketplace.mp
.mp	Martinique	http://www.nic.mq/
.mr	Mauritania	http://www.univ-nkc.mr/nic_mr.html
.ms	Montserrat	http://www.ms/
.mt	Malta	http://www.nic.org.mt
.mu	Mauritius	http://posix.co.za/mu/reg.txt
.mv	Maldives	None listed
.mw	Malawi	http://www.tarsus.net/
.mx	Mexico	http://www.nic.mx/
.my	Malaysia	http://www.mynic.net/
.mz	Mozambique	None listed
.na	Namibia	http://www.lisse.na/dns
.nc	New Caledonia	http://www.ird.nc

.ne	Niger	http://www.intnet.ne
.nf	Norfolk Island	http://www.names.nf/
.ng	Nigeria	None listed
.ni	Nicaragua	http://165.98.1.2/nic-for.html
.nl	Netherlands	http://www.domain-registry.nl/
.no	Norway	http://www.norid.no
.np	Nepal	http://www.mos.com.np
.nr	Nauru	http://www.cenpac.net.nr
.nu	Niue	http://www.nunames.nu/
.nz	New Zealand	http://www.domainz.net.nz/
.om	Oman	http://www.omantel.net.om
.pa	Panama	http://www.nic.pa/
.pe	Peru	http://www.nic.pe
.pf	French Polynesia	None listed
.pg	Papua New Guinea	None listed
.ph	Philippines	http://www.domreg.org.ph/
.pk	Pakistan	http://www.pknic.net.pk/
.pl	Poland	http://www.dns.pl/english/
.pm	St. Pierre and Miquelon	http://www.nic.pm/
.pn	Pitcairn Island	http://www.nic.pn/PnRegistry/ PnRegistry.htm
.pr	Puerto Rico	http://www.uprr.pr/domain/
.ps	Palestinian Territories	None listed

.pt	Portugal	http://www.dns.pt/
.pw	Palau	None listed
.py	Paraguay	http://www.nic.py
.qa	Qatar	http://www.qatar.net.qa/
.re	Reunion Island	http://www.nic.re/
.ro	Romania	http://www.rnc.ro/
.ru	Russian Federation	http://www.ripn.net/nic/
.rw	Rwanda	http://www.nic.cd/
.sa	Saudi Arabia	http://www.saudinic.net.sa/
.sb	Solomon Islands	http://www.nic.net.sb/
.sc	Seychelles	http://www.sc/
.sd	Sudan	http://www.sudatel.sd/
.se	Sweden	http://www.nic-se.se/
.sg	Singapore	http://www.nic.net.sg/
.sh	St. Helena	http://www.nic.sh/
.si	Slovenia	http://www.arnes.si/si-domene/
.sj	Svalbard and Jan Mayen Islands	http://www.uninett.no/navn/
.sk	Slovak Republic	http://www.sk-nic.sk
.sl	Sierra Leone	None listed
.sm	San Marino	http://www.intelcom.sm/Naming
.sn	Senegal	http://www.ucad.sn/nic.html
.so	Somalia	http://www.wcd.so/

.sr	Suriname	None listed
.st	Sao Tome and Principe	http://st-registry.tecnisys.net
.sv	El Salvador	http://www.svnet.org.sv
.sy	Syrian Arab Republic	None listed
.sz	Swaziland	http://www.iafrica.sz/domreg
.tc	Turks and Caicos	http://www.tc/
.td	Chad	http://www.tit.td/
.tf	French Southern Territories	http://www.tf/
.tg	Togo	None listed
.th	Thailand	http://www.thnic.net/
.tj	Tajikistan	http://www.nic.tj/
.tk	Tokelau	None listed
.tm	Turkmenistan	http://www.nic.tm/
.tn	Tunisia	http://www.ati.tn/Nic/
.to	Tongo	http://www.tonic.to/
.tp	East Timor	http://www.nic.tp
.tr	Turkey	http://dns.metu.edu.tr/
.tt	Trinidad and Tobago	http://ns1.tstt.net.tt/nic/
.tv	Tuvalu	None listed
.tw	Taiwan	http://rs.twnic.net.tw
.tz	Tanzania	http://www.psg.com/dns/tz/
.ua	Ukraine	http://nic.net.ua/
.ug	Uganda	http://www.nic.ug/

.uk	United Kingdom	http://www.nic.uk/
.um	US Minor Outlying Islands	http://www.nic.um
.us	United States	http://www.nic.us
.uy	Uruguay	http://www.rau.edu.uy/rau/dom/
.uz	Uzbekistan	http://www.noc.uz
.va	Vatican City	http://www.nic.va
.vc	Saint Vincent and the Grenadines	None listed
.ve	Venezuela	http://www.nic.ve/
.vg	Virgin Islands (British)	http://www.vg/
.vi	Virgin Islands (USA)	http://www.nic.vi
.vn	Vietnam	None listed
.vu	Vanuatu	http://www.vunic.vu
.wf	Wallis and Futuna Islands	http://www.nic.wf/
.ws	Western Samoa	www.samoanic.ws
.ye	Yemen	None listed
.yt	Mayotte	http://www.nic.yt/
.yu	Yugoslavia	http://www.nic.yu
.za	South Africa	http://www2.frd.ac.za/uninet/zadomains.html
.zm	Zambia	http://www.zamnet.zm
.zr	Zaire	None listed
.zw	Zimbabwe	None listed

Appendix 2

DATA PROTECTION SUPERVISORY AUTHORITIES OF THE EUROPEAN UNION MEMBER STATES

Country	Name of Supervisory Authority	Web Site of Supervisory Authority
Austria	Bundeskanzleramt Österreichische Datenschutzkommission	http://www.bka.gv.at/datenschutz/
Belgium	Commission de la protection de la vie privée	http://www.privacy.fgov.be/
Denmark	Datatilsynet	http://www.datatilsynet.dk/
Finland	Office of the Data Protection Ombudsman	http://www.tietosuoja.fi/
France	Commission Nationale de l'Informatique et des Libertés	http://www.cnil.fr/
Germany	Der Bundesbeauftragte für den Datenschutz	http://www.bfd.bund.de/
Greece	Hellenic Data Protection Authority	http://www.dpa.gr/
Ireland	Data Protection Commissioner	http://www.dataprivacy.ie/
Italy	Garante per la protezione dei dati personali	http://astra.garanteprivacy.it/ garante/HomePageNs
Luxembourg	Commission à la Protection des Données Nominatives	None available
Netherlands	Registratiekamer	http://www.registratiekamer.nl/
Portugal	Comissão Nacional de Protecção de Dados	http://www.cnpd.pt/
Spain	Agencia de Protección de Datos	https://www.agenciaprotecciondatos.org/
Sweden	Datainspektionen	http://www.datainspektionen.se/
United Kingdom	Office of the Information Commissioner	http://www.dataprotection.gov.uk/

Appendix 3

SELECT PRIVACY RESOURCES

1. Privacy Organizations

Entity	Web Site
American Civil Liberties Union – privacy resources	www.aclu.org/privacy
California Office of Privacy Protection	www.privacyprotection.ca.gov
Center for Democracy and Technology	www.cdt.org
Center of Digital Democracy	www.democraticmedia.org
Center for Media Education	www.cme.org
Computer Professionals for Social Responsibility	www.cpsr.org/dox/program/ privacy/privacy.html
Consumer Project on Technology	www.cptech.org/cpt.html
Cyber-Rights and Cyber Liberties	www.cyber-rights.org
Electronic Frontier Foundation	www.eff.org/pub/privacy
Electronic Privacy Information Center	www.epic.org
Foundation for Information Policy Research	www.fipr.org
Global Internet Liberty Campaign	www.gilc.org
Health Privacy Project	www.healthprivacy.org
Privacy Coalition	www.privacypledge.org
Privacy Exchange	www.privacyexchange.org
Privacy Foundation	www.privacyfoundation.org
Privacy Inc.	www.privacyinc.com
Privacy International	www.privacy.org/pi

Privacy News, Info & Action (EPIC & Privacy International)	www.privacy.org
Privacy Officers Association	www.privacyassociation.org
Privacy Rights Clearinghouse	www.privacyrights.org
Right to privacy	www.rightoprivacy.com
US Public Interest Research Group	www.pirg.org

2. Media

Entity	Web Site
Access Reports	www.accessreports.com
Computer Law and Security Report	www.compseconline.com
Full Disclosure	www.fulldisclosure.org
Privacy and American Business	www.pandab.org
Privacy Exposed	www.privacyexposed.com
Privacy Journal	www.townonline.com/privacyjournal
Privacy Laws and Business	www.privacylaws.co.uk
Privacy Times	www.privacytimes.com
US News & World Report – Privacy Pages	www.usnews.com/usnews/ nycu/tech/teprivacy.htm

3. Education

Entity	Web Site
Harvard Information Infrastructure Project	www.ksg.harvard.edu/iip/gateway
John Marshall Law School, Center for Information Technology and Privacy Law	www.jmls.edu

4. Governmental and Legal

Entity	Web Site
British Colombia, Canada Information and Privacy Commissioner	www.oipcbc.org
Canadian Office of the Privacy Commissioner	www.privcom.gc.ca
Federal Trade Commission	www.ftc.gov
New Zealand Office of Privacy Commissioner	www.knowledgebasket.co.nz/privacy
Office of the Australian Privacy Commissioner	www.privacy.gov.au
Ontario, Canada Information and Privacy Commissioner	www.ipc.on.ca
Parliamentary Commissioner for Data Protection and Freedom of Information	www.mkogy.hu/adatved/biztos/
THOMAS site for Federal Legislation	www.thomas.loc.gov/home/thomas.html
United States Code	www.law.cornell.edu/uscode

5. Privacy-Enhancing Services and Tools

Entity	Web Site
AdDelete Software	www.addelete.com
Anonmizer	www.anonymizer.com
Cookie Control	www.cookiecontrol.org
SafeWeb	www.safeweb.com
SpyChecker	www.spychecker.com
Zero Knowledge Systems	www.zeroknowledge.com

NOTES

CHAPTER 1: INTRODUCTION

1. See, e.g., *EC Outlines Strategy to Ensure Harmonized Market for Online Sale of Financial Services,* 6(8) ELECTRONIC COMMERCE & LAW REPORT 184 (2001), discussing the proposed strategy of the European Commission to address contractual differences among the Member States of the European Union in order to facilitate the growth of a harmonized market for on-line financial services throughout the European Union. This is but one example of how the European Commission has been working to harmonize certain aspects of Internet regulation. Outside the EU, other organizations such as the Organization for Economic Cooperation and Development have also been involved in efforts at harmonization.

2. *See* Children's Online Privacy Protection Act, Title XIII, Omnibus Consolidated and Emergency Supplemental Appropriations Act, 1999 Pub. L. 105-277, 112 Stat. 2681 (Oct. 21, 1998), *reprinted in* 144 Cong. Rec. HII240-42 (Oct. 19, 1998) [hereinafter COPPA].

3. *See* Digital Millennium Copyright Act, Pub. L. No. 105-304, 112 Stat. 2860 (1998) (to be codified at scattered sections of 17 U.S.C. § 1201).

4. SEC INTERPRETATIVE RELEASE ON USE OF ELECTRONIC MEDIA No. 33-7856, No. 34-42728 (Apr. 28, 2000).

5. *Id.*

6. *Dot.com Disclosures,* available on the Internet at http://www.ftc.gov/bcp/conline/pubs/buspubs/dtcom/index.html (accessed March 20, 2001).

7. *See, e.g.,* Reno v. American Civil Liberties Union, 521 U.S. 844, 849 (1997) (noting that the Internet is not a physical entity but rather "an international network of interconnected computers").

8. For more information on this point, see Shirley F. Sarna, *Advertising on the Internet: An Opportunity for Abuse?,* 11 St. John's J. Legal Comment. 683, 689 (1996), who contends that "without an enforceable set of rules to permit commercial predictability, certainty, and consumer confidence, the 'global market' will never achieve its potential."

CHAPTER 2: GETTING STARTED

1. The "look and feel" of the Web site can be understood to mean the overall appearance and presentation of the site, including only the nonliteral elements that make up the site's visual display, user interface, and screens (including their flow and sequencing), together with all patent rights, copyrights, trademarks, trade names, and other proprietary rights inherent therein or appurtenant thereto.

2. *See* 17 U.S.C. § 201(b).

3. Of course, you may also opt to host the site yourself. In addition, many Web site operators opt for contracting site development and hosting services at the same time from the same provider.

4. Privacy will be discussed in greater detail in chapter 4 of this book.

5. An IP address is a series of numbers used by networks to connect all computers on the Internet. A domain name may be up to 63 characters, consisting of letters, numbers, or the dash symbol.

6. *ICANN Announces Selections for New Top-Level Domains* (Nov. 16, 2000), available on the Internet at http://www.icann.org/announcements/icann-pr16nov00.htm (accessed Sept. 16, 2003).

7. Chris Lamorte, *Register Your Own Domain Name,* 12(1) Poptronics 10 (2000).

8. A listing of the accredited domain name registrars is available on the Internet at http://www.icann.org.

9. Kim Guenther, *What's in a Name? Usage and Registration of Domain Names,* 25(1) Online 73 (2001).

10. One definition of "cybersquatting" found in a 1999 report of the World Intellectual Property Organization is an "abusive registration" where (1) a domain name is identical or misleadingly similar to a trade or service mark of a complainant, who actually owns the mark; (2) the holder of the domain name has no rights or legitimate interests in the domain name; and (3) the registration and the use of the domain name have been in bad faith (World Intellectual Property Organization, *The*

Management of Internet Names and Addresses: Intellectual Property Issues: Final Report of the WIPO Internet Domain Name Process, Apr. 30, 1999, available on the Internet at http://wipo2.wipo.int/process1/report/finalreport.html [accessed Sept. 17, 2003]).

11. The Anticybersquatting Consumer Protection Act of 1999, 15 U.S.C. § 1125(d) (amending § 43(d) of the Trademark Act of 1946) [hereinafter Anticybersquatting Act].

12. *See* 15 U.S.C. § 1125(d)(1)(B).

13. *Id.*

14. 15 U.S.C. § 1125 (d)(1)(B)(i)(III).

15. 15 U.S.C. § 1125 (d)(1)(B)(i)(IV).

16. 15 U.S.C. § 1125 (d)(1)(B)(i)(V).

17. 15 U.S.C. § 1125 (d)(1)(B)(i)(VI).

18. 15 U.S.C. § 1125 (d)(1)(B)(i)(VII).

19. 15 U.S.C. § 1125 (d)(1)(B)(i)(VIII).

20. 15 U.S.C. § 1125 (d)(1)(B)(i)(IX).

21. 15 U.S.C. § 1116, § 1117(a).

22. 15 U.S.C. § 1125(d)(2)(A).

23. 15 U.S.C. § 1117(d).

24. 15 U.S.C. § 1125(d)(2)(A); see Quokka Sports Inc. v. Cup Int'l Ltd., No. C. 99-5076-DLJ (N.D. CA 1999), wherein a California company was found to have *in rem* jurisdiction over a New Zealand company. For a different outcome, see Alitalia-Linee Italiane S.p.A. v. Casinoalitalia.com, No. 00-394-A (E.D. Va. Jan. 19, 2001), where the Eastern District of Virginia ruled that the owner of the "Alitalia" mark could not proceed *in personam* against the alleged cybersquatter while also proceeding with an *in rem* proceeding against the allegedly infringing domain name. In this case, the court pointed out that the plain language of the Anticybersquatting Act limits the use of *in rem* jurisdiction to situations in which personal jurisdiction is not available. In this case, the court found that it had personal jurisdiction over Casinoalitalia.com based on the interactive nature of its on-line gambling Web site and the fact that its domain name infringed the Alitalia trademark.

25. While the *in rem* jurisdiction provisions of the Anticybersquatting Act have been somewhat controversial, the U.S. District Court for the Eastern District of Virginia recently ruled that they are not unconstitutional under the Fifth Amendment's due process clause, either facially or as applied to a Canadian citizen with no contacts with the United States except for the registration of a domain name with the Virginia-based Network Solutions, Inc. (Heathmount A.E. Corp. v. Technodrome.com, E.D. Va., Case No. CA-00-00714-A, 12/29/00).

CHAPTER 3: MANAGING RISKS THROUGH
WEB SITE TERMS OF USE

1. Determining jurisdiction for Web-based activities is an important issue that is not yet fully settled in the United States or on the global level. Further attention will be devoted to this controversial issue later in this chapter.

2. This section contains a considerable amount of sample language that is designed solely to illustrate the points discussed. Readers are cautioned that Internet law is a rapidly evolving area, and many concepts are not yet fully settled. Readers should seek the advice of counsel and not rely solely on any information contained in this book.

3. The argument that click-wrap agreements are enforceable stems from the Seventh Circuit's decision in Pro CD, Inc., v. Zeidenberg, 86 F. 3d 1447 (7th Cir. 1996), which upheld the enforceability of "shrink-wrap" licenses and contracts. In its decision, the court allowed licensers of computer software to condition the licensee's acceptance of the license agreement on some form of action indicating acceptance, such as using the product.

4. Carnival Cruise Line, Inc., v. Shute, 499 U.S. 585, 594 (1991).

5. Ticketmaster Corp. v. Tickets.com, 2000 U.S. Dist. LEXIS 12987.

6. The concept of deep linking refers to hyperlinks that are made into the internal pages of the Web site, as opposed to links that are made to the site's home page.

7. Ticketmaster's ten causes of action are (1) copyright infringement, (2) breach of contract, (3) passing off, (4) reverse passing off, (5) false advertising, (6) misappropriation, (7) state unfair business practices, (8) trespass, (9) unjust enrichment, and (10) tortious interference with prospective business advantage. *Id.* at 4.

8. Judge Hupp writes, "Many web sites make you click on 'agree' to the terms and conditions before going on, but Ticketmaster does not. Further, the terms and conditions are set forth so that the customer needs to scroll down the home page to find and read them." *Id.* at 8.

9. *Id.*

10. 2001 U.S. Dist. LEXIS 9073 (2001).

11. *Id.* at 5.

12. No. A092813 (Cal. App. Ct., June 21, 2001), *aff'd,* No. 827047-2 (Alameda County Super. Ct. Sept. 25, 2001) [hereinafter AOL Case].

13. California Civil Code §§ 1750–56.

14. See California Civil Code § 1751, stating: "Any waiver by a consumer of the provisions of this title is contrary to public policy and shall be unenforceable and void."

15. In responding to AOL's argument that California law favors contractual forum selection clauses, the appeals court countered: "Our law favors forum selection agreements only so long as they are procured freely and voluntarily, with the place chosen having some logical nexus to one of the parties or the dispute, and *so long as California consumers will not find their substantial legal rights significantly impaired by their enforcement*" (AOL Case at 20; italics mine).

16. Williams v. America Online, Inc., 2001 Mass. Super. LEXIS 11, 43 U.C.C. Rep. Serv. 2d (Callagan) 1101.

17. DIRECTIVE 99/93/EC OF THE EUROPEAN PARLIAMENT AND OF THE COUNCIL OF 13 DECEMBER 1999 ON A COMMUNITY FRAMEWORK FOR ELECTRONIC SIGNATURES, O.J. L 13/12, Jan. 19, 2000 [hereinafter the European E-Signature Directive].

18. *Id.* at Article 2(1).

19. *Id.* at Article 2(2).

20. UNCITRAL MODEL LAW ON ELECTRONIC SIGNATURES, United Nations Commission on International Trade Law (UNCITRAL), 34th Sess., June 25–July 13, 2001 (Vienna, Austria).

21. THE ACT ON ELECTRONIC SERVICE IN THE ADMINISTRATION 2000, at Section 3(6) (2000) (Finland). An unofficial English translation of the legislation is available on the Internet at http://www.om.fi/2838.htm (accessed Aug. 6, 2001).

22. Pub. L. No. 106-229, 114 Stat. 464 (2000) [hereinafter the E-Sign Act].

23. The E-Sign Act defines an "electronic signature" as "an electronic sound, symbol or process, attached to or logically associated with a contract or other record and executed or adopted by a person with an intent to sign the record." *Id.* at § 106(2).

24. *Id.* at § 101(a).

25. *Id.* at § 101(a)(1).

26. *Id.* at § 101(a)(2).

27. *Id.* at § 101(c)(1).

28. *Id.* at § 101(c)(1) (A).

29. *Id.* at § 101(c)(1) (B)(i).

30. *Id.* at § 101(c)(1) (B)(iii).

31. *Id.* at § 101(c)(1) (B)(iv).

32. *Id.* at § 101(c)(1) (C)(i).

33. *Id.* at § 101(c)(1) (C)(ii).

34. *Id.* at § 103.

35. *Id.* at § 102.

36. On June 28, 2001, the use of electronic signatures at all levels of

criminal case prosecution was approved in the United Arab Emirates. See *United Arab Emirates: E-signature for Legal Affairs Approved June 28, 2001,* available on the Internet at http://www.zawya.com/story.cfm?id= ZAWYA 2001 0628093017 (accessed Aug. 7, 2001).

37. In the Electronic Signatures Directive, "electronic signature" is defined as "data in electronic form which are attached to or logically associated with other electronic data and which serve as a method of authentication." European E-Signature Directive, *supra* note 15, at Article 2(1).

38. European E-Signature Directive, *supra* note 15, at Article 1.

39. The 15 Member States of the European Union are Austria, Belgium, Denmark, Finland, France, Germany, Greece, Ireland, Italy, Luxembourg, Netherlands, Portugal, Spain, Sweden, and the United Kingdom.

40. *See* David Griffith and Nicholas O'Neil, *Commission Proposes Directive on Digital Signatures,* 17(8) FINANCIAL REGULATION REPORT 13, 14 (1998). One of the first Member States of the European Union to pass a law concerning electronic signatures was Germany. GESETZ ZUR DIGITALEN SIGNATUR (SIGNATURGESETZ), v. (July 22, 1997) (BGBI. IS. 1870, 1872) (Germany). Although this law was passed in 1997, other Member States have still not passed legislation pertaining to the legal recognition of electronic signatures.

41. See European E-Signature Directive, *supra* note 15, at Recital 4, noting that "electronic communication and commerce necessitate 'electronic signatures' and related services allowing data authentication; divergent rules with respect to legal recognition of electronic signatures and the accreditation of certification-service providers in the Member States may create a significant barrier to the use of electronic communications and electronic commerce; on the other hand, a clear Community framework regarding the conditions applying to electronic signatures will strengthen confidence in, and general acceptance of, the new technologies."

42. *Id.* at Article 5(2).

43. *Id.* at Article 6.

44. The directive provides that Member States are required to ensure that certificates that are issued as qualified certificates to the public by a certification service provider established in a third country are recognized as legally equivalent to certificates issued by a certification service provider established within the Community if (1) the certification service provider fulfills the requirements laid down in this directive and has been accredited under a voluntary accreditation scheme established in a Member State; or (2) a certification service provider established within the

Community which fulfills the requirements laid down in this directive guarantees the certificate; or (3) the certificate or the certification service provider is recognized under a bilateral or multilateral agreement between the Community and third countries or international organizations. European E-Signature Directive, *supra* note 15, at Article 7(1).

45. *Id.* at Article 5(2).

46. *Id.* at Article 5(1)(b).

47. *Id.* at Article 4(2).

48. *Id.* at Article 4(1).

49. *Id.* at Article 6.

50. A certification service provider is defined by the directive as "an entity or a legal or natural person who issues certificates or provides other services related to electronic signatures." European E-Signature Directive, *supra* note 15, at Article 2(11).

51. *Id. supra* note 2, at Article 7.

52. *Id. supra* note 2, at Article 7(1).

53. *See* Anne Gallagher, *White House Frets over Possible Overseas Restriction on E-commerce Standards,* WASHINGTON TECHNOLOGY, Nov. 8, 1999, at 16.

54. European E-Signatures Directive, *supra* note 15, at Recital 16.

55. This observation has resulted from the fact that the directive "contains many open-ended exclusions and contradictory wording that invites various interpretations." Charles Bogino, *U.S. Wary but Optimistic as EU States Craft Own E-Signature Laws Based on EC Directive,* 5(1) ECLR 7 (Jan. 5, 2000).

56. *See* Richard Raysman and Peter Brown, *Yahoo! Decision Fuels E-commerce Sovereignty Debate,* NEW YORK LAW JOURNAL, Dec. 12, 2000, at 3.

57. The text of the code provides:

"Est puni de l'amende prévue pour les contraventions de la 5e classe le fait, sauf pour les besoins d'un film, d'un spectacle ou d'une exposition comportant une évocation historique, de porter ou d'exhiber en public un uniforme, un insigne ou un emblème rappelant les uniformes, les insignes ou les emblèmes qui ont été portés ou exhibés soit par les membres d'une organisation déclarée criminelle en application de l'article 9 du statut du tribunal militaire international annexé à l'accord de Londres du 8 août 1945, soit par une personne reconnue coupable par une juridiction française ou internationale d'un ou plusieurs crimes contre l'humanité prévus par les articles 211-1 à 212-3 ou mentionnés par la loi n° 64-1326 du 26 décembre 1964.

Les personnes coupables de la contravention prévue au présent article encourent également les peines complémentaires suivantes:

1. L'interdiction de détenir ou de porter, pour une durée de trois ans au plus, une arme soumise à autorisation;

2. La confiscation d'une ou de plusieurs armes dont le condamné est propriétaire ou dont il a la libre disposition;

3. La confiscation de la chose qui a servi ou était destinée à commettre l'infraction ou de la chose qui en est le produit;

4. Le travail d'intérêt général pour une durée de vingt à cent vingt heures.

Les personnes morales peuvent être déclarées responsables pénalement, dans les conditions prévues par l'article 121-2, de l'infraction définie au présent article.

Les peines encourues par les personnes morales sont;

1. L'amende, suivant les modalités prévues par l'article 131–41;

2. La confiscation de la chose qui a servi ou était destinée à commettre l'infraction ou de la chose qui en est le produit.

La récidive de la contravention prévue au présent article est réprimée conformément aux articles 132-11 et 132-15."

58. For an unofficial English translation of the ruling in this case, see http://gigalaw.com/library/france-yahoo-2000-11-2-0-lesecq.htm (accessed Mar. 11, 2001).

59. *See, e.g.,* Randall E. Stoss, *Pardon My French: If It's a World Wide Web, Why Is France Censoring Yahoo!?,* U.S. NEWS & WORLD REPORT, Feb. 12, 2001, at 41.

60. *See* John Markoff, *Online Service Blocks Access to Topics Called Pornographic,* N.Y. TIMES, Dec. 29, 1995, at A1. Subsequently, CompuServe reinstated all but five of the discussion groups and provided screening software to users. *See* Peter H. Lewis, *An Online Service Halts Restriction on Sex Materials,* N.Y. TIMES, Feb. 14, 1996, at A4.

61. *See* Nathaniel C. Nash, *Germans Again Bar Internet Access, This Time to Neo-Nazism,* N.Y. TIMES, Jan. 29, 1996, at D6.

CHAPTER 4: INTERNET PRIVACY ISSUES: THE LAW'S ALL OVER THE MAP

1. Video Privacy Protection Act, 18 U.S.C. § 2710.

2. Driver's Privacy Protection Act of 1994, 18 U.S.C. § 2721, available

on the Internet at http://www.epic.org/privacy/laws/drivers_privacy_bill.html (accessed Nov. 3, 2000).

3. Children's Online Privacy Protection Act of 1998, 15 U.S.C. 6501 (1999). On October 20, 1999, the FTC issued the final rule implementing COPPA. FTC, Children's Online Privacy Protection Rule; Final Rule 16 CFR Part 312 (1999). This final rule, along with the act, are referred to herein as COPPA.

4. 144 Cong. Rec. S12741 (Oct. 7, 1998) (statement of Senator Bryan).

5. Pursuant to COPPA, an operator is "any person who operates a website on the Internet or an online service and who collects or maintains personal information from or about the users of or visitors to such website or online service, or on whose behalf such information is collected or maintained, where such website or online service is operated for commercial purposes, including any person offering products or services through that website or online service, involving commerce—(i) among the several States or with 1 or more foreign nations; (ii) in any territory of the United States or in the District of Columbia, or between any such territory and (I) another such territory; or (II) any State or foreign nation; or (iii) between the District of Columbia and any State, territory or foreign nation." COPPA, *supra* note 3, at § 1302(2).

6. Under the terms of COPPA, the term "verifiable personal consent" means "any reasonable effort (taking into consideration available technology), including a request for authorization for future collection, use, and disclosure described in the notice, to ensure that a parent of a child receives notice of the operator's personal information collection, use, and disclosure practices, and authorizes the collection, use, and disclosure practices, and authorizes the collection, use, and disclosure, as applicable, of personal information and the subsequent use of that information before that information is collected from that child." *Id.* at § 1302(9).

7. COPPA defines disclosure in a rather broad manner. Under the act, disclosure, with respect to personal information, is said to constitute "(A) the release of personal information collected from a child in identifiable form by an operator for any purpose, except where such information is provided to a person other than the operator who provides support for the internal operations of the website and does not disclose or use that information for any other purpose; and (B) making personal information collected from a child by a website or online service directed to children or with actual knowledge that such information was collected from a child, publicly available in an identifiable form, by any means including by a public posting, through the Internet, or through (i) a home page of a web

site; (ii) a pen pal service; (iii) an electronic mail service; (iv) a message board; or (v) a chat room." *Id.* at § 1302(4).

8. *Id.* at § 1303(b)(1).

9. A copy of the complaint is available on the Internet at http://www.ftc.gov/os/1998:9898/geo-cmpl.htm (accessed Nov. 19, 1998).

10. *See* Federal Trade Commission, *Federal Trade Commission Announces Settlement with Web Sites That Collected Children's Personal Data without Parental Permission,* FTC Release (Apr. 19, 2001), available on the Internet at http://www.ftc.gov/opa/2001/01/girlslife.htm (accessed Feb. 17, 2003). Copies of the complaints and consent orders are available from the FTC's Web site at http://www.ftc.gov.

11. *See* Federal Trade Commission, *FTC Protecting Children's Privacy Online,* FTC Release (Apr. 22, 2002), available on the Internet at http://www.ftc.gov/opa/2002/04/coppaanniv.htm (accessed Aug. 1, 2002).

12. 15 U.S.C. §§ 6801–10.

13. Statute (Public Law 106-102, 15 U.S.C. § 6801) [hereinafter GLB Act].

14. A "consumer" is an individual who obtains or has obtained a financial product or service from a financial institution that is to be used primarily for personal, family, or household purposes, or that individual's legal representative.

15. A "financial institution" is any institution the business of which is engaging in financial activities as described in section 4(k) of the Bank Holding Company Act (12 U.S.C. § 1843(k)).

16. GLB Act, *supra* note 13, at §§ 313.14 and 313.15.

17. *Id.* at § 313.14(b).

18. FTC, Standards for Safeguarding Customer Information, Final Rule, 16 C.F.R. 314 (2002).

19. Public Law 104-191.

20. Standards for Privacy of Individually Identifiable Health Information, 45 C.F.R. Parts 160 and 164.

21. 45 C.F.R. § 164.501 (Definitions).

22. Security Standards, 45 C.F.R. Parts 160, 162, and 164.

23. 45 C.F.R. 164.308.

24. Id.

25. 15 U.S.C. §§ 1681, 1681a–1681t.

26. Consumer reporting agencies are entities that regularly engage in assembling or evaluating consumer credit information for the purpose of furnishing consumer reports to third parties (15 U.S.C. C. § 1681 a(f) (1988).

27. Electronic Communications Privacy Act, Pub. L. No. 99-508, 100

Stat. 1848 (1986) (codified at 18 U.S.C. 2510–21, 2701–10, 3117, 3121–26) (1986) [hereinafter ECPA].

28. ECPA defines "electronic communication" as "any transfer of signs, signals, writing, images, sounds, data, or intelligence of ant any nature transmitted in whole or in part by a wire, radio, electromagnetic, photoelectronic or photo-optical system that affects interstate or foreign commerce but does not include—

(A) the radio portion of a cordless telephone communication that is transmitted between the cordless telephone handset and the base unit;
(B) any wire or oral communication;
(C) any communication made through a tone-only paging device; or
(D) any communication from a tracking device." *Id.* at § 2510(12).

29. Codified at 18 U.S.C. §§ 2510–2521.

30. 18 U.S.C. §2501(1).

31. Laurie Thomas Lee, *Watch Your E-mail! Employee E-mail Monitoring and Privacy Law in the Age of the "Electronic Sweatshop,"* 28 J. Marshall L. Rev. 139, 144 (1994).

32. Codified at 18 U.S.C. §§ 2701–10.

33. *Id.* at § 2702.

34. *Id.*

35. Codified at 18 U.S.C. §§ 3117–26.

36. *Id.* at § 2707(b)(1).

37. *Id.* at § 2707(c).

38. *Id.* at § 2707(b)(3).

39. 18 U.S.C. § 2710.

40. Under the act, the term "video service provider" is defined as "any person, engaged in the business, in or affecting interstate or foreign commerce of rental, sale or delivery of prerecorded video cassette tapes or similar audio visual materials." 18 U.S.C. § 2710(a)(4).

41. Under the act, "personally identifiable information" includes information that identifies a person as having requested or obtained specific video materials from a videotape service provider. *Id.* at (a)(4).

42. 18 U.S.C. § 2710(b).

43. 18 U.S.C. § 2710(c).

44. *See* Alaska Const. art. I, § 22 ("[t]he right of the people to privacy is recognized and shall not be infringed"); Ariz. Const. art II, § 8 ("No person shall be disturbed in his private affairs, or his home invaded, without the authority of law"); Cal Const. art. I, §1 ("All people are by nature free and independent and have inalienable rights, among these are . . . pursuing and obtaining safety, happiness and privacy"); Fla. Const. art.

I, § 23 ("Every natural person has the right to be let alone and free from governmental intrusion into his private life except as otherwise provided herein"); HAW. CONST. art. I, § 6 ("The right of the people to privacy is recognized and shall not be infringed without a compelling interest. The legislature shall take affirmative steps to implement this right"); ILL. CONST. art I, § 6 ("The people shall have the right to be secure in their persons, houses, papers and other possessions against unreasonable searches, seizures, invasions of privacy or interceptions of communications by eavesdropping devices or other means"); LA CONST. art. I, § 5 ("Every person shall be secure in his person, property, communication, houses, papers, and effects against unreasonable searches, seizures or invasions of privacy. . . . Any person adversely affected by a search or seizure conducted in violation of this Section shall have standing to raise its illegality in the appropriate court"); MONT. CONST. art II, § 10 ("The right of individual privacy is essential to the well-being of a free society and shall not be infringed without the showing of a compelling state interest"); WASH. CONST. art I, § 7 ("No person shall be disturbed in his private affairs, or his home invaded, without authority of law").

45. The Constitution of California is somewhat notable in that its privacy rights language has been interpreted as being enforceable against private parties. *See* Hill v. NCAA, 865 P.2d 633, 641–44 (Cal. 1994).

46. *See, e.g.,* Ark. Code Ann. § 14-14-110(b) (Michie 1998); Haw. Rev. Stat. Ann. § 92F-14 (Michie 1996); Kan. Stat. Ann. § 72-6214 (1992); Mont. Code Ann. § 20-25 (1997); N.Y. Penal Law § 250.05 (McKinney 1989); W. Va. Code § 46A-2-126 (1998).

47. California Business and Professions Code §§ 350–52.

48. *Id.* at § 350(a).

49. TRUSTe, *Why Is Self-Regulating Privacy So Important?,* (2000), available on the Internet at http://www.truste.org/about/truste/about_faqs.html#self (accessed Dec. 10, 2000).

50. A complete listing of the TRUSTe participants is available on the Internet at http://www.truste.org/usrs/usrs_lookup.html.

51. For further information concerning this initiative, please refer to http://www.bbbonline.com.

52. A list of current participants in the BBBOnline privacy seal program can be found at http://www.bbbonline.com.

53. *See* http://www.webtrust.org.

54. *See* http://www.pwcbetterweb.com.

55. Organization for Economic Cooperation and Development, *Guidelines on the Protection of Privacy and Transborder Flows of Personal*

Data, Sept. 23, 1980, available on the Internet at http://www.oecd.org// dsti/sti/it/secur/prod/PRIV-EN.HTM.

56. COUNCIL DIRECTIVE NO. 95/46/EC OF 24 OCTOBER 1995 ON THE PROTECTION OF INDIVIDUALS WITH REGARD TO THE PROCESSING OF PERSONAL DATA AND ON THE FREE MOVEMENT OF SUCH DATA, O.J. L 281/ 31 (1995) [hereinafter Directive].

57. *Id.* at Art. 2(a).

58. *Id.* at Art. 4, which provides:

1. Each Member State shall apply national provisions it adopts pursuant to this Directive to the processing of personal data where:

(a) the processing is carried out in the context of the activities of an establishment of the controller on the territory of the Member State; when the same controller is established on the territory of several Member States, he must take the necessary measures to ensure that each of these establishments complies with the obligations laid down by national law applicable;

(b) the controller is not established on the Member State's territory, but in a place where the Member State's national law applies by virtue of international public law;

(c) the controller is not established on Community territory and, for purposes of processing personal data makes use of equipment, automated or otherwise, situated in the territory of the said Member States, unless such equipment is used only for purpose of transit through the territory of the Community.

59. Directive, *supra* note 51, at Art. 7(a).

60. *Id.* at Art. 7(b).

61. *Id.* at Art. 7(c).

62. *Id.* at Art. 7(d).

63. *Id.* at Art. 7(e).

64. *Id.* at Art. 7(f).

65. *Id.* at Art. 8(1).

66. *Id.* at Art. 8(2)(a).

67. *Id.* at Art. 8(2)(b).

68. *Id.* at Art. 8(2)(c).

69. *Id.* at Art. 8(2)(d).

70. *Id.* at Art. 8(2)(e).

71. *Id.* at Art. 8(2)(f).

72. *Id.* at Art. 8(2)(g).

73. *Id.* at Art. 18, requiring each Member State to "provide that one or

more public authorities are responsible for the application within its territory of the provisions adopted by the Member States."

74. A list of the supervisory authorities of the Member States and their Web site addresses is included in appendix 2.

75. Directive, *supra* note 51, at Art. 19(1)(a).

76. *Id.* at Art. 19(1)(b).

77. *Id.* at Art. 19(1)(c).

78. *Id.* at Art. 19(1)(d).

79. *Id.* at Art. 19(1)(e).

80. *Id.* at Art. 12(a).

81. *Id.*

82. *Id.* at Art. 17(1).

83. *Id.* at Art. 17(2).

84. *See Reglamento de Seguridad, Ultimas Noticias Sobre El Plazo Para Adoptar Las Medias de Nivel Alto Del Reglamento de Medias de Seguridad,* available on the Internet at https://www.agenciaprotecciondatos.org/novedad.htm (accessed June 25, 2002); and *Consultas mas frecuentes, 13 Consulta sobre medidas de seguridad,* available on the Internet at https://www.agenciaprotecciondatos.org/consulta13.htm (accessed June 25, 2002).

85. Directive, *supra* note 51, at 17(2).

86. *Id.* at 17(2).

87. COMMISSION DECISION 2000/519/EC OF 26.7.2000 PURSUANT TO DIRECTIVE 95/46/EC OF THE EUROPEAN PARLIAMENT AND OF THE COUNCIL ON THE ADEQUATE PROTECTION OF PERSONAL DATA PROVIDED IN HUNGARY—O.J. L 215/4 of 25.8.2000.

88. COMMISSION DECISION 2000/518/EC OF 26.7.2000 PURSUANT TO DIRECTIVE 95/46/EC OF THE EUROPEAN PARLIAMENT AND OF THE COUNCIL ON THE ADEQUATE PROTECTION OF PERSONAL DATA PROVIDED IN SWITZERLAND—Official Journal L 215/1 of 25.8.2000.

89. COMMISSION DECISION 2002/2/EC OF 20.12.2001 PURSUANT TO DIRECTIVE 95/46/EC OF THE EUROPEAN PARLIAMENT AND OF THE COUNCIL ON THE ADEQUATE PROTECTION OF PERSONAL DATA PROVIDED BY THE CANADIAN PERSONAL INFORMATION PROTECTION AND ELECTRONIC DOCUMENTS ACT—O.J. L 2/13 of 4.1.2002.

90. COMMISSION DECISION 2000/520/EC OF 26.7.2000 PURSUANT TO DIRECTIVE 95/46/EC OF THE EUROPEAN PARLIAMENT AND OF THE COUNCIL ON THE ADEQUACY OF THE PROTECTION PROVIDED BY THE SAFE HARBOR PRIVACY PRINCIPLES AND RELATED FREQUENTLY ASKED QUESTIONS ISSUED BY THE U.S. DEPARTMENT OF COMMERCE—Official Journal L 215/7 of 25.8.2000.

91. Further information about this program is available on the Web site of the United States Department of Commerce at http://www.export.gov/safeharbor, as well as on the Web site of the European Commission at http://europa.eu.int/comm/internal_market/en/dataprot/adequacy/index.htm.

92. The list of entities participating in the Safe Harbor initiative is available at http://web.ita.doc.gov/safeharbor/shlist.nsf/webPages/safe + harbor + list (accessed Sept. 22, 2003).

93. Directive, *supra* note 51, at Art. 26(2)(d).

94. *Id.* at recital 31.

95. *Id.* at Art. 26(2)(f).

96. *Id.* at Art. 26(3).

97. Bill C-6, assented to Apr. 13, 2000, available on the Internet at http://www.privcom.gc.ca./English/02?06_01_01.e.htm [hereinafter the Canadian Act].

98. "Personal information" is defined in Part I § 2(1) of the act as "information about an identifiable individual, but does not include the name, title or business address or telephone number of an employee of an organization." Commentary on the act further describes personal information as "information about an identifiable individual, and includes things such as race, ethnic origin, colour, age, marital status, religion, education, medical, criminal, employment or financial history, address and telephone number, numerical identifiers such as the Social Insurance Number, fingerprints, blood type, tissue or biological sample, and views or personal opinions" (*Building Trust in the Digital Economy,* available on the Internet at http://strategis.ic.ga.ca [accessed Jan. 18, 2001]).

99. Canadian Act, *supra* note 93, at Part 1, §3.

100. *Id.* at 1.

101. *Id.* at Part 1, Division 1 (Protection of Personal Information), Subdivision 7.(1) (a)–(d).

102. Confidential commercial information is not defined in the act.

103. Law No. 19628 of Aug. 30, 1999 (Chile).

104. Law No. 25, 326 (Argentina).

105. Law No. 8078, Sept. 11, 1990 (Brazil).

106. Law No. 7.232, Oct. 29, 1984 (Brazil).

107. Chapter of Laws (Cap) 383: 288, available on the Internet at http://www.justice.gov.hk.

108. The home page of the Office of the Privacy Commissioner in Hong Kong is http://www.pco.org.hk.

109. For example, a recent study undertaken by Cyber Dialog contended that consumer concerns about privacy are having a toll on e-

commerce. According to this study, 27 percent of the research participants had abandoned an on-line order because of privacy concerns. *See* Christopher Saunders, *Study: Web Privacy Concerns Cost $3.4 Billion,* INTERNET ADVERTISING REPORT, Nov. 8, 2001, available on the Internet at http://www.internetnews.com/IAR/article.php/12_920201 (accessed Jan. 8, 2002). Also, an August 2000 study of 1,017 Internet users in the United States revealed that 86 percent of the participants were concerned that the personal information they revealed on-line would end up in the possession of individuals and/or enterprises with whom they were not acquainted. S. Fox, *Trust and Privacy Online: Why Americans Want to Rewrite the Rules,* PEW INTERNET AND AMERICAN LIFE REPORT, Aug. 20, 2000, available on the Internet at http://www.pewinternet.org/reports/toc.asp?Report = 19 (accessed Nov. 20, 2000).

110. *See, e.g.,* Federal Trade Commission, *Online Privacy Policies Apply to Offline Data Practices,* ADVOCACY ISSUE BRIEFS, Dec. 13, 2001, available on the Internet at http://www.imarketing.org/advIssueBriefs.php (accessed June 26, 2002).

111. *Remarks of Howard Beales, Director, Bureau of Consumer Protection, Federal Trade Commission at the Promotional Marketing Association Annual Meeting, Dec. 5, 2001,* available on the Internet at http://www.ftc.gov/speeches/other/bealesconsumerprotectagenda.htm (accessed Dec. 12, 2002).

112. Federal Trade Commission, *FTC Announces Settlement with Bankrupt Website, Toysmart.com Regarding Alleged Privacy Policy Violations,* FTC Release (July 21, 2000), available on the Internet at www.ftc.gov/opa/2000/07/toysmart2.htm (accessed Aug. 20, 2001).

113. FTC v. Toysmart.com, LLC and Toysmart.com, Inc., Civil Action No. 00 = 11341-RGS, Stipulated Consent Agreement and Final Order, available on the Internet at http://www/ftc.gov/os/2000/07/toysmart consent.htm.

114. See *In the Matter of Eli Lilly & Co.,* No. 012 3214, Complaint, available on the Internet at www.ftc.gov/os/2002/01/lillycmp.pdf.

115. Federal Trade Commission, *Eli Lilly Settles FTC Charges Concerning Security Breach,* FTC Release (Jan. 18, 2002), available on the Internet at www.ftc.gov/opa/2002/01/elililly.htm (accessed June 10, 2002).

116. See *In the Matter of Eli Lilly & Co.,* No. 012 3214, Agreement Containing Consent Order, available on the Internet at www.ftc.gov/os/2002/01/lillycmp.pdf.

117. There are large number of resources pertaining to privacy. Appen-

dix 3 of this book contains links to a number of different Web sites concerning privacy.

CHAPTER 5: ON-LINE ADVERTISING AND MARKETING

1. A number of ISPs have been successful in legal actions against parties involved in spamming. *See, e.g.,* Cyber Promotions, Inc., v. America Online, Inc., C.A. No. 96-2486, 1996 WL 565818 (E.D. Pa. Sept. 5, 1996), *rev'd,* (3d Cir. Sept. 20, 1996), *partial summary judgment granted,* 948 F. Supp. 436 (E.D. Pa. Nov. 4, 1996) (on First Amendment issues), *reconsideration denied,* 948 F. Supp. 436, 447 (Dec. 20, 1996), *temporary restraining order denied,* 948 F. Supp. 456 (E.D. Pa. Nov. 26, 1996) (on antitrust claim), *settlement entered* (E.D. Pa. Feb. 4, 1997); CompuServe Inc. v. Cyber Promotions, Inc., No. C2-96-1070 (S.D. Ohio Oct. 24, 1996), *preliminary injunction entered,* 962 F. Supp. 1015 (S.D. Ohio Feb. 3, 1997, *final consent order filed,* (E.D. Pa. May 9, 1997) [hereinafter CompuServe v. Cyber Promotions]; Earthlink Network Inc. v. Cyber Promotions, Inc., No. BC 167502 (Cal. Super. Ct. L.A. County May 7, 1997) (preliminary injunction), *consent judgment entered,* (Mar. 30, 1998).

2. A listing of state laws concerning unsolicited commercial e-mail is available on the Internet at http://www.spamlaws.com/state/index/html.

3. California Business and Professional Code § 17511, and in particular, § 17538.45 (West 2000).

4. *See, e.g.,* Earthlinks Networks v. Cyber Promotions, Inc., No. BC 167502 (Cal. Super. Ct. L.A. County Mar. 30, 1998); Bigfoot Partners, L.P., v. Cyber Promotions and Sanford Wallace, No. 97 Civ. 7397 (S.D.N.Y. Oct. 6, 1997).

5. CompuServe v. CyberPromotions, *supra* note 1.

6. In this case, the court held that unauthorized transmission of electronic signals such as bulk e-mail is sufficient "contact" for purposes of the trespass claim. *Id.*

7. 24 Supp. 2d 548 (E.D. Va. 1998).

8. ELECTRONIC COMMUNICATIONS PRIVACY DIRECTIVE: DIRECTIVE CONCERNING THE PROCESSING OF PERSONAL DATA AND THE PROTECTION OF PRIVACY IN THE ELECTRONIC COMMUNICATIONS SECTOR—COMMON POSITION (EC) No. 26/2002, 2002 O.J. (C 113 E) 39 (Jan. 28, 2002); REPORT ON THE COUNCIL COMMON POSITION, No. A5-0130/2002 (Apr. 22, 2002; approved by Parliament May 30, 2002).

9. *Id.* at 13(1).

10. *Id.* at 13(2); italics mine.

11. CONSOLIDATED ACT NO. 600 of 17 July 2002 (Denmark) [herein-after the Danish Marketing Practices Act]. An English version of the act is available on the Internet at http://www.fs.dk/uk/acts/ukmfl.htm (accessed Aug. 12, 2002).

12. *Id.* at 6a(1).

13. *See* Ministry of Information Communications, *Statistics Show Cross Border Spam Mail on Decrease,* July 30, 2002, available on the Internet at http://www.mic.go.kr (accessed Aug. 17, 2002).

14. See *Law on Unsolicited Email Takes Effect,* July 1, 2002, available on the Internet at http://www.japantoday.com/e/?content = news&cat = 2&id = 221054 (accessed Aug. 17, 2002).

15. *Id.*

16. *Spam Losses,* THE CONTROLLER'S REPORT, July 2002, at 9.

17. See *Frying Spam,* CORPORATE COUNSEL, *July 2001,* at 33.

18. Robert Lemos, *Spam Could Soon Be Majority of E-mail: Report,* ZDNet, Aug. 30. 2002, available on the Internet at http://www/zdnet.com/au/newstech/ebusiness/story/0,2000024981,20267797,00,htm (accessed Sept. 6, 2002).

19. Up to 10 percent of all U.S.-based telemarketing is fraudulent. Annual losses from fraudulent telemarketing in the United States have been estimated at up to $40 billion. *See* Telemarketing and Consumer Fraud and Abuse Prevention Act, 15 U.S.C. 6101(3) (1994) ("Consumers and others are estimated to lose $ 40 billion a year in telemarketing fraud"); COMMITTEE ON GOV'T OPERATIONS, THE SCOURGE OF TELEMARKETING FRAUD: WHAT CAN BE DONE AGAINST IT?, H.R. REP. NO. 102-421, at 7 (1991). A more recent report from the National Consumers League (NCL) reported that consumers lost more than $3.2 million dollars in Internet fraud in 1999. This figure was based only on incidents of fraud that were reported to the NCL and represents an increase of 38 percent from 1998. National Consumers League, *National Consumers League Warns Consumers Millions Are Lost to Internet Fraud,* press release, Feb. 16, 2002, available on the Internet at http://www.fraud.org/internet/99 final.htm (accessed Mar. 28, 2002).

20. National Consumers League, *National Consumers League Warns Consumers Millions Are Lost to Internet Fraud.*

21. *See Timothy R. Bean,* 121 F.T.C. 772, 781 (1996); *Robert Serviss,* 121 F.T.C. 820, 831 (1996).

22. *See Sherman G. Smith,* 121 F.T.C. 807, 817 (1996).

23. *See Bryan Coryat,* 121 F.T.C. 784, 795 (1996).

24. *See* FTC v. Chappie (Infinity Multimedia), No. 96-6671-CIV-Gonzalez (S.D. Fla. filed June 24, 1996).

25. *See* FTC v. Intellicom Servs., Inc., No. 97-4572 TJH (Mcx) (C.D. Cal. filed June 23, 1997).

26. *See, e.g.,* FTC v. Cano, No. 97-7947-CAS-(AJWx) (C.D. Cal. filed Oct. 29, 1997); FTC v. JewelWay Int'l, Inc., No. CV97-383 TUC JMR (D. Ariz. filed June 24, 1997); and FTC v. Fortuna Alliance, L.L.C., No. C96-799M (W.D. Wash. filed May 23, 1996).

27. For instance, in one survey, 75 percent of respondents said that unknown reliability of on-line businesses was a key factor in their decision whether to engage in on-line commerce. See *E-Commerce Survey: Business Reliability Ranks Near Transaction Security in Public Trust in Online Purchasing,* REP. ELEC. COMM., Feb. 10, 1998, at 3.

28. 15 U.S.C. §571(a)(1)(B).

29. Examples of such rules and guides include Guides for the Nursery Industry (16 C.F.R. Part 18); Guides for the Rebuilt, Reconditioned, and Other Used Automobile Parts Industry (16 C.F.R. Part 20); Guides for the Jewelry, Precious Metals, and Pewter Industries (16 C.F.R. Part 23); Guides for Select Leather and Imitation Leather Products (16 C.F.R. Part 24); Tire Advertising and Labeling Guides (16 C.F.R. Part 228); Guides against Deceptive Practices (16 C.F.R. Part 223); Guides against Bait Advertising (16 C.F.R. Part 238); Guides for the Advertising or Warranties and Guarantees (16 C.F.R. Part 239); Guides for the Household Furniture Industry (16 C.F.R. Part 250); Guide concerning Use of the Word "Free" and Similar Representations (16 C.F.R. Part 251); Guides for Private Vocational and Distance Education Schools (16 C.F.R. Part 254); Guides concerning Use of Endorsements and Testimonials in Advertising (16 C.F.R. Part 255); Guides concerning Fuel Economy Advertising for New Automobiles (16 C.F.R. Part 259); Guides for the Use of Environmental Marketing Claims (16 C.F.R. Part 260); Rules and Regulations under the Wool Products Labeling Act of 1939 (16 C.F.R. Part 300); Rules and Regulations under Fur Products Labeling Act (16 C.F.R. Part 301); Rules and Regulations under the Textile Fiber Products Identification Act (16 C.F.R. Part 303); Rule concerning Disclosures regarding Energy Consumption and Water Use of Certain Home Appliances and Other Products Required under the Energy Policy and Conservation Act (16 C.F.R. Part 305); Rule concerning Automotive Fuel Ratings, Certification, and Posting (16 C.F.R. Part 306); Labeling Requirements for Alternative Fuels and Alternative Fueled Vehicles (16 C.F.R. Part 309); Telemarketing Sales Rule (16 C.F.R. Part 310); Deceptive Advertising as to Sizes of Viewable

Pictures Shown by Television Receiving Sets (16 C.F.R. Part 410); Retail Food Store Advertising and Marketing Practices (16 C.F.R. Part 424); Use of Prenotification Negative Option Plans (16 C.F.R. Part 425); Power Output Claims for Amplifiers Utilized in Home Entertainment Products (16 C.F.R. Part 432); Preservation of Consumers' Claims and Defenses (16 C.F.R. Part 433); Mail or Telephone Order Merchandise Rule (16 C.F.R. Part 435); Credit Practices Rules (16 C.F.R. Part 444); Used Motor Vehicle Trade Regulation Rule (16 C.F.R. Part 455); Labeling and Advertising of Home Insulation (16 C.F.R. Part 460); Interpretations of Magnuson-Moss Warranty Act (16 C.F.R. Part 700); Disclosure of Written Consumer Product Warranty Terms and Conditions (16 C.F.R. Part 701); Pre-sale Availability of Written Warranty Terms (16 C.F.R. Part 702); and Informal Dispute Settlement Procedures (16 C.F.R. Part 703).

30. *See also* Federal Trade Commission, *Federal Trade Commission Policy Statement on Deception,* appended to *Cliffdale Associates, Inc.,* 103 F.T.C. at 174 (1984).

31. *See also* Federal Trade Commission, *Federal Trade Commission Policy Statement on Unfairness,* appended to *International Harvester Co.,* 104 F.T.C. 949, 1070 (1984).

32. The FTC has produced a guidance document concerning the on-line advertising and, specifically, the proper use of disclosures for on-line advertisements. The document, entitled *Dot.com Disclosures,* is available at on the Internet at http://wwww.ftc.gov/bcp/conline/pubs/buspubs/dtcom/index.html (accessed Mar. 20, 2001).

33. The FTC may seek civil penalties from any person or company that violates a rule "without actual knowledge or knowledge fairly implied on the basis of objective circumstances that such act is unfair or deceptive and is prohibited by such rule." 15 U.S.C. §45(m)(1)(A). The FTC may also seek redress for consumers. 15 U.S.C. §57(b)(a)(1).

34. Green Paper on Commercial Communications in the Internal Market, COM(96)192 final (European Commission) [hereinafter the Green Paper].

35. *See* Directive 97/55/EC of the European Parliament and of the Council of 6 October 1997, *amending* Directive 84/450/EEC concerning Misleading Advertising so as to Include Comparative Advertising, 1997 O.J. (L 290) 18, *corrected at* 1998 O.J. (L 194) 54.

36. Council Directive 84/450/EEC of 10 September 1984 on the Approximation of the Laws, Regulations, and Administrative Provisions of the Member States concerning Misleading Advertising.

37. It is important to note, however, that European regulators are continuing follow-up work related to these issues. On March 10, 2000, the commission submitted a report to the Council and the European Parliament on consumer complaints in respect of distance selling and comparative advertising. The report resulted from the request from the European Parliament and Council to conduct a study on the feasibility of establishing effective means to deal with consumers' (cross-border) complaints regarding distance selling and comparative advertising. In the report, the Commission outlines the current status of consumer complaints across the EU as a whole and assesses the situation in light of the provisions contained in the EC Treaty, as well as the various initiatives under way concerning consumer access to justice.

38. See Jenna D. Beller, *The Law of Comparative Advertising in the United States and around the World: A Practical Guide for U.S. Lawyers and Their Clients,* 29 INT'L LAW. 917, 925–43 (1995), for a discussion of the laws concerning comparative advertising in a number of jurisdictions around the world. Although the article predates the Comparative Advertising Directive, Beller presents an interesting discussion of some of the different approaches that have been adopted to regulate the use of comparative advertising.

39. Green Paper, *supra* note 34 at 23.

40. Danish Marketing Practice Act, *supra* note 11 at 6(1).

41. DIRECTIVE 95/58/EC OF 29.11.95 OF THE EUROPEAN PARLIAMENT AND OF THE COUNCIL AMENDING 79/581.EEC ON CONSUMER PROTECTION IN THE INDICATION OF PRICES OF FOODSTUFFS AND DIRECTIVE 88/314/EEC ON CONSUMER PROTECTION OF PRICES OF NON-FOOD PRODUCTS (O.J. L299 of 12.21.1995).

42. COUNCIL DIRECTIVE 76/768/EEC OF 27.7.1976 ON THE APPROXIMATION OF LAWS OF THE MEMBER STATES RELATING TO COSMETIC PRODUCTS (O.J. L262 OF 27.9.1976), *amended by* DIRECTIVE 79/661/EEC (O.J. L192 OF 31.7.1979), DIRECTIVE 82/368/EEC (O.J. L167 OF 15.6.1982), DIRECTIVE 83/574/EEC (O.J. L332 OF 28.11.1983), DIRECTIVE 88/667/EEC (O.J. L382 OF 21.12.1998), DIRECTIVE 89/679/EEC (O.J. L398 OF 20.12.89), DIRECTIVE 93/35/EEC (O.J. L151 OF 23.6.1993), *and* DIRECTIVE 97/18/EC (O.J. L114 OF 1.5.1997).

43. DIRECTIVE 96/74/EC OF THE EUROPEAN PARLIAMENT AND OF THE COUNCIL OF 16.12.1996 ON TEXTILE NAMES (O.J. L32 of 3.2.1997), *amended by* DIRECTIVE 97/37.EC (O.J. L169 of 27.6.1997).

44. COUNCIL DIRECTIVE 92/28/EEC OF 31 MARCH 1992 ON THE ADVERTISING OF MEDICINAL PRODUCTS FOR HUMAN USE (O.J. L113).

45. Council Directive 90/314/EEC of 13.06.1990 on package travel, package holidays, and package tours (O.J. L158 of 23.06.1990).

46. Council Directive 85/577/EEC of 20.12.1985 to Protect the Consumer in Respect of Contracts Negotiated Away from Business Premises—"Door to Door Selling" (O.J. L372 of 31.12.1985).

47. Council Directive 87/102/EEC of 22.12.1986 on the Approximation of Laws, Regulations, and Administrative Provisions of the Member States concerning Consumer Credit (O.J. L42 of 12.02. 1987), *as amended.*

48. Directive 97/7/EC of the European Parliament and of the Council, of 20.05.97, on the Protection of Consumers in Respect of Distance Contracts (O.J. L144 of 04.06.1997).

49. Directive 90/384/EC of the Council on the Harmonization of the Laws of the Member States Relating to Non-automatic Weighing Instruments.

50. Directive 94/47/EC of the European Parliament and the Council 26.10.1994 on the Protection of Purchasers in Respect of Certain Aspects of Contracts Relating to the Purchase of the Right to Use Immovable Properties on a Time-Share Basis (O.J. L280 of 29.10.1994).

51. Green Paper, *supra* note 34 at 26.

52. *Id.* at 27.

53. *Id.* at 27–28.

54. *Id.* at 28.

55. Nabil Freif, *Localize Your Products to Globalize Your Business,* Mass. High Tech, Mar. 23–29, 1998, at 16.

56. *See* Mike King, *Language Police Patrolling Internet Sites,* Montreal Gazette, June 14, 1997, at A1.

57. Michael Geist, *Quebec Forms Language Law-Challenge Tests E-Jurisdiction,* Lega Media, July 30, 2002, available on the Internet at http://www.legamedia.net/column/2002/02-06/0206-geist-michael-quebec-language-law (accessed Aug. 14, 2002).

58. Attorney General of Quebec v. HyperInfo Canada, Inc. (Nov. 1, 2002), Hull 550-61-000887-014 (C.Q.); For a summary of the case, see Bradley J. Freedman, *Quebec's Charter of the French Language and the Internet: Case Comment on Attorney General of Quebec v. Hyperinfo Canada, Inc.,* The Continuing Legal Education Society of British Columbia, Mar. 7, 2002, available on the Internet at http://www.cle.bc.ca/CLE/Analysis/Collection/02-quebec-internet (accessed Aug. 14, 2002).

59. *Id.*

60. King, *supra* note 56.

CHAPTER 6: PROTECTING PROPERTY ON-LINE

1. See 17 U.S.C. § 102(a), providing:

Copyright protection subsists, in accordance with this title, in original works of authorship fixed in any tangible medium of expression, now known or later developed, from which they can be perceived, reproduced or otherwise communicated, either directly or with the aid of a machine or device. Works of authorship include the following categories:

(1) literary works;
(2) musical works, including any accompanying words;
(3) dramatic works, including any accompanying music;
(4) pantomimes and choreographic words:
(5) pictoral, graphic and sculptural works:
(6) motion pictures and other audiovisual work;
(7) sound recordings; and
(8) architectural works

2. If the databases contain personally identifiable information of Web site users, the potential application of the numerous privacy laws and regulations must also be considered.

3. 149 F.3d 1368 (Fed. Cir. 1998), *cert. denied* 199 S.Ct. 851 (1999).

4. Wynn Coggins, *The Evolution of the Business Method Patent and Update on the Business Method Action Plan,* USPTO TODAY, Dec. 2000, at 8, available on-line at http://www.uspto.gov/web/offices/ac/ahrpa/opa/ptotoday/ptotoday12.pdf (accessed Sept. 10, 2003).

5. *See* 416 University Computing Co. v. Lykes-Youngstown Corp., 504 F.2d 518 (5th Cir. 1974).

6. See, generally, ICC Commercial Crime Services, *A Brief Overview of Counterfeiting,* available on the Internet at http//www.iccwbo.org/ccs/cib_bureau/overview.asp (accessed Sept. 9, 2002), for an overview of the magnitude and the effects of counterfeiting.

7. 75 F. Supp. 2d 1290, 1999 U.S. Dist. LEXIS 19103 (D. Utah 1999).

8. Utah Lighthouse Ministry, *Settlement Signed by All Parties,* available on the Internet at http://www.utlm.org/underthecoverofflight/signedsettle mentandthankyou.htm (accessed Sept. 9, 2002).

9. No. 96/048 (District Court of the Hague, June 9, 1999).

10. Tribunal de Commerce de Paris, ordonnanceder référé, 26 Dec. 2000.

11. 87 Civ. 3055 (C.D.Cal. filed Apr. 28, 1997).

12. Edinburgh, Scotland, Court of Session, Oct. 24, 1996 (Lord Hamilton).

13. Copyright Act 1998, § 17.

14. *Id.* § 20.

15. No. 92 CV 01190 (SDNY filed Feb. 22, 1997).

16. Washington Post Co. v. Total News, Inc., No. 97 Civ. 1190 (PKL) (SDNY, complaint filed Feb. 20, 1997). A copy of the complaint is available on the Internet at http://ljx.com/internet/complain.html (accessed Feb. 5, 1999) [hereinafter TotalNEWS Complaint].

17. *Id.* at Paragraph 40.

18. *Id.* at Paragraph 40.

19. *Id.* at Paragraph 49.

20. *Id.* at Paragraph 58.

21. *Id.* at Paragraph 59.

22. *Id.* at Paragraph 62.

23. The violations were alleged to have occurred under the common law of the state of New York and N.Y. Gen. Bus. Law § 368-e.

24. Total News Complaint, *supra* note 16, at Paragraph 64.

25. The acts were alleged to be in violation of the New York Anti-dilution Statute, N.Y. Gen. Bus. Law § 368-d.

26. The relevant provisions of the state law were N.Y. Gen. Bus. Law. §§ 349–50.

27. Washington Post Co. v. Total News, Inc., No. 97 Civ. 1190 (PKL) (SDNY, Stipulation and Order of Settlement and Dismissal). A copy of the Stipulation and Order of Settlement and Dismissal is available on the Internet at http://ljx.com/internet/totalse.html (accessed Feb. 5, 1999).

28. Futuredonics, Inc., v. Applied Anagramatics, Inc., No. 97 Civ. 567-11, filed July 23, 1998 (9th Cir. 1998).

29. Under U.S. law, one of the most common exclusive rights of copyright law is the right to create derivative works from, or, in the language of the statute, "recast, transform or adapt," the copyrighted work. See 17 U.S.C. 106. In most framing cases, the framers take copyrighted works appearing on other sites and combine them with content of their own at their Web sites. The resulting page, as a whole, may be argued to be a derivative work of the other site's copyrighted content and thus an infringement.

30. 839 F. Supp. 1552 (M.D. Fla. 1993).

31. *Id.* at 1561.

32. Public Law 105-304.

33. 17 U.S.C. § 512(k)(1)(B).

34. 17 U.S.C. § 512(i)(1). "Standard technical measures" are measures adopted by an industry and embedded in copyrighted materials to protect them from copying and alteration.

35. 17 U.S.C. § 512(c)(2).

36. 17 U.S.C. § 512(d).

37. The full title of this directive is the Directive 2000/31/EC of the European Parliament and of the Council of 8 June 2000 on Certain Legal Aspects of Information Society Services, in Particular Electronic Commerce, in the Internal Market [hereinafter the E-commerce Directive].

38. *Id.* at Article 13.

39. *See Id.* at Recital 40, providing, in part: "Both existing and emerging disparities in Member States' legislation and case law concerning liability of service providers acting as intermediaries prevent the smooth functioning of the internal market, in particular by impairing the development of cross-border services and producing distortions of competition."

40. *Id.* at Recital 42.

41. *Id.* at Article 22(1). As an example of one nation's implementation of the requirements of Article 13 of the E-commerce Directive, consider Section 18 of the Electronic Commerce (EC Directive) Regulations 2002 of the United Kingdom, which provides:

Caching

18. Where an information society service is provided which consists of the transmission in a communication network of information provided by a recipient of the service, the service provider (if he otherwise would) shall not be liable for damages or for any other pecuniary remedy or for any criminal sanction as a result of that transmission where—

   (a) the information is the subject of automatic, intermediate and temporary storage where that storage is for the sole purpose of making more efficient onward transmission of the information to other recipients of the service upon their request, and

   (b) the service provider—

   (i) does not modify the information;

   (ii) complies with conditions on access to the information;

   (iii) complies with any rules regarding the updating of the information, specified in a manner widely recognised and used by industry;

   (iv) does not interfere with the lawful use of technology, widely recognised and used by industry, to obtain data on the use of the information; and

(v) acts expeditiously to remove or to disable access to the information he has stored upon obtaining actual knowledge of the fact that the information at the initial source of the transmission has been removed from the network, or access to it has been disabled, or that a court or an administrative authority has ordered such removal or disablement. When comparing the provisions contained in the E-Commerce Regulations 2002 with those contained in the E-Commerce Directive, it is apparent that the provisions of the E-Commerce Directive that concern caching address civil and criminal liability simultaneously. In the E-Commerce Regulations 2002, they are addressed separately. On the one hand civil liability is limited and on the other hand, service providers are provided with a defence against criminal liability. The UK government has instructed that this was done "solely because separating the treatment of civil and criminal liability is standard drafting practice for UK legislation." Electronic Commerce (EC Directive) Regulations 2002, Public Consultation—Government Response, July 31, 2002.

42. 18 U.S.C.§ 1030 (1984) [hereinafter CFAA].

43. Under the CFAA, the term "protected computer" refers to a computer "(A) exclusively for the use of a financial institution or the Unites States government, or, in the case of a computer not exclusively for such use, used by or for a financial institution or the United States government, and the conduct constituting the offense affects that use by or for the financial institution of the government; or (B) which is used in interstate or foreign commerce or communication." 18 U.S.C. § 1030(c).

44. It is important to note that under (3) and (4), the damage must cause physical injury, or a threat to health or public safety, or a monetary loss to one or more persons exceeding (in the aggregate) $5,000 over a one-year period.

45. 18 U.S.C. § 1028.

46. Pursuant to 18 U.S.C. § 1028(a)(7), "means of identification included electronic information that may be used to identify a person or a group of persons."

47. 18 U.S.C. § 1831.

48. 18 U.S.C. § 2701.

49. State laws concerning computer crime include the following: Ala. Code §§ 13A-8-100 to 13A-8-103; Ariz. Rev. Stat. Ann. §§ 13-2301(E), 13-2316; Ark. Code §§ 5-41-101 to 5-41-107; Cal. Penal Code §§ 484j, 499c, 502, 502.01, 502.7(h), 503, 1203.047, 2702; Colo. Rev. Stat. §§ 18-5.5-101 to 18-5.5-102; Conn. Gen. Stat. §§ 53a-250 to 53a-261; Del. Code Ann. tit. 11, §§ 931–39; Fla. Stat. ch. 775; Ga. Code Ann. § 16-7-22;

Haw. Rev. Stat. §§ 708-891 to 708-893; Idaho Code §§ 18-2201 to 18-2202, 26-1220, 48-801; Ill. Rev. Stat., ch. 38, §§ 16D-1 to 16D-7; Iowa Code §§ 716A.1 to 716A.16; Kan. Stat. Ann. § 21-3755; Ky. Rev. Stat. Ann. §§ 434.840 to 434.860; La. Rev. Stat. Ann. §§ 14:73.1 to 14:73.5; Me. Rev. Stat. Ann. tit. 17-A, ch. 18, §§ 431–33; Md. Code Ann., Crim. Law §§ 27-45A, 27-145, 27-146, 27-340; Mass. Gen. L. ch. 266, §§ 30, 60A; Mich. Comp. Laws §§ 752.791 to 752.797; Mo. Rev. Stat. §§ 569.093 to 569.099; Mont. Code Ann. §§ 45-1-205(4), 45-2-101, 45-6-310, 45-6-311; Neb. Rev. Stat. §§ 28???-1341 to 28-1348; Nev. Rev. Stat. § 603.050; N.J. Stat. Ann. §§ 2A:38A-1 to 2A:38A-1-6, 2C:20-1, 2C:20-23 to 2C:20-34; N.M. Stat. Ann. §§ 30-45-1 to 30-45-7; Various Sections of N.Y. Penal Law; N.C. Gen Stat. §§ 14-453 to 14-457; N.D. Cent. Code §§ 12.1-06.1-01, 12.1-06.1-08; Ohio Rev. Code Ann. §§ 2901.01(J), (M); 2901.1(I); 2901.12; 2912.01(F), (L)-(R), (T); 2913.04 (B), (D); 2913.42; 2913.81; 2933.41(A)(7); Okla. Stat. Ann. tit. 21, §§ 1951–58; Or. Rev. Stat. § 164.377; Penn. Cons. Stat. § 3933; R.I. Gen. Laws §§ 11-52-1 to 11-52-8; S.C. Code Ann. §§ 16-16-10 to 16-16-40; S.D. Codifed Laws Ann. §§ 43–43B-1 to 43–43B-8; Tenn. Code Ann. §§ 39-14-601 to 39-14-603; Tex. Penal Code Ann. §§ 33.01??? to 33.05; Utah Code Ann. §§ 76-6-701 to 76-6-705; Va. Code §§ 18.2-152.1 to 18.2-152.14; W. Va. Code §§ 61-3C-1 to 61-3C-21; Wis. Stat. § 943.70; Wyo. Stat. § 6-3-401.

50. Council of Europe Convention on Cybercrime, Budapest 23.X1.2001, available on the Internet at http://convention.coe.int/Treaty/en/HTMl/185.htm (accessed Sept. 20, 2002).

51. *Id.* at Preamble.

52. *Id.* at Chapter II, Section 1.

53. *Id.* at Chapter II, Section 1, Title 1.

54. *Id.* at Chapter II, Section 1, Title 2.

55. *Id.* at Chapter II, Section 1, Title 3.

56. *Id.* at Chapter II, Section 1, Title 4.

57. *Id.* at Chapter II, Section 2.

58. *Id.* at Chapter III.

59. *Id.* at Chapter II, Section 3.

60. European Commission's Proposal for a Council Framework Decision on Attacks on Information Systems, COM (2002) 173 Final 2002/086 (CNS) [hereinafter the Framework Decision].

61. *Id.* at Article 1.

62. *Id.* at Article 3. "Information systems" are defined under the Framework Decision as "computers and electronic communications networks, as well as computer data stored, processed, retrieved or transmitted by

them for the purposes of their operation, use, protection and maintenance."
Id. at Article 2(d).

    63. *Id.* at Article 4.
    64. *Id.* at Article 9.
    65. *Id.* at Article 10.
    66. *Id.* at Article 11.
    67. *Id.* at Article 12.

SELECTED BIBLIOGRAPHY

416 University Computing Co. v. Lykes-Youngstown Corp., 504 F.2d 518 (5th Cir. 1974).

1990 CODE OF CONSUMER PROTECTION AND DEFENSE, Law No. 8078 (Sept. 11, 1990) (Brazil).

THE ACT ON ELECTRONIC SERVICE IN THE ADMINISTRATION 2000, at Section 3(6) (2000) (Finland). An unofficial English translation of the legislation is available on the Internet at http://www.om.fi/2838.htm (accessed Sept. 10, 2003).

Alitalia-Linee Italiane S.p.A. v. Casinoalitalia.com, No. 00-394-A (E.D. Va. Jan. 19, 2001).

American Online, Inc., v. IMS, 24 Supp. 2d 548 (E.D. Va. 1998).

America Online, Inc., v. Mendoza, No. A092813 (Cal. App. Ct. June 21, 2001), *aff'd,* No. 827047-2 (Alameda County Super. Ct. Sept. 25, 2001).

Anticybersquatting Consumer Protection Act of 1999, 15 U.S.C. § 1125(d) (amending § 43(d) of the Trademark Act of 1946).

Attorney General of Quebec v. HyperInfo Canada, Inc. (1 Nov. 2002), Hull 550-61-000887-014 (C.Q.).

Bank Holding Company Act (codified at 12 U.S.C. § 1843(k)).

Beller, Jenna D., *The Law of Comparative Advertising in the United States and around the World: A Practical Guide for U.S. Lawyers and Their Clients,* 29 INT'L LAW. 917, 925–43 (1995).

Bigfoot Partners, L.P., v. Cyber Promotions and Sanford Wallace, No. 97 Civ. 7397 (S.D.N.Y. Oct. 6, 1997).

Bogino, Charles, *U.S. Wary but Optimistic As EU States Craft Own E-signature Laws Based on EC Directive,* 5(1) ECLR 7 (Jan. 5, 2000).

Bryan Coryat, 121 F.T.C. 784, 795 (1996).

Building Trust in the Digital Economy, available on the Internet at http://strategis.ic.ga.ca (accessed Jan. 18, 2001).

California Civil Code §§ 1750–56.

Carnival Cruise Line, Inc., v. Shute, 499 U.S. 585, 594 (1991).

Children's Online Privacy Protection Act, Title XIII, Omnibus Consolidated and Emergency Supplemental Appropriations Act, 1999 Pub. L. 105-277, 112 Stat. 2681 (Oct. 21, 1998), *reprinted in* 144 Cong. Rec. HII240–42 (Oct. 19, 1998).

Church of Scientology v. Spaink, No. 96/048 (District Court of the Hague, June 9, 1999).

Coggins, Wynn, *The Evolution of the Business Method Patent and Update on the Business Method Action Plan,* USPTO TODAY, Dec. 2000, at 8, available on-line at http://www.uspto.gov/web/offices/ac/ahrpa/opa/ptotoday/ptotoday12.pdf (accessed Sept. 10, 2003).

COMMISSION DECISION 2000/519/EC OF 26.7.2000 PURSUANT TO DIRECTIVE 95/46/EC OF THE EUROPEAN PARLIAMENT AND OF THE COUNCIL ON THE ADEQUATE PROTECTION OF PERSONAL DATA PROVIDED IN HUNGARY— O.J. L 215/4 of 25.8.2000.

COMMISSION DECISION 2000/518/EC OF 26.7.2000 PURSUANT TO DIRECTIVE 95/46/EC OF THE EUROPEAN PARLIAMENT AND OF THE COUNCIL ON THE ADEQUATE PROTECTION OF PERSONAL DATA PROVIDED IN SWITZER-LAND—Official Journal L 215/1 of 25.8.2000.

COMMISSION DECISION 2002/2/EC OF 20.12.2001 PURSUANT TO DIRECTIVE 95/46/EC OF THE EUROPEAN PARLIAMENT AND OF THE COUNCIL ON THE ADEQUATE PROTECTION OF PERSONAL DATA PROVIDED BY THE CA-NADIAN PERSONAL INFORMATION PROTECTION AND ELECTRONIC DOC-UMENTS ACT—O.J. L 2/13 of 4.1.2002.

COMMISSION DECISION 2000/520/EC OF 26.7.2000 PURSUANT TO DIRECTIVE 95/46/EC OF THE EUROPEAN PARLIAMENT AND OF THE COUNCIL ON THE ADEQUACY OF THE PROTECTION PROVIDED BY THE SAFE HARBOR PRI-VACY PRINCIPLES AND RELATED FREQUENTLY ASKED QUESTIONS IS-SUED BY THE U.S. DEPARTMENT OF COMMERCE—Official Journal L 215/7 of 25.8.2000.

COMMITTEE ON GOV'T OPERATIONS, THE SCOURGE OF TELEMARKETING FRAUD: WHAT CAN BE DONE AGAINST IT?, H.R. REP. NO. 102-421, at 7 (1991).

CompuServe Inc. v. Cyber Promotions, Inc., No. C2-96-1070 (S.D. Ohio Oct. 24, 1996), *preliminary injunction entered,* 962 F. Supp. 1015 (S.D. Ohio Feb. 3, 1997), *final consent order filed* (E.D. Pa. May 9, 1997).

The Computer Fraud and Abuse Act of 1984, 18 U.S.C. § 1030 (1984).

CONSOLIDATED ACT NO. 600 of 17 July 2002 (Denmark). An English version of the act is available on the Internet at http://www.fs.dk/uk/acts/ukmfl.htm (accessed Aug. 12, 2002).

COPYRIGHT ACT 1988 (U.K.).

COUNCIL DIRECTIVE 76/768/EEC OF 27.7.1976 ON THE APPROXIMATION OF LAWS OF THE MEMBER STATES RELATING TO COSMETIC PRODUCTS (E.G., L262 OF 27.9.1976), *amended by* DIRECTIVE 79/661/EEC (O.J. L192 OF 31.7.1979), DIRECTIVE 82/368/EEC (O.J. L167 OF 15.6.1982), DIRECTIVE 83/574/EEC (O.J. L332 OF 28.11.1983), DIRECTIVE 88/667/EEC) OJ L382 OF 21.12.1998), DIRECTIVE 89/679/EEC (OJ L398 OF 20.12.89), DIRECTIVE 93/35/EEC (OJ L151 OF 23.6. 1993), *and* DIRECTIVE 97/18/EC (OJ L114 OF 1.5.1997).

COUNCIL DIRECTIVE 84/450/EEC OF 10 SEPTEMBER 1984 ON THE APPROXIMATION OF THE LAWS, REGULATIONS, AND ADMINISTRATIVE PROVISIONS OF THE MEMBER STATES CONCERNING MISLEADING ADVERTISING.

COUNCIL OF EUROPE CONVENTION ON CYBERCRIME, Budapest 23.X1.2001, available on the Internet at http://convention.coe.int/Treaty/en/HTMl/185.htm (accessed Sept. 20, 2002).

Cyber Promotions, Inc., v. America Online, Inc., C.A. No. 96-2486, 1996 WL 565818 (E.D. Pa. Sept. 5, 1996), *rev'd* (3d Cir. Sept. 20, 1996), *partial summary judgment granted,* 948 F. Supp. 436 (E.D. Pa. Nov. 4, 1996) (on First Amendment issues), *reconsideration denied,* 948 F. Supp. 436, 447 (Dec. 20, 1996), *temporary restraining order denied,* 948 F. Supp. 456 (E.D. Pa. Nov. 26, 1996) (on antitrust claim), *settlement entered* (E.D. Pa. Feb. 4, 1997).

Digital Millennium Copyright Act, Pub. L. No. 105-304, 112 Stat. 2860 (1998) (codified at scattered sections of 17 U.S.C. § 1201).

DIRECTIVE CONCERNING THE PROCESSING OF PERSONAL DATA AND THE PROTECTION OF PRIVACY IN THE ELECTRONIC COMMUNICATIONS SECTOR—COMMON POSITION (EC) No. 26/2002, 2002 O.J. (C 113 E) 39 (Jan. 28, 2002); REPORT ON THE COUNCIL COMMON POSITION, No. A5-0130/2002 (Apr. 22, 2002; approved by Parliament May 30, 2002).

DIRECTIVE 85/577/EEC OF 20.12.1985 TO PROTECT THE CONSUMER IN RESPECT OF CONTRACTS NEGOTIATED AWAY FROM BUSINESS PREMISES—"DOOR TO DOOR SELLING" (O.J. L372 OF 31.12.1985).

DIRECTIVE 87/102/EEC OF 22.12.1986 ON THE APPROXIMATION OF LAWS, REGULATIONS, AND ADMINISTRATIVE PROVISIONS OF THE MEMBER STATES CONCERNING CONSUMER CREDIT (O.J. L42 OF 12.02. 1987), *as amended.*

DIRECTIVE 90/314/EEC OF 13.06.1990 ON PACKAGE TRAVEL, PACKAGE HOLIDAYS, AND PACKAGE TOURS (OJ L158 OF 23.06.1990).

DIRECTIVE 92/28/EEC OF 31 MARCH 1992 ON THE ADVERTISING OF MEDICINAL PRODUCTS FOR HUMAN USE (OJ L113).

DIRECTIVE 94/47/EC OF THE EUROPEAN PARLIAMENT AND THE COUNCIL 26.10.1994 ON THE PROTECTION OF PURCHASERS IN RESPECT OF CERTAIN ASPECTS OF CONTRACTS RELATING TO THE PURCHASE OF THE RIGHT TO USE IMMOVABLE PROPERTIES ON A TIME-SHARE BASIS (O.J. L280 of 29.10.1994).

DIRECTIVE NO. 95/46/EC OF 24 OCTOBER 1995 ON THE PROTECTION OF INDI-
VIDUALS WITH REGARD TO THE PROCESSING OF PERSONAL DATA AND
ON THE FREE MOVEMENT OF SUCH DATA, O.J. L 281/31 (1995).

DIRECTIVE 95/58/EC OF 29.11.1995 OF THE EUROPEAN PARLIAMENT AND OF
THE COUNCIL, amending 79/581.EEC ON CONSUMER PROTECTION IN
THE INDICATION OF PRICES OF FOODSTUFFS AND DIRECTIVE 88/314/EEC
ON CONSUMER PROTECTION OF PRICES OF NON-FOOD PRODUCTS (OJ L
299 OF 12.21.1995).

DIRECTIVE 96/74/EC OF THE EUROPEAN PARLIAMENT AND OF THE COUNCIL OF
16.12.1996 ON TEXTILE NAMES (O.J. L32 of 3.2.1997) *amended by* DI-
RECTIVE 97/37/EC (O.J. L169 of 27.6.1997).

DIRECTIVE 97/7/EC OF THE EUROPEAN PARLIAMENT AND OF THE COUNCIL, OF
20.05.1997, ON THE PROTECTION OF CONSUMERS IN RESPECT OF DIS-
TANCE CONTRACTS (O.J, L144 of 04.06.1997).

DIRECTIVE 97/55/EC OF THE EUROPEAN PARLIAMENT AND OF THE COUNCIL OF
6 OCTOBER 1997, *amending* DIRECTIVE 84/450/EEC CONCERNING MIS-
LEADING ADVERTISING SO AS TO INCLUDE COMPARATIVE ADVERTISING,
1997 O.J. (L 290) 18, *corrected at* 1998 O.J. (L 194) 54.

DIRECTIVE 99/93/EC OF THE EUROPEAN PARLIAMENT AND OF THE COUNCIL OF
13 DECEMBER 1999 ON A COMMUNITY FRAMEWORK FOR ELECTRONIC
SIGNATURES, O.J. L 13/12, Jan. 19, 2000.

DIRECTIVE 2000/31/EC OF THE EUROPEAN PARLIAMENT AND OF THE COUNCIL
OF 8 JUNE 2000 ON CERTAIN LEGAL ASPECTS OF INFORMATION SOCIETY
SERVICES, IN PARTICULAR ELECTRONIC COMMERCE, IN THE INTERNAL
MARKET.

Dot.com Disclosures, available at on the Internet at http://wwww.ftc.gov/bcp/
conline/pubs/buspubs/dtcom/index.html (accessed Mar. 20, 2001).

Driver's Privacy Protection Act of 1994, 18 U.S.C. § 2721, available on the
Internet at http://www.epic.org/privacy/laws/drivers_privacy_bill.html
(accessed Nov. 3, 2000).

Earthlink Network Inc. v. Cyber Promotions, Inc., No. BC 167502 (Cal. Super.
Ct. L.A. County May 7, 1997) (preliminary injunction), *consent judgment entered* (Mar. 30, 1998).

*EC Outlines Strategy to Ensure Harmonized Market for Online Sale of Financial
Services,* 6(8) ELECTRONIC COMMERCE & LAW REPORT 184 (2001).

*E-commerce Survey: Business Reliability Ranks Near Transaction Security in
Public Trust in Online Purchasing,* REP. ELEC. COMM., Feb. 10, 1998,
at 3.

Economic Espionage Act, 18 U.S.C. § 1831.

THE ELECTRONIC COMMERCE (EC DIRECTIVE) REGULATIONS 2002 (U.K).

Electronic Communications Privacy Act, Public Law No. 99-508, 100 Stat. 1848
(1986) (codified at 18 U.S.C. 2510–21, 2701–10, 3117, 3121–26) (1986).

Electronic Signatures in Global and International Commerce Act, Public Law
No. 106-229, 114 Stat. 464 (2000).

EUROPEAN COMMISSION'S PROPOSAL FOR A COUNCIL FRAMEWORK DECISION ON ATTACKS ON INFORMATION SYSTEMS, COM (2002) 173 Final 2002/ 086 (CNS).

Federal Trade Commission, *Online Privacy Policies Apply to Offline Data Practices,* ADVOCACY ISSUE BRIEFS, Dec. 13, 2001, available on the Internet at http://www.imarketing.org/advIssueBriefs.php (accessed June 26, 2002).

Federal Trade Commission, *Federal Trade Commission Announces Settlement with Web Sites That Collected Children's Personal Data without Parental Permission,* FTC Release (Apr. 19, 2001), available on the Internet at http://www.ftc.gov/opa/2001/01/girlslife.htm (accessed Feb. 17, 2003).

Federal Trade Commission, *Federal Trade Commission Policy Statement on Deception,* appended to *Cliffdale Associates, Inc.,* 103 F.T.C. at 174 (1984).

Federal Trade Commission, *Federal Trade Commission Policy Statement on Unfairness,* appended to *International Harvester Co.,* 104 F.T.C. 949, 1070 (1984).

Federal Trade Commission v. Cano, No. 97-7947-CAS-(AJWx) (C.D. Cal. filed Oct. 29, 1997).

Federal Trade Commission v. Chappie (Infinity Multimedia), No. 96- 6671-CIV-Gonzalez (S.D. Fla. filed June 24, 1996).

Federal Trade Commission v. Fortuna Alliance, L.L.C., No. C96-799M (W.D. Wash. filed May 23, 1996).

Federal Trade Commission v. Intellicom Services., Inc., No. 97-4572 TJH (Mcx) (C.D. Cal. filed June 23, 1997).

Federal Trade Commission v. JewelWay Int'l, Inc., No. CV97-383 TUC JMR (D. Ariz. filed June 24, 1997).

Fox, S., *Trust and Privacy Online: Why Americans Want to Rewrite the Rules,* PEW INTERNET AND AMERICAN LIFE REPORT, Aug. 20, 2000, available on the Internet at http://www.pewinternet.org/reports/toc.asp?Report = 19 (accessed Nov. 20, 2000).

Freedman, Bradley J., *Quebec's Charter of the French Language and the Internet: Case Comment on Attorney General of Quebec v. Hyperinfo Canada, Inc.,* THE CONTINUING LEGAL EDUCATION SOCIETY OF BRITISH COLUMBIA, Mar. 7, 2002, available on the Internet at http://www.cle.bc.ca/CLE/ Analysis/Collection/02-quebec-internet (accessed Apr. 20, 2002).

Freif, Nabil, *Localize Your Products to Globalize Your Business,* MASS. HIGH TECH, Mar. 23–29, 1998, at 16.

Frying Spam, CORPORATE COUNSEL, July 2001, at 33.

Futuredonics, Inc., v. Applied Anagramatics, Inc., No. 97 Civ. 567-11, filed July 23, 1998 (9th Cir. 1998).

Gallagher, Anne, *White House Frets over Possible Overseas Restriction on E-commerce Standards,* WASHINGTON TECHNOLOGY, Nov. 8, 1999, at 16.

Geist, Michael, *Quebec Forms Language Law: Challenge Tests E-Jurisdiction,* LEGA MEDIA, July 30, 2002, available on the Internet at http://www.

legamedia.net/column/2002/02-06/0206-geist-michael-quebec-language-law (accessed Aug. 15, 2002).

Gesetz zur digitalen Signatur (Signaturgesetz), v. (July 22, 1997) (BGBI. IS. 1870, 1872) (Germany).

Gramm-Leach-Bliley Act, Public Law 106-102 (codified at 15 U.S.C. § 6801.)

Green Paper on Commercial Communications in the Internal Market, COM(96)192 final (European Commission).

Griffith, David, and Nicholas O'Neil, *Commission Proposes Directive on Digital Signatures,* 17(8) Financial Regulation Report 13, 14 (1998).

Guenther, Kim, *What's in a Name? Usage and Registration of Domain Names* 25(1) Online 73 (2001).

Heathmount A.E. Corp. v. Technodrome.com, E.D. Va., Case No. CA-00-00714-A, (12/29/00).

Hill v. NCAA, 865 P.2d 633, 641–44 (Cal. 1994).

ICANN Announces Selections for New Top-Level Domains (Nov. 16, 2000), available on the Internet at http://www.icann.org/announcements/icann-pr16nov00.htm (accessed Dec. 11, 2001).

ICC Commercial Crime Services, *A Brief Overview of Counterfeiting,* available on the Internet at http//www.iccwbo.org/ccs/cib_bureau/overview.asp (accessed Sept. 9, 2002).

Identity Theft and Assumption Deterrence Act, 18 U.S.C. § 1028.

The Informatics Law of 1984, Law No. 7.232, Oct. 29, 1984 (Brazil).

Intellectual Reserve, Inc., v. Utah Lighthouse Ministry, Inc., 75 F. Supp. 2d 1290, 1999 U.S. Dist. LEXIS 19103 (D. Utah 1999).

King, Mike, *Language Police Patrolling Internet Sites,* Montreal Gazette, June 14, 1997, at A1.

Lamorte, Chris, *Register Your Own Domain Name,* 12(1) Poptronics 10 (2000).

Law on Unsolicited Email Takes Effect, July 1, 2002, available on the Internet at http://www.japantoday.com/e/?content = news&cat = 2&id = 221054 (accessed Aug. 17, 2002).

Law for the Protection of Private Life, Law No. 19628 of Aug. 30, 1999 (Chile).

Lee, Laurie Thomas, *Watch Your E-mail! Employee E-mail Monitoring and Privacy Law in the Age of the "Electronic Sweatshop,"* 28 J. Marshall L. Rev. 139, 144 (1994).

Lewis, Peter H., *An Online Service Halts Restriction on Sex Materials,* N.Y. Times, Feb. 14, 1996, at A4.

Markoff, John, *Online Service Blocks Access to Topics Called Pornographic,* N.Y. Times, Dec. 29, 1995, at A1.

Nash, Nathaniel C., *Germans Again Bar Internet Access, This Time to Neo-Nazism,* N.Y. Times, Jan. 29, 1996, at D6.

National Consumers League, *National Consumers League Warns Consumers Millions Are Lost to Internet Fraud,* press release, Feb. 16, 2002, available on the Internet at http://www.fraud.org/internet/99final.htm (accessed Mar. 28, 2002).

Organisation for Economic Co-operation and Development, *Guidelines on the Protection of Privacy and Transborder Flows of Personal Data,* Sept. 23, 1980, available on the Internet at http://www.oecd.org//dsti/sti/it/ secur/prod/PRIV-EN.HTM (accessed Sept. 8, 2001).

PERSONAL INFORMATION PROTECTION AND ELECTRONIC DOCUMENTS ACT, (Canada), available on the Internet at http://www.privcom.gc.ca./English/ 02?06_01_01.e.htm (accessed Sept. 22, 2003).

Playboy Enterprises v. Frena, 839 F. Supp. 1552 (M.D. Fla. 1993).

PRIVACY DATA PROTECTION LAW, Law No. 25, 326 (Argentina).

Pro CD, Inc., v. Zeidenberg, 86 F. 3d 1447 (7th Cir. 1996).

Quokka Sports Inc. v. Cup Int'l Ltd., No. C. 99-5076-DLJ (N.D. CA 1999).

Raysman, Richard, and Peter Brown, *Yahoo! Decision Fuels E-commerce Sovereignty Debate,* NEW YORK LAW JOURNAL, Dec. 12, 2000, at 3.

Remarks of Howard Beales, Director, Bureau of Consumer Protection, Federal Trade Commission at the Promotional Marketing Association Annual Meeting, Dec. 5, 2001, available on the Internet at http://www.ftc.gov/ speeches/other/bealesconsumerprotectagenda.htm (accessed Dec. 12, 2002).

Reno v. American Civil Liberties Union, 521 U.S. 844, 849 (1997).

Robert Serviss, 121 F.T.C. 820, 831 (1996).

Sarna, Shirley F., *Advertising on the Internet: An Opportunity for Abuse?,* 11 ST. JOHN'S J. LEGAL COMMENT. 683, 689 (1996).

Saunders, Christopher, *Study: Web Privacy Concerns Cost $3.4 Billion,* INTERNET ADVERTISING REPORT, Nov. 8, 2001, available on the Internet at http://www.internetnews.com/IAR/article.php/12_920201 (accessed Jan. 8, 2002).

SEC INTERPRETATIVE RELEASE ON USE OF ELECTRONIC MEDIA No. 33-7856, No. 34-42728 (Apr. 28, 2000).

Sherman G. Smith, 121 F.T.C. 807, 817 (1996).

Shetland Times Ltd. v. Wills, Edinburgh, Scotland, Court of Session, Oct. 24, 1996 (Lord Hamilton).

SNC Havas Numerique v. SA Kelijob, Tribunal de Commerce de Paris, ordonnanceder référé, 26 Dec. 2000.

Spam Losses, THE CONTROLLER'S REPORT, July 2002, at 9.

Specht v. Netscape Communications Corp., 2001 U.S. Dist. LEXIS 9073.

State Street & Trust Co. v. Signature Financial Group, Inc., 149F.3d 1368 (Fed. Cir. 1998), *cert. denied,* 199 S. Ct. 851 (1999).

Statistics Show Cross Border Spam Mail on Decrease, Ministry of Information Communications, July 30, 2002, available on the Internet at http:// www.mic.go.kr (accessed Aug. 17, 2002).

Stoss, Randall E., *Pardon My French: If It's a World Wide Web, Why Is France Censoring Yahoo!?,* U.S. NEWS & WORLD REPORT, Feb. 12, 2001, at 41.

Telemarketing and Consumer Fraud and Abuse Prevention Act, 15 U.S.C. 6101(3) (1994).

Ticketmaster Corp. v. Microsoft Corp., 87 Civ. 3055 (C.D.Cal. filed Apr. 28, 1997).

Ticketmaster Corp. v. Tickets.com, 2000 U.S. Dist. LEXIS 12987.

Timothy R. Bean, 121 F.T.C. 772, 781 (1996).

UNCITRAL MODEL LAW ON ELECTRONIC SIGNATURES, United Nations Commission on International Trade Law (UNCITRAL), 34th Sess., June 25–July 13, 2001 (Vienna, Austria).

United Arab Emirates: E-signature for Legal Affairs Approved June 28, 2001, available on the Internet at http://www.zawya.com/story.cfm?id = ZAWYA 2001 0628093017 (accessed Sept. 14, 2002).

Video Privacy Protection Act (codified at 18 U.S.C. § 2710).

Washington Post Co. v. Total News, Inc., No. 92 CV 01190 (S.D.N.Y. filed Feb. 22, 1997).

Williams v. America Online, Inc., 2001 Mass. Super. LEXIS 11, 43 U.C.C. Rep. Serv. 2d (Callagan) 1101.

World Intellectual Property Organization, *The Management of Internet Names and Addresses: Intellectual Property Issues: Final Report of the WIPO Internet Domain Name Process,* Apr. 30, 1999, available on the Internet at http://wipo2.wipo.int/process1/report/finalreport.html (accessed Sept. 20, 2002).

INDEX

About the Author

JACQUELINE KLOSEK is an attorney and Senior Associate in the Intellectual Property Practice Area of Goodwin Procter LLP in Roseland, New Jersey.